Verdun to the

Impressions of the War o

Frontier of France

Gerald Campbell

Alpha Editions

This edition published in 2024

ISBN : 9789362925374

Design and Setting By
Alpha Editions
www.alphaedis.com
Email - info@alphaedis.com

As per information held with us this book is in Public Domain.
This book is a reproduction of an important historical work. Alpha Editions uses the best technology to reproduce historical work in the same manner it was first published to preserve its original nature. Any marks or number seen are left intentionally to preserve its true form.

Contents

PREFACE .... - 1 -
CHAPTER I LONDON TO DIJON .... - 5 -
CHAPTER II DIJON TO BELFORT .... - 10 -
CHAPTER III IN ALSACE .... - 16 -
CHAPTER IV ROBBERY UNDER ARMS .... - 23 -
CHAPTER V BELFORT TO NANCY .... - 27 -
CHAPTER VI ÉTAT-DE-SIÈGE IN NANCY .... - 33 -
CHAPTER VII THE FRENCH OFFENSIVE .... - 41 -
CHAPTER VIII OCCUPATIONS OF MULHOUSE .. - 49 -
CHAPTER IX MORHANGE .... - 55 -
CHAPTER X GENERAL DUBAIL'S STAND .... - 62 -
CHAPTER XI THE MARTYRED TOWN .... - 70 -
CHAPTER XII BATTLE OF THE GRAND COURONNÉ. I - 77 -
CHAPTER XIII BATTLE OF THE GRAND COURONNÉ. II .... - 87 -
CHAPTER XIV BATTLE OF THE GRAND COURONNÉ. III .... - 95 -
CHAPTER XV LUNÉVILLE .... - 108 -
CHAPTER XVI NEWSPAPER CORRESPONDENTS .... - 117 -
CHAPTER XVII A DAY WITH A PREFECT .... - 124 -
CHAPTER XVIII THE ATTACK ON THE RIVER FORTS .... - 132 -
CHAPTER XIX THE "SOIXANTE-QUINZE" .... - 147 -
CHAPTER XX SIEGE WARFARE .... - 158 -
EPILOGUE .... - 178 -

PREFACE

At the beginning of September, 1914, I was commissioned by *The Times* to go to France as its representative on the eastern frontier, and it so happens that, during the war, no other English newspaper correspondent has been stationed for any length of time on the long section of the front between Verdun and Belfort. One or two paid flying visits to Lorraine after I was settled there, but they were birds of passage, and were off again almost as soon as they arrived. In collecting the material for my despatches and letters I was helped more than I can say by my colleague, Monsieur Fleury Lamure, a French journalist who had already worked for *The Times* in Belgium, where he spent some exciting days in August dodging about in front of the armies of von Kluck, von Bulow, and von Hausen as they advanced on Charleroi and Namur. Before the war he had served two years as an engineer officer in the French and Russian navies, and had also worked in Manchuria and the Near East, first as interpreter to General Silvestre, the French military *attaché* at Kuropatkin's headquarters, and then as correspondent of the *Novoe Vremya*, with the Servians, in the second Balkan war. In the course of our wanderings together we found that the French military and civil authorities highly appreciated the fact that the newspaper which most of them consider the greatest of English journals had associated a Frenchman with me in the work of writing about the operations of their frontier force. From the first our path was smoothed by what they looked upon as a graceful and sensible act on the part of the Editor. At a later stage in the war my French colleague, who has been twice *réformé* as unfit for the active exercise of his profession, offered himself at the Admiralty in Paris for one of the auxiliary forces, but was told that the best thing he could do for his country was to go on working for *The Times*.

From September, 1914, to January, 1915, after which no correspondents were allowed in the zone of the armies, we made our headquarters at Nancy. Between us, at various times, we visited a large part of the front from Verdun to Ferette, close to the Swiss frontier, and only fifteen or twenty miles from the Rhine. Sometimes we were in the trenches, *à bout portant* of the enemy's rifles, and for four months hardly a day or a night passed when we did not hear the sound of the guns. From what we saw and from what we heard from those who took an active part in it, we were able to get what is, I believe, a fairly correct idea of the general run of the fighting on both sides of the frontier. We were well placed, not only for judging the temper of the civil population of the invaded provinces, but also the spirit and fighting qualities of their defenders.

Before we came to Lorraine we had both seen a little of the early fighting in Belgium—at Namur and Mons, and Charleroi and Dinant. But it was at Nancy that I really got to know something of French soldiers and learnt to admire the wonderful cheerfulness and courage of the XXth Army Corps and the other splendid troops who talked with the enemy in the gate of France, and blocked the passage with their dead bodies.

All that is long ago, though not so long as it seems after the weary waiting of more than a year's work in the trenches. But the end is not yet. Those army corps, or their successors—for nearly all of the original officers and men are dead or wounded—are still steadily pressing the enemy back, almost on the same ground as when we were there, and, though the full story cannot be told even now, it is neither too late nor too soon for an Englishman to try and give some idea of the debt which England owes to the French armies of the east.

But I should like to say a word about England too. It is always difficult to see ourselves as others see us. Till long after I had gone abroad for this war—to be quite frank, till the end of 1915—I had no real idea of the view which other nations held at the beginning of the chances of our taking a hand in it. I knew, of course, that many Germans had declared since it began that they for their part had never believed that we would draw the sword. I knew from Englishmen who were in Berlin two days, and even I believe one day, before we did declare war, that Englishmen at that time were received in the streets with cries of "Vive l'Angleterre," or rather "Hoch! England!" and that the bitter revulsion of feeling against us only began when we had thrown down the glove. But that—as I then thought—extraordinary miscalculation and misunderstanding of our national temper, the infuriated reaction from which found vent in the "Gott strafe England" campaign and the "Song of Hate," I put down to an inexplicable blindness peculiar to the German nation, and to the sort of fury to which we are all liable when other people on important occasions do not act as we wish and expect that they will. Since then—but only lately—I have learnt better, from the vantage ground of a neutral nation.

It is a fact that not only the Germanophil but the Francophil Swiss were genuinely and deeply astonished when they learnt—from the official *communiqués*—that we intended to intervene in the war because the soil of Belgium had been invaded. When the thing was done they accepted it as a fact. They were bound to. But they did not anticipate it. They found it hard to believe that with an army, as they thought—and they were not so far wrong—of only 150,000 men, with nothing to gain and everything to lose, we would be so quixotic as to throw ourselves into a contest in which we were not directly concerned, and to send our "contemptible little army" (even smaller than their own) to fight in a foreign country the battles of another state against the overpowering military might of Germany.

It is also a fact—and to me a still more astounding revelation—that a month after the war had begun there were people in France, and among them soldiers of high standing, who were honestly surprised at what we had already done in the war, as well as profoundly grateful, and who even then honestly doubted whether we really meant to put our backs into it to any purpose.

One can understand their astonishment at what we have done since. Even an Englishman may say, without excessive national conceit, that the work of our Navy, the huge volunteer armies raised in a year from the Mother-country and our Dominions and Colonies and India, and our subsequent if only partial acceptance of the principle of National Service, are not everyday affairs. But the initial Swiss doubt or scepticism as to our possible action, once the neutrality of Belgium had been violated, and the fears of our friends in France at the beginning, that having set our hand to the plough we might turn back before the furrow was finished, are not so easy for us Englishmen to comprehend. We had thought that they knew us better. No matter what Government had been in power, once the Germans had declared their intention of passing through the country of the Belgians, we must inevitably have drawn the sword to defend or avenge them; more than that, even if Belgium had not been invaded, we must no less have put our sword at the disposal of invaded France, for the one wrong was in reality as great as the other. And, no matter what Government may be in power to-morrow or the day after, the spirit of England will not change. We stand by the side of France and our other Allies to the end. And by now, I fancy, the French have found that out.

But do we, even now, realize fully what the war means, and what, as a nation, we have got to do before we can expect to win it? I have just come back to England after an absence of a year and a half. I find that though Parliament and the great mass of the people in all ranks have accepted the principle of National Service, there are still in some quarters powerful organizations which are vehemently opposed to it. I find that in spite of all the warnings that have been issued in the Press and by other means as to the imperative necessity of thrift, and in spite of all the efforts made by countless individuals and large sections of the community to model their lives in accordance with those warnings, other individuals and other sections of the community pay no attention to them at all. Money is being earned in unexampled and hitherto undreamt-of profusion, and is being spent with reckless prodigality. Thrift there is on all sides, but cheek by jowl and hand-in-hand with it there is appalling waste.

We have got to get rid of that word thrift altogether. At the best it is an affair of calculation, and can never inspire us to great deeds or counteract the personal and ignoble motives by which human nature, even in the greatest crises, is too often swayed. There is nothing lofty or idealistic or spiritual about it. We must get into an altogether higher region than that of economics. We must learn the lesson not of thrift but of self-sacrifice. Only that can save us. Without it, even though we have the dreaded ships and the splendid men and the all-necessary money too, we shall be in this war as sounding brass or a tinkling cymbal. With it, bearing all things, believing all things, hoping all things, enduring all things, we shall move mountains and overcome the world—the world of the powers of darkness. It is the lack of it, and nothing but the lack of it, which is at present preventing us from winning the war and putting an end to its intolerable misery and evil.

G. C.

LONDON,

March, 1916.

CHAPTER I
LONDON TO DIJON

We left London on the evening of September the 8th with passports viséd for Dijon, and a faint hope that, if we were lucky, we might succeed some day in getting to Belfort, the immediate object of our journey. In ordinary times, and even now, after more than a year of the war, that is not a very difficult undertaking. In the second week of September, 1914, it was in its way quite a little adventure. Everything was obscure, everybody was in the dark. For all that most of us knew the retreat that had begun at Mons three weeks before was still going on. The possibility of the enemy pressing on to Paris was by no means at an end, and even in the eyes of those who had some inside knowledge of what was happening on the different fields of battle the risk was still so great that the French Government had left that capital for Bordeaux some days before.

Nowadays we rattle gaily along in the trains between Paris and Boulogne or Dieppe, safe in the assurance that though the Germans are not so very much further off there is between them and us a great gulf of entrenchments fixed, as well as two huge French and English armies, to say nothing of King Albert and the Belgians. There were practically no trenches in those days, and the enemy were in almost overpowering force. General French's army, though not so contemptible as the German Emperor believed, was certainly little. There was still good reason for anxiety about the possible fate of Paris. After I left Belgium in the middle of August I had spent some time in Holland, where I saw a good deal of a young Prussian engineer, who had offices in London, and was also an officer in the Imperial Flying Corps. He had to report himself at headquarters in Germany, but had been given short leave to go to Flushing, and there wait for his English wife, who was to follow him from London. That was the story he told me, and I believe it was true, as far as it went, though it is possible that he may also have been connected with the Intelligence Department of the German army, or what is commonly termed a spy. In any case there was no doubt about his own intelligence, which was remarkable, or his fund of information, which was extensive. Day after day, at the time when the retreat from Mons had begun and afterwards, he predicted to me (with many apparently genuine expressions of sympathy for the evil fate that was in store for the British army and for England) what the next step in the victorious German advance would be, and day after day he proved to be right. It was not till I had left Holland and was well on my way to Belfort that I had the satisfaction of knowing that some of his prophecies were beginning to go wrong.

I find it interesting to recall now what they were, because they undoubtedly represented at the time the German plan of campaign, as it was mapped out by the General Staff, and confidently anticipated by most of the thinking rank and file of the German army. The great drama, as everyone knows now, was to be preceded by the violation of Belgium as the *lever de rideau*. But the plot of the front piece was felt to be weak, and it had to be strengthened. So the fiction was invented that French soldiers were already in Belgium before the war began, and that evidence had been discovered in Brussels of a promise by the Belgian Government to allow the Allies free passage into Germany through their territory. The proofs of this conspiracy (the alleged story of which was not so widely known then as it is now) would, my young Prussian assured me, be produced at the end of the war. Without that *pièce justificative* there could be, he admitted, no excuse for Germany's preliminary step. He knew other things that were not at the end of August common property—outside Germany and the Germans—about Zeppelins and guns and submarines and other not-to-be-divulged surprises which were to be sprung on us during the course of the war. He was able, for instance, to tell me all about the mammoth 42-centimetre guns, served not by ordinary artillerymen but by specially and secretly trained artificers from Krupp's works, which were to batter down the vaunted French fortresses as they had smashed the forts of Liége. They looked, he said, less like cannons than huge unwieldy antediluvian animals compounded of wheels and levers. They had been assigned an important part in the final act of the drama to be played in front of Paris, which was timed to finish by the end of the year. More in sorrow than in anger he explained how Paris would be reached. The armies of the German right wing which had poured through Belgium (von Kluck's and the rest) would be rushed forward in irresistible masses and by incredibly rapid stages so as to envelop the French and English left wing from the north. At the same time a corresponding hook (he was continually talking of this "hook" as the be all and end all of German strategy) would take place from the south. Under the command of von Haeseler, the idol of the German troops (a man of iron will with ribs of silver which he wore in the place of those he lost in the Franco-Prussian War), the left wing were to advance through the Vosges, Lorraine, and La Woevre, crushing the cupolas of Belfort and Epinal and Toul and Verdun on their way like so many egg-shells, and, with the Crown Prince's army as the connecting link between them and the northern hook, to round up the whole of the French and British armies, on or near the plain of Châlons. Meanwhile a specially detached army was to march on Paris and inform the Government and its inhabitants that unless the terms of peace proposed by Germany were immediately signed the city would be bombarded, and the French, he assured me, sooner than see their beloved Paris reduced to ruins by the 42-centimetre mammoths, would certainly comply, and leave Germany free to turn her attentions and the super-mammoths which she was preparing for their especial benefit to London and England.

To-day all this sounds very fantastic and foolish—the idle vapourings of an irresponsible young man of no importance. But that it was in outline the German plan there is no doubt, and, but for the heroic resistance of de Castlenau and Foch and Dubail on the eastern frontier and the taxi-cab march of Gallieni's Paris army and the other circumstances which caused that curious flank march of von Kluck's on the north at the moment when his part in the programme was on the eve of completion, it might have gone near to succeeding. We know that if it had it would not have ended the war, for the French would undoubtedly have sacrificed Paris and fought to the bitter end, rather than agree to the proffered peace. But up to the end of the Battle of the Marne no one could say with any approach to certainty that they would not be put to the test.

That was the position when we started for Paris. The whole ordered course of modern civilized life had been upset, and anxiety and uncertainty had taken its place. Telephones and telegraphs were only used by the official world, who were nearly as much in the dark as the rest of us. Channel boats were few and far between. Long-distance trains were either not running at all or were restricted to not more than two journeys in the twenty-four hours, and they felt their way like skirmishers advancing over open country, stopping and making a prolonged halt at every single station. The journey from Havre in a carriage dimly lit by a single candle seemed as if it would never end, and I had plenty of time to reflect with mixed feelings on certain articles which had recently been published in *The Times* pointing out the crying necessity of reducing the time of the whole journey between the two capitals to something under seven hours. This time it took rather over thirty. I was beginning to learn the first lesson of the war, the sovereign virtue of patience.

In Paris we had to put up with another day's delay. There was, of course, no question of taking the *ceinture* or driving straight across to the Gare de Lyon. Instead we had to dawdle about from five in the morning till ten at night, getting passports viséd and buying tickets (a two hours' job), and then sitting in the train for another two hours before it started so as to keep the places which by good luck and the help of a friendly police official, after a series of humiliating rebuffs from about half a dozen other commissaires and commandants, all of them harassed and suspicious, we had had the luck to secure. That was the second lesson, afterwards many times repeated—never to expect to get a *laisser passer* or a *permis de voyage* or *séjour* or any other necessity of a journalist's existence, until you had approached at least three of the powers that be.

When at last we started, at midnight, the atmosphere of the crowded carriage was so suffocating that I migrated to the corridor and tried to sleep, with a suit case for a pillow, on the floor, while other restless passengers walked about on various parts of my body. Once more we stopped at every station with a violent bumping and jolting, repeated at each fresh start, and due to the combined facts that the train was about a quarter of a mile long, that it was made up of a job lot of carriages, and that the understudies of the regular drivers and stokers mobilized for active service were not very well up in their parts. Still, all things considered, we were uncommonly lucky to reach Dijon in thirteen hours instead of in five; and, all things considered, we knew quite well that we had nothing to complain of. As the Battle of the Marne was being fought at an average distance of about seventy miles from the line on which we were travelling, the wonder was that passenger trains were running at all. When the real history of the war is written a good deal will have to be said of the splendid way in which the railwaymen of France have done their important but trying and dreary share of the country's work in the country's hour of need.

We were not, as I wrote at the time, a cheerful crowd. Many of us had come long distances, some even from America. The compelling hand of the war was on everyone in the train. Except in the deserted streets of Paris during the few hours that I spent there the day before, I had never seen such uniform sadness on so many faces at once. The women especially, bravely as they tried to face their grief and their anxieties, kind and helpful as they were to one another and the tiny babies that some of them had with them, were indescribably pathetic.

These people were not refugees, like the trainloads one had seen lately in Belgium and Holland. They were going to the scene of the war instead of away from it. Most of them were reservists or the wives and children of reservists, bound for their old homes near the various headquarters to which the men had been called up. Some of them were nurses of the Croix Rouge, middle-aged women and quite young girls; some were on their way to visit wounded relations. Each and all carried the same heavy burden. Not one but many of those near and dear to them were at the front. They knew in some cases that they were already among the dead or wounded or missing. But generally they knew nothing at all except that, if they were still alive, they were there somewhere on one of the many battlefields on the long line of the Allies' front, face to face with the enemy and death.

We made many friends of different conditions in life during the slow hours between dawn and midday, and all had the same story to tell. But there was no need to ask. It was written in their faces. The natural vivacity of these sorrowing women of France was gone. They talked, when they did talk, quietly and sadly, and of only one subject. More often they sat with unseeing eyes, looking far off into the darkness of the unknown future, fearful of the fate that waited for the men by their side, and appalled by the thought of the ruin and suffering that threatened their homes and their children. The tragedy that has brought sorrow to the women of half the world had come upon them with the suddenness of a bomb from a Taube, and some of them were wounded and all were stunned by its effect. That was when we were still in the dark about the result of the great battle that had begun to rage on the left wing near Paris, before the German retreat began. On the second day of our stay in Dijon there was a sudden change in the emotional atmosphere. Directly I left the hotel in the evening I felt that good news had come. Relief and happiness were in the air. In the railway station, in the streets, in the cafés, on the pavements outside the newspaper offices where the daily news of the war was posted up, the look of the people was absolutely different. For the moment personal griefs and losses were hidden and forgotten. General Joffre's general order of September 11th had been published to the troops, and from them the news had spread so quickly that in half an hour everyone seemed to know what had happened.

It was the first real success of the war, the first time since its very early days that the French had begun to lose the feeling of apprehension produced in their minds by the steady retreat of the allied troops from the Belgian frontier, after the battles of Charleroi and Mons. Even the officers at Dijon were affected by it. Up till then, though they spoke confidently enough of eventual success, the subject uppermost in their minds and their conversation was always the wonderful perfection of the German organization. That was a nightmare which they had not so far been able to shake off. Now suddenly it was gone. In a day it had become evident that France and England had their organization too, as well as the common enemy, and that the strategy of the allied forces was beginning at last to tell. And the really hopeful sign of it all was, if I may venture to say so, the English way in which Dijon and France received the good news. They behaved, in fact, much better than some English had done in similar circumstances in past days. There was no mafficking and no hysterical excitement, but only a more determined resolution than ever to see the thing through to the end, a strengthening of the national spirit of unity, and a fuller realization of the value and sincerity of the alliance with England and of the fine fighting qualities of our troops.

CHAPTER II
DIJON TO BELFORT

In Paris, when we passed through it, it was still possible for inoffensive travellers to feel themselves free men. At Dijon we had our first real taste of the restrictions on personal liberty imposed by the war in the zone of the armies. Each time that we came to a new place we had to get at least three separate signed and stamped permits (from three or more officials) empowering us to leave the station, to stay, even for an hour, in the town, and to go into the station again, or anywhere outside the town, when our business was done. To all such applications the attitude of officialdom, entrenched behind barriers and supported by bayonets, and vindictive or regretful according to the temperament of the individual representative of the law and the degree of exasperation to which he had been brought by previous encounters with the public, was, as a rule, one of uncompromising refusal. At first that kind of thing, even when it has become a commonplace of one's existence, is rather trying. The shock to one's self-esteem and the sense of confinement are both extremely galling. It is not pleasant day after day to put yourself in a position in which you are liable to be treated like a naughty schoolboy, nor to feel that you are as restricted in your walks abroad as a Dartmoor convict. From the abominable feeling of being shut up in a cage there was, with rare exceptions, no escape, any more than there is for the lions at the Zoo. But we soon found that the chase after permits, if we treated it as a kind of game, was tolerable and even exciting, because each time we played it, though with *The Times* as our trump card we almost invariably won, we stood a good chance of losing. The real skill consisted in knowing when it was wise and safe to play it. Our opponents, destined in time to become our friends, were generals, staff officers, gendarmes, station guards and their commandants, military police commissaires, civil police "*agents*," and other officials of all sorts and sizes. Most of them started by being suspicious of us and our mission, and generally speaking the more humble their post the more they wanted humouring before they could be brought to see that the rules of the game might perhaps be slightly relaxed in our favour. But once they had reached that point, as soon, that is to say, as they got to know us for what we said we were, they were ready to do anything in their power, because we were allies and representatives of *The Times*—which has not yet been burnt, and never will be, on any Bourse in the east of France. With the exception of a fierce-moustachioed warrior who had a holy horror of German spies (and therefore, if you see the connexion, of English journalists) the only French officials, high or low, who persistently refused anything important for which we asked them, were a distinguished General Officer and his Chief of Staff, who always dealt with us through their subordinates. If only we could have seen and known the General himself I firmly believe that he would have been as kind as all the rest. But he had other things to do, or else he never got our cards and letters.

Having got into Dijon, and having received reluctant permission to stay there, first for a night, and then for as much longer as we liked, the next thing was to get out of it, using it, if it would allow itself so to be used, as a stepping stone to higher things. It was occupied at that time by the 20th (Reserve) Army Corps, which had its staff headquarters at the hotel where we put up. Both before and after we received the news of the Battle of the Marne all the officers whom we met there were chafing to be at the front, and openly envious of our poor little chance of getting there before them. They little knew how slender it was. However, in General Brissaud, the Governor of the town, we found after a time a real friend, and from him we got a personal *visa* as far as Besançon, which was the limit of his jurisdiction, together with a verbal recommendation that we should be passed on to Belfort. At Besançon we had a bad quarter of an hour, as the station-commandant hesitated a long time before he agreed to let us go on, and we only just escaped being sent back to Paris. Something, however, turned the scale in our favour, and at last, though with rather a wry face, he sent us on our way rejoicing, greatly relieved at our escape, but careful not to show it till we were safe in our carriage.

It was long after dark when we got to Belfort. There was nowhere for us to sleep in the station, and no return train. Otherwise I think the little knot of officers who shook their heads doubtfully over our passports on the dimly lit platform would certainly have packed us into it straight away. There were some grounds for their hesitation. We had reached one of the chief of the gates of France, and were getting near the enemy. The Trouée de Belfort, the wide flat opening between the foothills of the Vosges and the Jura mountains, had to be defended from possible foes within as well as without. War, as the warrior with the fierce moustachios remarked to me a month or two later, is a serious matter, and nowhere were the French taking it more seriously than in the war-worn outpost fortress that stands sentinel in front of the Belfort gap, linked to the heart of the Republic by the long chain of lonely sentries that guarded the railway night and day all the way to Paris. Outside it very little was known at that time—in England nothing at all—of its then condition. Even the Germans knew nothing, so they, or their newspapers, invented lies about it, and said that it was closely invested. But though no German soldier, except in an aeroplane, ever got within miles of it, the state of siege proclaimed by the Governor was enforced with rigid strictness, and the whole of the civil population, except those who catered for the needs of the garrison, had been evacuated some days before we got there. At the best, therefore, however genuine our passports and however innocent our appearance, we were two *bouches inutiles* who would have to be fed; at the worst, as journalists, the chances were that we should be indiscreet (that is the normal view); and anyhow it was very doubtful if we had any right to be there at all. But there, undeniably, we were, and so—well, perhaps after all the best way out of the difficulty was to send us to the Governor's headquarters and leave him to deal with our case. So to the General's quarters, the heart of the fortress, which we were as anxious as any German to reach, we set out, under the escort of Private Jouanard, election agent and newspaper correspondent, a convinced socialist and anti-militarist, but, like his idol Jaurès, a Frenchman first of all, and therefore an ardent soldier of France, a warm admirer of England, and a bitter enemy of the Boche and all his works.

I suppose that long before this book is published England will have at last realized the truth of the creed of French soldiers like Private Jouanard, and will have demanded as one man to be put, like France, on the footing of national service. But I may be too sanguine; we may have to grapple with the industrial revolution threatened by Mr. J. H. Thomas, M.P. In any case I should like to quote once more a proclamation written by Private Jouanard for *l'Humanité*, which, before our acquaintance was twelve hours old, he gave me for publication in *The Times*. It was addressed "Aux Camarades Socialistes," and signed "L. J. A mobilized comrade."

"We are now at the parting of the ways. After having fought stubbornly against that human scourge—war, the insatiable ambition of a despot forces us to take up arms. Despite the immense sorrow that grips us at the thought of being the involuntary murderers of those Germans and Austrians who have the same communion of ideas, in their name and in our own, for humanity, socialism, right against the arbitrary, civilization against barbarism, in the name of all these sacred principles, our brothers of England, of Belgium, of Russia, and ourselves have answered 'Present' with one voice to the call of our native land. Each one filled with emotion and confident in the justice of our cause, we have flown to arms at the cry of Liberty, like the great revolutionaries of '93.

"Socialists of the allied armies, we have not to weep, but to avenge the death of the martyr of the Idea, our great friend Jaurès, our guide and our light in difficult moments. Humanity loses in him a great defender, the indirect victim of the unmitigated Teuton aggression.

"The most competent among us are giving a manly example by entering the Governments of the Allies, thus taking, in the eyes of their countries, a position of responsibility for the Party which they represent. More than others we socialists must prove the error of this monstrous accusation of anti-patriotism. Let us prove, in defending ourselves, that we are firmly resolved to fight to the end for our national independence.

"Forward, comrades! Take heart, take courage, and the bar of red, which mingles with the two other colours, forming a trinity symbolic of liberty, peace, and labour, will not be defiled by the bloody hands of the bandits who would make us slaves! May the furrows, sprinkled with our blood, bring forth the ear of corn beneath the branch of olive, symbolizing fruitful labour in eternal peace."

"Out of the mouths of babes and sucklings hast Thou ordained strength, because of Thine enemies, that Thou mightest still the enemy and the avenger." Out of the mouth of a French *simple soldat* the Englishmen who are still holding back as I write from the supreme sacrifice or privilege of national service, the Britons who never, never, never will be slaves, are condemned. A year of the war has passed, and hundreds of thousands of their fellow subjects of all classes have given up their professions and their positions, their pleasures and their ease, their wives and their families, and have freely offered themselves on the field of battle as part of the strength by which the enemy can be stilled. But they themselves have done none of the things for which their French socialist comrade unhesitatingly gave them credit. They have not—up to October, 1915—realized that we are at the parting of the ways, they have not with one voice answered "Present" to the call of their native land, they have not flown to arms at the cry of liberty, they have not proved by defending themselves that they mean to fight to the end for their national independence. Instead, they sit at home and strike—not for freedom, but for higher wages and less work—and prate of Conscripts and a Capitalists' War and a Capitalists' Press, and all the other labour shibboleths which have lost whatever sense they had before the war and become mere nonsense, because the war is different from all other wars and has changed everything in the world. It is a Capitalists' War, of course. It was made by the Prussian Junkers and the business men of Germany with no other object than that of increasing their capital and destroying that of the Allies and particularly of England. It is a war fought by "conscripts" (though I should like to hear Mr. J. H. Thomas, M.P., use that term to Private Jouanard) in the case of every country engaged in it except England. And it is also, because of these two undeniable premises, the greatest strike against selfishness in high places that has ever taken place, and the conscript brothers who are fighting or working for it are the champions of freedom, and the men who refuse to stand by their side are, without knowing it, the blackest blacklegs in the history of the world. And no one knows better than they and the newspapers and politicians who support them what blacklegs are. They are the men who in the wars of labour refuse to submit to the Compulsory Service of trade-unionism, which is sometimes the most servile service and the most autocratic and deadening compulsion that ever was enforced in a free country, and the badge and livery and alpha and omega of the god with the feet of clay before which they bow down and worship.

Though it was a clear starlight night when we walked up to General Thévenet's quarters, the moon had not risen and the town was wrapped in silence and dense darkness. Not a lamp was lit in the streets, not a chink of light escaped through the closely shuttered windows, not a sound was to be heard but the steady tramp of a distant patrol and the clatter of our feet on the cobbles. Afterwards, in Toul, and Epinal, and Commercy, and Nancy, and Lunéville, and other towns near the front, we got used to the conditions of a state of siege after *couvre feu*, when people go to bed at eight or nine o'clock—the deathly night stillness, broken only by the barking of dogs, the shrill despairing shrieks peculiar to French engine whistles, and the dull boom of cannon, and, in the empty streets, walled in by tall houses teeming with unseen human life, the solid blackness of the grave. In time you get used to it and forget to wonder whether the Germans too can hear the howling of that far-off dog that is baying the moon. You even crack jokes with the heavy-footed sentries and stealthy police *"agents"* who loom up uncannily out of the darkness and may or may not request you to follow them to the *"poste."* But that first night in Belfort, before I had seen the miles and miles of solid entrenchments that lie between it and the frontier, the effect of it all, and the thought of the long line of millions of men, stretching almost from our feet far away for five hundred miles across France and Belgium to the Channel, thousands of them watching and waiting and fighting and suffering under the wide canopy of the quiet night, was curiously eerie. You seemed to hear Europe sighing and groaning in her sleep.

Suddenly, out of the unseen came a sharp challenge—"Qui vive? Halte là! Avancez à l'ordre! Le mot!"—and we stopped dead, as it is wise to do when you meet a night patrol in a town in *état de siège* if you are anxious to go on living. Then, one by one, we walked forward, gave the word, handed our papers to the corporal to be examined by the light of his lantern, and finally, after a few more challenges, half blinded by the dazzling glare of the lamps of a motor-car standing in the courtyard in front, were ushered into General Thévenet's business-like office. Our reception was as different from what had gone before as the abrupt change from darkness to light. At last we had struck a man of real authority and decision. After a word or two of explanation—who we were and what we had come for—we were welcomed as warmly as if we had been the whole British army, horse, foot, guns, and aeroplanes, instead of two troublesome journalists. We had come at a happy moment. England and *The Times* would in any case have been passports enough for the General and his staff. But we shone also with the reflected glory of the common endurance of the retreat from Mons and the common triumph of the Battle of the Marne, which had brought our two countries closer together than they had been since Balaclava and Inkermann. And when we had explained the immediate purpose of our mission—to publish the truth and to contradict the lying reports spread by the enemy about Belfort and Verdun and Nancy—the General at once promised us all the help in his power.

CHAPTER III
IN ALSACE

Next morning the General was as good as his word. A note was brought to our hotel by an orderly to say that if we would be round at his quarters after lunch we should be able to see *des choses intéressantes*, and by half-past one, in a motor-car driven by an Alsatian sergeant (who, like many others in the same position, had preferred service in the French army to his pre-war occupation as a German private), we were driving between the outlying forts on our way to the frontier, with Captain de Borieux of the Headquarters Staff as our guide and friend. Lie number one was soon disposed of. It was quite evident that the German claim that they were investing Belfort, and had even taken two of its forts, was false. Till we reached the frontier, after passing for eight miles over a wide, rolling plain, which even then was scarred in all directions with line upon line of French entrenchments and other formidable defences, there was not a sign of them, and even then it was only the negative sign that the boundary post erected by the Germans after 1870 was now rebaptized with the colours of France. A yard further, and I was in Alsace, the first of the very few Englishmen who since the beginning of the war have crossed into the part of the annexed provinces which had been won back from the enemy.

Photograph by Libert-Fernand, Nancy.

LES HALLES, RAON L'ETAPE—VOSGES.

We stopped first at Montreux Vieux, the German name for which was Alt Munster—a little town a mile or so beyond the frontier on the Rhine-Rhone Canal, just before it takes a turn to Dannemarie and Altkirch—in which a month before there had been some brisk fighting. In their attack on the town, which suffered pretty severely from their guns, the Germans pushed forward their infantry as far as the canal, about two hundred yards across the fields from the French sandbag defences in front of the station. That was the nearest point to Belfort which they reached. Before they got to the movable bridge over the canal a sergeant who was on guard in the bridge-house, ran out under heavy fire and turned the wheel by which it is raised and lowered till it stood erect on the French side. "*Il était temps que j'y aille, mon Colonel,*" he said afterwards to his commanding-officer, when the enemy had been finally driven back from the canal banks to the woods round Romagny, a scattered village a mile or two off which we visited later in the afternoon. The Germans visited it too, on the same day that they failed to get into Montreux Vieux, and vented their spite on its feeble inhabitants (their own fellow-subjects) in the now familiar way, bombarding church and houses from a distance of a few hundred yards, and then setting fire to a quarter of its cottages and homesteads, in none of which were there any French soldiers. I have often thought since of the two pictures—the quiet sergeant by the canal bridge and those smoking piles of rubbish that once were peasants' homes—though the destruction in Romagny was nothing at all compared with the wholesale ruin and desolation which we saw afterwards in Meurthe et Moselle and other departments further north. They seem to me typical illustrations of the difference between the French and German conceptions of making war. For we know now that one of the normal features of the much-vaunted German organization (till the deadlock of the trenches made it impossible) was the organized burning by squads of disciplined men of defenceless villages, peopled, as a rule, only by old men and women and children. Even for the malign fits of bad temper which found vent in these wanton acts of incendiarism, the mailed fist of the drill sergeant gave the signal, and the men, acting under his orders and those of his superiors, carried them out, working shoulder to shoulder, as part of the regular system. There was nothing systematic about the act of the French sergeant at the bridge-house. He just did his duty, as he saw it himself, and on his own initiative, when he felt that it had to be done. The German soldier, for all his courage, is part of a mass, a cog or a nut in an unthinking machine. The Frenchman, for all his discipline, remains an individual, and the French army is made up not of men burning with the spirit of *la revanche*, but of patriots who have gone to the defence of their country because they thought it time.

That night, five weeks after the war had begun, we penetrated a good deal further into Alsace, to within about twenty miles of the Rhine. It was before the hard-and-fast line of the trenches had been drawn, and between the outposts on either side there was a wide stretch of No-Man's land in the Sundgau (the corner of the Rhine plain in the angle between the ranges of the Vosges and the Bernese Jura) which was constantly traversed by both French and Germans. Colonel Quais, the officer commanding the brigade stationed at Montreux Vieux, had arranged for the following day a reconnaissance in force as far as Ferette, which lies close to the Swiss frontier a little way west of Basle. Part of his object was to round up the German troops by which it was tenanted, as they had been making themselves a nuisance to his cavalry patrols. His force consisted of two regiments of infantry and two batteries of 75's, with detachments of dragoons and bicyclists. From Montreux Vieux to Pfetterhausen, to which they had marched that evening, was only eleven miles, and from Pfetterhausen to Ferette another seven or eight. But night marches are leisurely affairs, and to be on the ground in good time in the morning, we had to start before midnight. So after a very early dinner with the Colonel and his staff we turned in at eight o'clock on the shake-downs which he provided for us, and, after three hours' sleep and a hasty snack, five of us packed into a smallish car and set off for what he called his little *fête*, with high hopes of what the morrow might bring forth. Unfortunately, for all of us—our kind host as well as ourselves—the promised fight did not come off, but for all that the trip was well worth making. It is not every night in the war that English journalists get a chance of a forty-mile march into German territory with an escort of between two and three thousand French troops.

On the way to Pfetterhausen we were challenged several times by sentries posted at different barriers on the road. At each stop the car slowed down and was pulled up, the officer sitting next the driver got down and opened the slide of his lantern—the night was pitch dark, with only a thin crescent moon high up in the cloudy sky—gave the word, advanced to the barrier, showed our papers, and finally turned the lantern in our direction to show that we might come on. Once or twice he must have found the pauses before the sentries would let him walk up to the muzzles of their loaded and levelled rifles uncomfortably long. We were cutting across the narrow strip of French territory which lies between Montreux Vieux and Pfetterhausen, and their lonely posts were quite close enough to the frontier to make the question of dealing with an unknown motor, arriving suddenly in the dead of night, rather a nervous problem. They could not know for certain, till they had examined the permits—even the Acting-Brigadier had to have one—whether we were friends or foes, and to fire first and inquire afterwards might have seemed to them the better part of discretion if not of valour. That did happen more than once to harmless travellers like ourselves while we were driving about Belgium, where the sturdy patriots of the *troisième ban*, who guarded the barriers with ancient weapons that looked as if they had been dug up on the field of Waterloo, were a real terror by night. But these sentries were disciplined French soldiers, not ignorant Wallachian peasants, and gave one quite a pleasant feeling of security—once we had passed them. No German scouts were likely to be prowling about within, at any rate, a mile or two of their posts.

When we had left the last of them behind and had turned into Alsace again we seemed to be alone in the quiet night, when, all of a sudden, startlingly close beside us, there was the clink of a chain and the stamp of a horse's hoof, and we could just see that we were abreast of a long line of horses and guns and men drawn up along the side of a narrow lane, barely leaving room for us to pass on to the cross-roads of the village. Here there was a long wait while the officers of the different units got their orders from the Brigadier. The men, who were drawn up along the roads leading to the village, were curiously quiet. They spoke very little and only in whispers, and even the tramp of their feet when the column began to get on the move soon after two o'clock had struck, with the Colonel marching with the infantry at its head and the dragoons darkly silhouetted against the grey walls of the houses, made hardly a sound. We gave them a long start and then followed on in the car, continually overtaking and passing different bodies of the long column, horse and foot. At one time, at a moment when we happened to be out of touch with any part of it and were rather afraid that we might have lost our way, we roused a scared German villager out of his bed and took him on board to show us the road. We were not anxious to come upon the enemy unawares, and when we sighted and caught up another body of troops, it was distinctly comforting to see in the dawning light that the colour of their trousers was red and not grey. Just after that, in the middle of a thick wood, the car stuck for a time in some boggy ground as we were trying to get past a couple of trees which the Germans had felled the day before and dragged across the road—a likely enough place for an ambush. Nothing, however, happened, and a mile or two further on, as the sun rose in front of us beyond the Rhine, a quickly-fading picture of gorgeous rose and crimson and deep blue, we overtook the head of the column, picked up the Colonel, as fresh and eager as a boy for all his sixty-two years, and five minutes later were eating bread and cheese and other good things in the orchard which was to be his headquarters in the battle of Ferette. And after all, there was no battle. The batteries took up their position in our rear, the infantry deployed in open order over the fields, the cyclists and dragoons exchanged snap-shots with the enemy's vanishing scouts and skirmishers far away on the left flank, and gradually the town, which nestles among the wooded hills of the Bernese Jura, was surrounded. But not a German soldier was left in it, and the only result of the reconnaissance was to prove that in that part of Alsace there was no body of enemy troops strong enough to risk an attack on our half-brigade.

If the Colonel had been a German officer he would probably have treated Ferette as the enemy had Romagny, by way of revenge and as an object-lesson in terrorism to the Alsatian villagers. There was nothing and no one to prevent him. He had the men and the guns and at a pinch could have improvised the fire-lighters which the Frenchman does not carry ready-made in his haversack, like the Boche. But that is not the French way. They fight like soldiers, not with women and children, and they do not wantonly destroy property. At the same time I am bound to say that just to show what the 75's, though served by territorials, could do, they were allowed to fire one shot at the ruined castle which stands on one of the wooded heights above the town. The range was about three miles, the target was invisible to the gunners, the observation officer was perched in a tree three or four hundred yards from the battery, and yet the shell struck the wall exactly in the middle of the panel above the central window, making a neat little extra window, absolutely round, which was even an improvement on the original architect's design.

It was a trifling little incident, but it was very characteristic of the light-hearted boyish way in which the French set about the business of war. The nearer you get to the front the more that fact strikes you. Behind the armies, far away from the trenches, war is a dreary affair. The office-clerks, the road-menders, the men who guard canals and bridges and lines of communication, or are scattered about in little *postes* of twenty or thirty, in ugly suburbs and out-of-the-way villages, and all the other hosts of soldiers (including most of the *embusqués*), who have never come face to face with an enemy, except, perhaps, a disarmed prisoner—these are the real unfortunates of the war. They only see its unpicturesque side, where if there is little danger there is also no glory and no excitement, and are apt to lose heart and take a gloomy view of its prospects. The optimists and the real light-hearted children of the nation are the fighting men who suffer its horrors and its hardships day and night, summer and winter, at the front. Their life, as was said shortly before his death by an Eton boy and gallant English soldier, is a glorified picnic—a picnic with an object. They live the open-air existence, which is the proper environment of the natural man. It is better fun to ride and march through the night to Ferette, with a chance of a scrap with the Boches at the end of it, than to put on a stiff collar and hard hat to crawl to a stuffy office day after day in a crowded suburban train. It is better fun, as well as a more dignified calling, to be a soldier fighting your country's battles than a waiter or a flunkey or a billiard-marker or a rich idler with no real work to do. That is how the French soldier at the front takes the war, in spite of its hardships and sufferings and its deadly home-sickness, the aching separation from those he loves, which is the worst thing that the soldier has to bear. For a long year now in the east of France his home for the most part has been in the big woods that, in the Vosges and Lorraine and La Woevre, lie almost everywhere behind the lines, and it is because he is a boy at heart that when he has built his leafy wigwam or his wooden or stone hut, or hollowed out and roofed his cave in the ground—just the things that boys love to do—he is able to keep lively and cheerful. He surrounds his new home with little paths and garden-beds—generally with coloured stones arranged in patterns instead of borders and flowers—he decorates it with war trophies, and, if he is an artist, with war pictures and even frescoes, he collects round it young boars and owls and other live mascots (which boys would call pets), he builds his own fires and has picnic meals in the open, he is constantly doing things with his hands, he goes to bed early and sleeps like a top (when he is not in the trenches), his relaxations, which he has to invent for himself, are simple and clean, and, officer or man, although he is living constantly face to face with death, he manages somehow, but chiefly because he is a Frenchman, to be nearly always gay and young-hearted.

I remember once coming to a nearly roofless village near Thiaucourt, which was held as part of the front line of trenches by an infantry battalion of territorials. An enemy aeroplane was whirring overhead, and occasional shells were dropping not very far off. It was an off-time, and the men were mostly in the street, playing with their baby *sanglier* and posing for a snap-shotting photographer. When the Taube came "over" they all bolted for cover like a lot of cheerful rabbits, and in half a minute came running out again, laughing and joking like schoolchildren, and crowding together in front of the camera to be taken in a regimental group. The spirit of the officers was just the same. Four young lieutenants were just starting to play tennis on a vilely bad mud court, and, Taube or no Taube, they went on with their game. But the Colonel, portly and middle-aged, was the real joy. He had just invented and rigged up an ingenious system of taps and pulleys and cisterns and boilers, thanks to which his men could enjoy the luxury of hot as well as cold shower-baths. As he was showing it off he stopped for a moment to listen to the scream of an approaching shell, then said, "Ce n'est pas pour nous," and went on enthusing over the merits of his new toy. Apparently he had not a thought of war in his head.

That is one side of the character of French soldiers as I have seen it in this war. But there is another, which almost seems to have been born during the war, some little time after it had begun. I only speak from a very slight experience, but some of the French as well as the Belgian officers whom we met right at the beginning gave me the idea of being nervous and rattled of knowing nothing about their own plans or the enemy's whereabouts, and of being generally in a state of mental confusion and irritable uncertainty, which looked extremely likely to lead to disaster. When I came to France later on I saw an extraordinary change, or perhaps my original diagnosis was entirely wrong. Bad mistakes were certainly made at the beginning, and probably the greatest service rendered by General Joffre to France was the way in which, quietly and without unnecessary publicity, but with perfect firmness, he weeded out the men, whatever their rank, whom he held to be at fault. But these, perhaps, were exceptions. The spirit and training of the great bulk of the army may have been as admirable from the first as it is now, and that spirit may have been in existence before the war, and not produced by it and by the example and warning of the preliminary failures. At all events, there is no doubt about it now. The confusion and uncertainty and nervous apprehension, if they ever existed to an extent greater than what was naturally caused by the suddenness of Germany's unprovoked attack, are gone—were already gone when we arrived in Belfort. Even in those anxious times, when we had only just begun to throw back the impetuous rush of the enemy, there was everywhere order, and method, and quiet confidence, and a fixed determination to go on, neither unduly elated by success nor troubled by failure, to the absolutely certain end. No one was in a hurry, but every one was quick and alert. The army, officers and men, seemed to be an army of real soldiers, masters of their profession, and not a collection of bunglers. If mistakes had been made, or should be made, they would have to be rectified. But no mistakes and no defeats, and no possible combination of circumstances, would alter the final issue, because France and her Allies were fighting for the cause of the liberty of the world, the triumph of which was absolutely certain. That was the spirit of the French a year ago, and it is so now more than ever. For all their light-heartedness they are taking the war as seriously as a religion, and out of the travail of it a new France has been born.

CHAPTER IV
ROBBERY UNDER ARMS

Between Montreux Vieux and Pfetterhausen there is a little French village called Suarce, which, on the very eve of the war, was the scene of an incident almost as dramatic from a historical point of view as the violation of Belgium two days later. At the end of July, for some days before the war began, the French had withdrawn their troops to a distance of six miles from the frontier all along the line from Luxembourg to the point, a mile from Pfetterhausen, which is the meeting-place of the boundaries of France, Switzerland, and Alsace. They were acting, I believe, partly at the suggestion of the English Government, and certainly with their warm approval. A few frontier posts, consisting chiefly of douaniers and gendarmes, had to be left, but, short of their recall, everything possible was done to remove temptation from the path of swashbuckling Uhlan patrols, and so to diminish the risk of incidents likely to precipitate the declaration of war.

Unfortunately, these precautions were thrown away, and were even turned to France's disadvantage. Before war had begun, Germany had sent a number of small patrols across the frontier with roving commissions, to promote the very incidents which France had tried to avoid. After it was declared, in part of the border district between Metz and Luxembourg, she gained valuable time by the ease with which her troops advanced in the neutral zone which France had created. France, hoping against hope for peace, had played the game: Germany, bent on war, had broken the rules before it began.

There were nineteen of these deliberate acts of trespass by armed men on the soil of a friendly power between Longwy and Belfort, twelve of them, on Sunday, August 2nd, in the Belfort district, the rest, either on the Sunday or the Monday, at Cirey and other places further north. The number of them and the wide extent of ground which they covered, were in themselves enough to prove that they were part of a premeditated scheme, and not merely the casual acts of a few irresponsible and excitable individuals. But there were facts about the affair at Suarce which made it different from the others and established beyond question that the German soldiers concerned in it (and therefore in the other eighteen cases) were acting under the orders of their superior officers.

The affray in which the first lives were lost on each side took place at Joncherey, close to Delle on the Swiss frontier, five miles nearer to Belfort than Suarce. A glowing account of it was given in the *Elsasser Kurier*, a paper published at Colmar, which not only acknowledged the raid and the date (August 2, 1914), but deliberately gloried in the achievement of its leader, Lieutenant Mayer, of the 5th Chasseurs. He was, it says, when he received his orders from the general officer commanding the brigade to reconnoitre in the direction of Belfort, "full of joy and the lust of fighting, and proud to be the first to teach the enemy the might of the German trooper." When he and his patrol of six or seven crossed the frontier into France they found, according to the same authority, that the numerous French cavalry and infantry detachments which had patrolled the district for some days before had disappeared—in obedience, of course, to the orders of their Government. On the way to Delle they saw, however, two sentinels posted on the road. "Like a flash of lightning," wrote the Colmar enthusiast, "Lieutenant Mayer overtook them, and with the first stroke of his German sabre cleft to the breast the head of a French *pioupiou*, who was almost paralyzed by terror. At the same time, just as quickly, first-class trooper Heize thrust his lance with such fury into the breast of the other private that he could not withdraw his weapon from the body which he had pierced ("overtaken" is the word used), and was obliged to continue his ride with his sabre (and not his lance) in his hand." The German story then goes on to tell how the little troop proceeded to gallop through a company of fifty French infantry without losing a man, how Lieutenant Mayer was shot down after they had passed them, and how first-class trooper Heize then took command and finally reached the German lines with a further loss of three men. As a matter of fact, the feats of arms of the gallant lieutenant and first-class trooper Heize were not quite so charmingly mediæval as the story makes out. What really happened was that when they came upon the French post, consisting of a corporal and four men, Lieutenant Mayer, by way of answer to Corporal Peugeot's challenge, fired three shots at him with his revolver, one of which wounded him mortally, and was himself hit and killed by three bullets fired by the guard. (He was afterwards buried at Joncherey with full military honours, and a wreath was placed on his grave by the French.) The rest of the German account, except the appearance on the scene of the fifty worst shots in the French army, is fairly correct. In any case it is near enough to the truth to prove without need of further witness that the raid was not a mere youthful indiscretion on the part of the unfortunate Lieutenant Mayer.

FRENCH ADVANCE IN VILLAGE STREET OF MAGNIÈRES, MEURTHE ET MOSELLE.
From *"En Plein Feu."* By kind permission of M. Vermot, Rue Duguay-Trouin, Paris.

But the affair at Suarce is the most really damning piece of evidence supplied by any of these pre-war violations of French territory. It is not necessary to depend on the testimony of a Colmar newspaper, which might possibly be still further mistaken in its statements, to make the complicity of the German *haut commandement* historically certain. Early in the morning of the same fateful date (August 2, 1914), two cyclists and seven troopers of the German 22nd regiment of Dragoons rode into the village and informed the inhabitants that it was conquered territory. Later in the day an officer, a non-commissioned officer, and twelve troopers of the same regiment appeared, and after breaking up the telephone apparatus, forced a provision convoy, consisting of nine men, two waggons, and twenty-two horses, on its way to Belfort, to turn round and accompany them to Germany. The waggons and horses were taken as loot; the men were presumably the first specimens of the new kind of civil prisoner which, during the war, the Germans have been pleased to label as "hostages." But in time of peace it is not the custom of civilized nations to take either loot or hostages from their neighbours, and, since there were no soldiers engaged in the affair on the French side, and therefore no fighting, the act could not be defended as an act of retaliation. Nor is there any question of the officer having done what he did merely on his own responsibility. You cannot take a troop of French horses and waggons and men into Germany and hide them under a bushel. The officer would not, in fact, have dared to commit the crime of international robbery and kidnapping, and then carried off his spoil with him to barracks, unless he had known that it would be condoned by his superior officers. In other words, like the Roman centurion, he was a man set under authority, and only did what he was told to do. The facts of the incident, as I have given them, are indisputable. If, at the time when the British cabinet was weighing the reasons for and against joining in the war, there were any of its members who doubted the extent of Germany's guilt, the story of Suarce may well have played (as I have heard it did) an important part in helping them to make up their minds. For it was possibly the earliest positive evidence which proved beyond a shadow of doubt Germany's deliberate intention of going to war. As far as I know, the story has not previously been published, at all events in any detail, and therefore it may be of a certain amount of historical interest to give the names of the nine Frenchmen who were made prisoners of war before war was declared. They were: Edouard Voelin (58 years of age), Eugène Mattin (52), François Verthe (66), Isidore Skup (57), Céléstin Fleury (55), Henri Féga (53), J. Pierre Marchal (51), Charles Martin (29), and Emile Mouhay (29). The last two had been passed as "bons pour l'armée" in the class of 1914. The rest were obviously far beyond the military age. Two of the nine have died during their indefensible imprisonment in Germany.

CHAPTER V
BELFORT TO NANCY

Our first direct news of Nancy was given us by an army-surgeon whom we met in Dijon. He had just been invalided home suffering from septic poisoning as the result of an operation which he had performed in one of its many hospitals. In these days very little information was getting through from the Lorraine front. The general situation was so obscure that at one time some of the map-drawers of the English newspapers, probably owing to a too naïf confidence in the accuracy of the statements published by the Wolff bureau, actually placed the line showing the position of the German front on the west side of Nancy, as though it had been occupied by the enemy. Fortunately they were mistaken. Though the capital of Lorraine had been lightly bombarded on the night of September 9, two days before the médecin-major left it, it was then, as it has since remained, in spite of the enemy's persistent efforts to reach it, *Nancy l'Inviolée*. But though the Germans, after three weeks of incessant fighting, during which they suffered very heavy losses, had been driven back, they were still only a few miles away, and when we got back to Belfort from Alsace, we had already decided that, if it could be managed, Lorraine was the place for us to go to.

Even if we could have got leave to stay in Belfort the outlook there, from our point of view, was not promising. The field defences between it and the frontier, without taking into account the troops stationed at Montreux Vieux and in other parts of Alsace, were enough to convince us that there was little chance of the enemy getting anywhere near it. The lessons of Liége and Namur had not been thrown away. It was pathetic now to remember how when we were in Belgium everyone had gone about repeating the parrot cry, "Namur est imprenable" (just as they had said "Les forts de Liége tiennent, et ils tiendront toujours"), when, except inside the girdle of the forts, it was not protected by a single earthwork of any value. The confidence of the French in Belfort was better founded. The commanders of the garrison had learnt very early in the war that forts, to be of any use in modern warfare, must themselves be flanked, as golf-architects guard their greens, with an interminable network of bunkers. Acting on that principle they had constructed a position of such formidable strength that not even the German generals, who had shown such a complete disregard of losses in their advance after Charleroi, would be likely to face the huge waste of life which a frontal attack on the Vosges fortress would have entailed.

A year has passed since then, and instead of getting nearer to it they are miles further back than the place where Lieutenant Mayer met his death. Pfetterhausen and Montreux Vieux and Dannemarie and a good slice of Alsace are still in the hands of the French, and the siege of Belfort (unless the enemy try the desperate expedient of a flanking movement through Switzerland) is more unlikely than ever. So confident are the authorities of their security that most of the civil inhabitants who had been evacuated at the time of our first visit have now been allowed to return, and the life of the town is becoming almost normal again. That is a healthy sign. It is one of the numerous proofs that the apparent deadlock at the front is really a signal victory for the Allies. For it means that for all their carefully prepared organization and their calm disregard of the conventions of war by which the other nations consider themselves bound, the original plans of the enemy have broken down. The cupolas of the forts of Belfort, which were to have been so easily crushed, are still intact; their guns have not yet fired a shot, except at aeroplanes. As in 1870, no German soldier has set foot within its walls. Its famous lion is still a lion *couchant*.

Just before starting on our way back to Dijon we paid a visit to M. Goublet, the Civil Governor and Préfet of the Territoire de Belfort (who has rejoined his old service, the Navy, and is now in command of a small cruiser), another warm friend and admirer of England and *The Times*. During the war M. Goublet and all his fellow-préfets of the border provinces have been most valuable servants of the State. No men in France, except perhaps the ministers and the great chiefs of the army, have had heavier responsibilities on their shoulders or more anxious duties to perform, and no account of the way in which France has faced the invader can be anything like complete which does not give some idea of their share in the common work.

We have nothing in England that corresponds to the office of the French prefect, who, as the direct representative of the Government in his Department, plays a very important part in the civil administration of the country. The eighty-six Departments, each governed by its Prefect, are divided into sub-districts under the sous-préfets, and the sub-districts into Communes or Mayoralties. The Mayor, as with us, is a municipal officer, and looks after only what concerns his own commune, which is called, in the case of the big towns, an Arrondissement. In his Department the Prefect is supreme. Every civilian official in it—the Sous-Préfets, the Mayors and their subordinates, and all the minor officers of the State, such as the gendarmerie and the special police commissaires whom he controls himself—is under his orders. He is saluted not only by all these civilian officials and employés, but by the officers and soldiers of the army. He ranks with the Generals commanding army-corps, and in time of peace even takes precedence of them. When a new General comes into a Department he calls on the Prefect, and by him is introduced to the civil authorities, and in the same way all the official calls on New Year's Day are paid first to the Préfecture. Even in time of war, because the State is greater than its army, it is only in strictly military matters that the Generals in his Department are his superiors. Thus a proclamation by a General to the people can only be issued through the Prefect and over his signature, and he has the power, subject of course to the General's right of appeal to the Généralissime and the Minister of War, to refuse to sanction any decree affecting the civil population which the military authority might wish to enforce. There has been one striking instance of the exercise of this power during the present war. By an agreement between the Prefect and the Military Governor the population of an important town near the frontier were evacuated in the early days when it appeared very probable that it would be besieged by the Germans. After a time, as nothing happened and all fear of an investment seemed to be at an end, the inhabitants began gradually to come back, and no notice was taken of their return till suddenly the Military Governor issued a second proclamation, without consulting the Prefect, ordering them once more to leave the town. To this the Prefect objected, on the ground that his sanction had not been asked. He announced that they might stay, and the action which he had taken was upheld by the Minister of the Interior.

The Prefect, therefore, acts either as the channel, or (if he thinks it necessary), as the barrier between the military authorities and the people of his Department, and is therefore a standing safeguard against the militarism, which, according to some English critics, is bound to arise in a country which has a "conscript" army. The mere fact of the existence of the office, with its extraordinary powers, is a sufficient guarantee that in France the militarism of which these people make a bugbear can never make any real headway.

Amongst his other duties the Prefect is responsible for the care of the main roads and State monuments (such as cathedrals) in his Department; for the holding of *Conseils de Révision* (the periodical assemblies of the young men of the nation, at which they are finally examined, in classes dependent on the year of their birth, to see if they are physically and mentally fit for service in the army); for the provisioning and lighting of the towns and villages in his district; and for the control of the Press, or what is commonly termed the censorship, which, in time of war, he exercises jointly with the military authorities. In the invaded districts the importance of each of these several duties is obvious, and no praise can be too high for the way in which they have been carried out, all along the battle-line from Belfort to Briey, by M. Goublet (Territoire de Belfort), M. Linarès (Vosges), M. Léon Mirman (Meurthe et Moselle), M. Aubert (Bar le Duc) and the sous-préfets of Lunéville, Toul, and Briey, M. Minier, M. Mage, and M. Magre. To the sorely tried people under their charge these men have set a fine example of unity, hard work, self-sacrifice, confidence, and courage, with a leaven of the less ornamental virtue of common-sense. They have unflinchingly carried out the often risky work of visiting, as soon as the enemy was driven back from one position after another, the burnt and ruined villages which he left behind him. They have been the stand-by of the brave mayors who have stuck to their posts in the hour of danger, they have cheered the wounded in the hospitals, they have cared for the homeless and destitute refugees, and they have stimulated and encouraged the whole population by giving them a true and lofty ideal of what the war means for France and the world, and of the way in which Frenchmen and French women and children should face its perils and its inevitable sufferings and distress. And—*si parva licet componere magnis*—those of them whom we have been fortunate enough to know have been exceedingly kind and helpful to two grateful journalists from London.

Woelflin, Nancy, phot.

M. LEON MIRMAN, PREFECT OF MEURTHE ET MOSELLE.

At this particular moment, however, it was the military, rather than the civil authorities, who were able to help us on our way. By the *service de renseignements*, or military intelligence department, at Belfort, we were given a special pass to go to Nancy by way of Dijon and Chalindrey (the direct route by Epinal being impossible), and when we got back to Dijon General Brissaud himself *viséd* our passports for the same destination.

Armed with these double credentials we started from Dijon on what in ordinary times is a journey of six hours, instead of which it took us from three o'clock in the afternoon till half-past eight next morning. The first big check was at Chalindrey, close to Langres, where we had a three hours' wait during which we saw two interesting little sidelights on the war. In those days all station-restaurants had been taken over for the use of the army, and as we were not allowed to stay on the platform or to sit in the train, we thought at first that we should have to kick our heels till midnight in the station yard. It was a dark and chilly prospect. However, by the help of a friendly private and persistent knocking at a back door, we did at last force our way into the refreshment room, and on the strength of being English were allowed to order some supper. While we were eating it a taciturn sergeant demanded our papers and carried them off into the outer darkness. Then there was a long pause. We waited and waited, each moment getting more and more afraid that they were not going to get us through after all, when the door opened and out of the *ewigkeit*, nearly two hundred miles from the nearest English troops, two Red Cross Tommies, an Australian and a Lanarkshire miner, walked into the room. They were under the escort, not to say the arrest, of the Station Commandant, who wanted to confront them with us to see if the story they told was true. It was, as a matter of fact, rather lame. They said that after the Battle of the Marne they had lost the rest of their detachment somewhere near Compiègne, and being tired of hospital work were trying to reach the front, in the hope of being allowed to do some fighting. Whether they were deserters or not they certainly had their full share of Scotch and Australian mother-wit, or they could never have got so far without being arrested. Three months later, by some miracle, for they spoke no French and had only their ordinary soldiers' passes, they turned up in Nancy, still on their own, and were taken to Toul, this time, I believe, under close arrest. As they were the unconscious means of doing us a good turn, I rather hope that they were not impostors, and that they were not too hardly dealt with. Hearing me talking to them, a French officer, Commandant Chesnot of the 360th Regiment of the Reserve, introduced himself as an ardent admirer of England, and invited us to make the rest of the journey in the reserved carriage which he shared with another officer. They were old schoolfellows belonging to the same regiment, who had been knocked over by the same shell three weeks before at Réméréville, and were now returning to duty, still limping from the effect of their wounds. Like every wounded French officer and soldier whom we met, their one idea was to get out of the surgeon's hands and back again to the front as soon as possible. It was lucky for us that they were so keen.

At Toul, where we had to wait for another three hours, we sat with them in the waiting-room reserved for soldiers, instead of being herded with the civilian crowd next door, and from Champigneul, beyond which no passenger trains had been running for some time, we travelled as their friends in one of the familiar trucks built to accommodate forty men or eight horses, sitting on bundles of sacking filled with the disinfected uniforms of dead soldiers. Since the service had been suspended at the beginning of the war, we were, I believe, the first civilians who made their entry into Nancy by train.

CHAPTER VI
ÉTAT-DE-SIÈGE IN NANCY

Our start in Nancy was not encouraging. We reported ourselves first at the Place, the military headquarters of the town, and were ushered by mistake into the room of an officer (we never knew his name), who was not the Military Governor, and was just packing up to go elsewhere. Therefore he said he could do nothing for us himself, though he had had friendly relations with Printing House Square, and he much doubted whether any one would give us leave to stay in the town for more than a night. The only General who possibly might was, according to him, a strong stern man who had a rooted objection to journalistic enterprise, and he earnestly advised us to keep out of his way. So we went off to lunch, in rather low spirits—and sat down at the next table to a third General, who looked particularly human and friendly. He was, the waiter informed us in a whisper, General de la Massellière, the Commandant d'Armes, and in about two minutes M. Lamure had introduced himself and me and explained our business, and we had received a polite invitation to present ourselves and our credentials at the *Place* at two o'clock. By a quarter-past we had a *permis de séjour* for one night, next day it was extended to four nights (with the understanding that we must go at once if the enemy resumed their abortive bombardment of the 9th), a day or two afterwards it was prolonged "till further notice," and eventually we stayed for four months.

Our second visit was to the Préfet, M. Mirman, and our third to the Mayor, M. Simon, and, thanks to the warm welcome which they gave us, we went to bed that first night hoping for the best and feeling that we had already made three very good friends.

Both M. Mirman and M. Simon were appointed to their posts *ad hoc* on the outbreak of hostilities, and Meurthe et Moselle and Nancy very soon found out that they had got the right men in the right places. M. Mirman had served his time in the ranks of the army as a Chasseur-à-pied, while he was the Député for Reims and still a very young man, and was known in his constituency and Paris as the *député soldat*. Before the war he was *Directeur de l'Assistance Publique* in Paris, at the Ministry of the Interior, but resigned that post when fighting began in order to get as near to the front as possible. At Nancy he had his wish even without leaving the Préfecture. During part of August and September it was only five miles from the German lines, and just near enough to the Cathedral, supposing that the bombs of the enemy airmen missed one of their favourite targets by a short hundred yards, to be one of the danger-spots of the town. Madame Mirman came with him to Lorraine, and was followed soon afterwards by her daughters, all under twenty, and her young son. Their presence in Nancy greatly helped M. Mirman in a very important part of his work as Prefect. Apart from the compassionate services which they rendered to the wounded and the refugees, the mere fact of their being there was a constant encouragement to the townspeople in the dark and critical days at the beginning of the war. It meant, presumably, that the Prefect thought that the apparently imminent danger would be averted, or at least that he expected them not to run away from it. As a matter of fact, except the Post Office employés, who bolted in a body (I believe in obedience to orders), surprisingly few of the Nancéiens did run away, either after the Germans had rained shells on the town for an hour at the end of the fierce battle which poured streams of wounded into its hospitals day and night for three weeks, or later on when they had come to look upon Taubes and Aviatiks as a sort of gratuitous cinema show, and had further been roused from their sleep on Christmas Eve by the first Zeppelin that ever dropped bombs on an open town.

Dufey, Nancy, phot.

M. SIMON, MAYOR OF NANCY.

The people of Nancy, like all Lorrainers and all border-races, are by nature a hard-plucked breed. Their fathers and their fathers' fathers before them for many generations have stood in the great gap of western Europe and fought for their liberty against Huns and Romans and Germans and half a dozen other tribes and nations, till war and all its ghastly consequences have been burnt into their bones. They come, therefore, of a fighting stock, and it was to be expected that they would show a brave front to the enemy. But for all that it was largely owing to the example of M. Mirman and M. Simon (a true Nancéien, who looks like a fighter all over, and was unanimously chosen by his municipal colleagues as the right man to be Mayor of Nancy in time of war) that the town kept its head and its *bonne humeur* through the anxious weeks when the enemy was pounding at its gates.

When we arrived there were still gaping holes in the houses that had been struck by the German shells, and every here and there heaps of broken glass and timber and masonry piled up on the pavement. All through the day convoys of prisoners and long columns of marching troops, horse, foot, and guns, and strings of carts and ambulances, carrying provisions, ammunition and wounded men, were constantly passing through the streets. At night, like Belfort, Epinal, Commercy, Toul, and Verdun, the town was in complete darkness, and hardly a soul was stirring. And all day and all night there was the sound of the guns, rumbling and roaring with monotonous regularity. Every few seconds the thunder of them kept breaking out, dull, angry, and continuous, pressing with leaden weight on one's ears and head, like the banging of a furious wind roaring down a gaping chimney. You heard it as you went to sleep, you heard it whenever you woke up in the night and the first thing in the morning, and you heard it all day long. And after a time you took no notice of it. You heard it less than the rattle of the tramcars, except when it burst into particularly furious claps, and then you turned to your neighbour and said, "Ça tape," and went on with what you were doing. But in spite of it all—the noise of battle and the sad and stirring sights of the wounded and the soldiers, the shattered roofs, the war proclamations on the walls and the war-pictures and war-accoutrements (even to a suit of chain armour) in the shop windows—it was difficult to believe that the enemy were so close and that actually as well as technically Nancy might at any moment be in a state of siege. For apparently the life of the place, except for the wounded and the number of women who were dressed in black, was very little different from the normal life of an ordinary garrison town. The streets were crowded and lively, the tramcars were running, and motor-cars dashing about in all directions; the shops and cafés were open, and though most people looked thoughtful, no one was gloomy. Every one had his share of the common work to do, and did it cheerfully and unselfishly. Come what might, they would not despair of the Republic. Come what might, they felt that they were going to win, because their cause was just and God would defend the right. Above all, they were a united people. Soldiers and citizens, governors and governed, were all one. At the Préfecture, at the Place, at the Mairie, in the Press, there was only one spirit and only one aim—to sink all differences and jealousies and work shoulder to shoulder for France and for freedom. There was no question of one authority setting himself up against another; the times were too serious. Party feeling was dead—or peradventure it slumbered. State and Church had buried the hatchet. No one talked or thought of politics except to hope and believe that the politicians in Paris would continue to preserve the peace.

All the time we were in Lorraine I never once heard a soldier or a Churchman or a freethinker or an editor or a politician of any complexion say a word about his personal political views. For all I knew from the men themselves they might have had none; except by inference it was impossible to tell what they were. The war and the common danger had wrought a miracle. France had been born again, and the watchwords of Liberté, Egalité, and above all Fraternité, were become lifegiving spiritual facts.

We did not grasp all this the first day we were in Nancy, though we felt it, for it was in the air. But little by little we began to know the people, largely owing to the kind offices of M. Mirman, M. Slingsby, the President of his council, and other members of his staff. The Press we met in a body twice at the Préfecture, once at a dinner given in honour of our own newspaper and England, and once when we were all formally presented to M. Viviani. For each of us the then Prime Minister had a ready and graceful remark. "*Le Times*," he said to me, "est toujours si bien renseigné"—possibly, I think, with a little touch of self-consciousness. For no one knew better than he the restrictions under which the Press had suffered, in its quest of information, during the war. The five excellent newspapers which supply the needs of Nancy's 100,000 inhabitants—*L'Est Republicain, l'Eclair de l'Est, l'Etoile de l'Est, l'Impartiale*, and the *Journal de la Meurthe*—have been particularly severely treated. There have been times when their editors have not been allowed to announce even the fact of some local incident (such as the visit of the Zeppelin, which was naturally known at once to every one in the town) till the news had been published in the Paris newspapers and telegraphed back to Nancy. Often they have suffered the mortification of being forbidden to say things which could not possibly have given information to the enemy and would certainly have been of real service to the community. But their loyalty has never wavered. Like the rest of the Lorraine world they have put their country and the need for unity before everything else, and have done excellent service to the State, not only in keeping before their readers the sufferings and necessities of the wounded, the refugees, and other victims of the war in the town, but in holding up to every one a lofty ideal of patience and courage.

More obvious in the streets than the work of the Nancy press, because nothing is more conspicuous than the Red Cross flag, was the work of the Nancy hospitals. In the early days of the war the arrangements for picking up and bringing in the wounded were to a large extent inadequate and primitive. We talked with many French soldiers who, during the great battle in front of Nancy, lay on the field for two, three, and even four days without food or water, suffering from their wounds, before the ambulance men could come to their assistance. That was largely the fault—or the crime—of the Germans, who often lay hid in the woods commanding the scene of a recent fight and fired on every man lying there who stirred a limb as well as on the stretcher-bearers who tried to carry the wounded away. When at last those who were still alive could be got at, large numbers of them had to be carried to the hospitals in clumsy rickety country waggons, the jolting of which, to men in their condition, was almost past endurance. A large proportion of the deaths which took place in the hospitals were due to one or both of these causes—the days and nights of exposure on the battlefield, and the long-drawn-out torture of the slow journey to the rear—and some of the men who survived them both told me that for sheer agony of suffering the second was the harder to bear. Nowadays that has been altered. In the summer of 1915 I saw near Commercy some English motor-ambulances sent to supplement the French Red Cross service at the front, which, for arrangement and comfort and swiftness, were as good as anything to be found. But in the early days there is no question that the provision for the transport of the wounded from the field was painfully deficient.

In Nancy itself full preparations had been made from the beginning. Besides the regular hospitals a large number of supplementary establishments were organized by the Union des Femmes de France, the Commission Municipale des Hospices, the Société des Secours aux Blessés, and other more or less temporary agencies of the Red Cross. The Union des Femmes de France in particular showed praiseworthy forethought. Soon after the fighting began they had twenty or more temporary hospitals in working order in Nancy and the surrounding towns, and also provided a motor convoy for collecting the wounded, which was quickly taken off their hands by the Army Medical Service. All of these hospitals were arranged in buildings temporarily converted from other uses. The most important of them, wonderfully well supplied with everything needed by the wounded, were those administered by M. Lespines, in the Lycée Poincaré, and by General Schneider and his wife and some of their friends from Paris, in a training-school for teachers.

In the two big permanent hospitals, the Military and the Civil, the arrangements, at all events to my nonprofessional eye, appeared to be perfect. The first is probably one of the best equipped hospitals in Europe. There is plenty of cubic space and plenty of air in its long, well-lighted corridors and roomy wards. Storerooms of all kinds, pharmaceutical, bacteriological, and chemical laboratories, radiograph rooms, operating rooms, baths, laundries, kitchens, disinfecting chambers—everything that is necessary for the care and the cure of the wounded and the sick—have their appointed place, and are furnished with the best appliances that surgical and scientific skill can devise. When I visited the hospital the members of the regular military staff who work there in time of peace had gone to the front. Among the men who had taken their places were some of the foremost physicians and surgeons of the city. Some of them belonged to Nancy's own famous school of medicine, some came from Paris and other headquarters of science in different parts of the country, and all of them, whether they were mobilized or had volunteered their services, had become part of the military organization of the State, and were freely giving for the benefit of the wounded and of generations yet unborn the fruits of their life experience as civilian doctors. In the Civil Hospital, since the war began a civil hospital in name only, another wonderfully well-equipped and well-officered institution, there was everywhere the same spirit of devotion and self-sacrifice for the good of the nation and the same high level of surgical and scientific attainment among the members of the staff.

Of the sisters of mercy and the nurses in all these hospitals, also in very many cases volunteers, it would be difficult to speak too highly. The loving care with which they tend and mother the wounded—"mes garçons" they call them—and the grateful affection with which they are rewarded by their patients, are unspeakably touching. I was never in one of the Nancy hospitals during the trying time—far more exacting for the nurses than any operation—when the men's wounds are being dressed and the agonized cry of some sufferer will sometimes spread its infecting example from bed to bed through almost a whole ward. But no one who has seen at ordinary times the fortitude and cheerfulness with which the French bear their sufferings and talk of their wounds and of the day when they will be able to get up and go to fight again for their beloved country could ever forget the sight of those rows of quiet beds, so different from the wards in an ordinary hospital. There were no horrible diseases, nothing repulsive or unclean, nothing that is the result of decay and sin. A few hours or days or weeks before these weak and helpless sufferers had been young and strong and vigorous, the physical pick of the manhood of France. Now, when they were not talking or reading or smoking, they lay with closed eyes and uncomplaining wistful faces or looked at one like dumb animals with a marvellous inarticulate patience that seemed to ask what it all meant, and why, when diplomatists differ and nations go to war, it is their poor bodies that have to pay the price.

War and wounds certainly have the effect of putting the human body in its right place and of doing away with all the false shame and prudery with which we are so apt to surround it. When these thousands of men are well and strong again—or as well and strong as they can ever be—it hardly seems possible that they can ever forget the frank purity of their sweet-faced, tender-handed nurses and sisters of mercy, or the lessons of the dignity of the body and of life which they have unconsciously learnt from them.

One day I saw some of the sisters kneeling in the little chapel in the grounds of the Civil Hospital. The choir was singing some kind of a litany, the burden of which was the words "Sauvez la France," repeated over and over again. It was one of those days when the sound of the guns, from some trick of the wind, as well as from their actual nearness, was more than usually loud, and each time that the three words of the prayer rang out through the open door of the chapel they were followed without a moment's pause by the booming roar of the heavy shells. And of the two, the cannon that had shattered their limbs or the kneeling women who had soothed and tended them, there was not, I think, much doubt in the minds of the wounded men who were well enough to sit about in the sunny courtyard outside the chapel as to which was the finer force—and the stronger.

THE
FRENCH FRONTIER
FROM
VERDUN TO THE VOSGES.

CHAPTER VII
THE FRENCH OFFENSIVE

There is no denying the importance of the German territorial gains in Belgium and France, even with the smaller acquisitions of the French in Haut Alsace as a set-off. But the effect which they will have on the final results of the war has been much exaggerated, not only by the Germans, but by the States which call themselves neutral, the wavering small Powers in the Balkans, and our own faint-hearted pessimists at home. All of these people habitually forget or ignore that practically the whole of this advantage was gained in the first month of the war, and that since then the tide has hardly ever stopped flowing, however slowly, the other way. Once the immediate effects of the first surprise shock had spent themselves and the war had settled down into its long-distance stride, it was the Allies who, army for army, proved themselves the better men. Other things being equal—and what inequality is likely to arise in the future is in our favour—the conclusion is that little by little the enemy will inevitably be driven to his own side of the frontier which he has violated and invaded. If before that time comes there is any serious talk of peace proposals and neutral intervention, based on the relative positions of the combatants on the western front, it will be difficult for the would-be peacemakers to go on ignoring all that has happened since the first month of the war.

Looked at from this point of view, the offensive in Alsace and Lorraine, with which the campaign on the eastern frontier opened, was not the mistake which it was considered at the time by many of General Joffre's French and English and German critics. France could not in honour invade her great neighbour to the north of Longwy, because of the neutral barriers of Luxembourg and Belgium. But to the south of that point, or at least south of the obstacle of Metz and its defences, she could and did. Along the line where the frontiers of France and Germany march there were no considerations of loyalty to treaty obligations to deter her from attacking instead of waiting to be attacked. And that was the course on which General Joffre decided. His offensive was twofold. The advance north of the barrier of the Vosges failed. But south of them, in front of the Trouée de Belfort, intersected by the Rhine-Rhone canal and the tributaries of the Doubs and the Ill, it so far succeeded that the scene of action has remained ever since in the enemy's country. The consequent moral and strategical gains to France are enormous. The position of the Germans would have been infinitely better than it was (even without taking into account the possibility of a consequent further advance) if they had been able to dig the almost stationary line of trenches which they have occupied since the middle of September, 1914, in the soil of France instead of in the Sundgau.

After the French had mobilized their armies, their great difficulty was that they could not be sure where to expect the main attack. For many years the military experts and prophets of both countries had asserted confidently that it would come by way of Belgium; on the other hand, it was a traditional belief of the great mass of the French public that it would be made through Lorraine. Both routes were possible, both had to be taken into account, but to a certain extent, from a lingering belief in Germany's honour as well as out of deference to the popular expectation (which, on sentimental and political grounds the French Government could hardly afford to ignore), greater provision was made for resisting the possible invasion on the eastern frontier than further north.

It came, as a matter of fact, by both routes at once, but of the two main assaults, which culminated at Charleroi and Nancy on the same day, the more important and dangerous was that delivered in Flanders, where the French had relatively the smaller defensive force.

In the north the first meeting between the French and German armies did not take place till August 15th at Dinant. In the east they were in continual contact from the first day of the war. At first, in this sector of the front, things went well for our allies. In front of the three great fortresses of Belfort, Epinal, and Toul, the vanguards of three armies began at once to strike towards the frontier, the first into Alsace, by the plain of the Sundgau, the second through the passes of the Vosges, and the third across the boundary river, the Seille, into the flat country between the Vosges and Metz.

On the exposed part of the frontier guarded by these armies the opening period of the war lasted for three weeks. At the end of that time, on August 24th, the French were in apparently desperate straits. Their extreme left was driven back at Charleroi, in the centre they were just beginning, with a defeated army, the defence of Nancy, and on the right they had been obliged by the imminent danger on the left, to withdraw their forces from Mulhouse for the second time. But up till then, or at least till the disaster at Morhange on August 20th, they had on the Eastern sector done much better than they probably expected. The Verdun army, though not strong enough to adopt an effectively vigorous offensive, had been able to keep the enemy from attacking its forts, and south of Metz the commands of de Castelnau and Dubail had advanced well into German territory.

In the Metz, Verdun, Longwy triangle, bisected by the valley of the Orne running directly east from Verdun to the Moselle, the fighting was at first not very important. Conflans, Maugiennes, Spincourt, and several other towns and villages were early victims of German savagery, both sides scored moderate local successes, and the net result was that the enemy secured no advantage except what was due to their surprise invasion of the strip of territory from which the French withdrew their troops on the eve of the war. They would have advanced further and more quickly (as they confidently expected to do) but for two unforeseen obstacles. In the first place, there was the Verdun field-force, which, instead of falling back under the protection of its forts, persisted in coming out into the open; in the second, there was Longwy. Its defender, Colonel Darche, had only one battalion under his command, and consequently was not strong enough to follow the example of the Verdun field-army. But with his slender force he could and did hold up a whole German army till August 27th, three weeks after the Crown Prince had arrogantly summoned him to surrender. That officer's failure to take the town at the first time of asking was a bitter disappointment to the Germans, as his army was intended to form the connecting-link between the two great offensives through Belgium and Lorraine, and orders had actually been given to German reservists to report themselves at Verdun in the second week of August. It was the first of the many misfortunes which have since dogged his footsteps, and it is not surprising that it brought him into disfavour with his Imperial father. For the heroic resistance of Longwy, like the defence of Liége and of Nancy, was one of the determining incidents of the early part of the war.

In the meantime, while Verdun and Longwy were proving that "its dogged as does it," to the south of them the characteristic *élan* of the French troops was having its fling from the Moselle to Mulhouse, along a front of over a hundred miles. The strengthening of the forces in this region and the consequent weakening of the armies on the Belgian frontier was partly, as I have said, due to political considerations. But there were also sound military reasons for this distribution of the available forces, and for the subsequent French offensive in Alsace and Lorraine. For forty-four years the garrison and field armies of the rival pairs of fortresses—Verdun and Metz, Toul and Saarburg, Epinal and Strassburg—had been waiting like kennelled watchdogs, ready, once they were let loose, to fly at one another's throats. Primarily the French troops were intended not for attack—which was the German *métier*—but for defence. Both by training and tradition they were the frontier force of the Republic. In time of peace they held the post of honour on the vulnerable border-line between Luxembourg and the Swiss frontier, always ready for war, as their ancestors before them had been for generations. Most of the best generals of France had served their apprenticeship in one of these famous frontier army corps, and ever since 1870 officers and men, nearly all of them children of the soil, had been bound more and more closely together, at first by the war-cry of *la revanche*, and later by the nobler feeling that, when the threatened and expected invasion came, the task and the glory of repelling it would be theirs. They were the flower of the French army, and they looked upon the post of honour as their birthright.

When the blow fell at last there were several reasons which justified General Joffre in using them for purposes of offence instead of in the *rôle* which French and Germans alike expected of them. Being a soldier and not a politician, he realized that he could not afford to wait and see. It was a clear gain that his action should be the exact opposite of what the Germans looked for. They were so overwhelmingly sure of their military superiority that they practically counted on a walk-over. Besides Verdun, other towns far behind the line of the frontier fortresses, such as Besançon and Dijon, were the appointed rendezvous at an early date in August of the German soldiers who could not be ready to join the colours at the outset, and even the officials who were to have governed these towns after their expected conquest had received their commissions well in advance of the declaration of war. The Kaiser and his advisers had made the common mistake of despising the enemy they were sent to attack. Both in *morale* and in men the armies of the east proved far stronger than they had expected.

The consequent upsetting of their original plan of campaign was in itself a strong vindication of General Joffre's policy. But he had another object in view. The first point was to have enough troops on the eastern frontier to prevent the Germans from breaking through the line of fortresses. The second—no less important, once the march through Belgium had begun—was to keep a large part of the enemy's forces busily employed at a distance from the northern theatre of operations. That was the reason and the justification of the offensive in Alsace and Lorraine.

Up to a point this forward movement of the French was successful. From Metz the frontier runs south-east for about sixty miles, up the valley of the river Seille, to the Donon, a mountain just over 3000 feet high at the north end of the Basses Vosges, and from there, a trifle west of south along the crests of the range and across the Trouée of Belfort for about the same distance to Pfetterhausen on the Swiss frontier. The Vosges half of this line, practically parallel with the course of the Rhine, is divided into three sections, from the Donon to the Climont (12 miles), from the Climont to the Col de Schlucht (20 miles), and from the Col de Schlucht to the Ballon d'Alsace (18 miles).

In the northern section the range is broken by the valley of the Bruche, commanded from the north by the Donon, which runs from south-west to north-east past Saales and Schirmeck towards Strassburg.

In the central section, steep on the French side, but on the east sloping gently down to the valley of the Ill, the chief passes are Ste. Marie aux Mines and the Col du Bonhomme, with a narrow wooded crest seven miles long at an average altitude of 3000 feet between them.

In the southern section the slope is easier on the French side and more abrupt on the east, and besides the Col de Schlucht the chief pass is the Col de Bussang. The summit and eastern slopes of the range command, of course, an uninterrupted view across the plain to the Rhine, about fifteen miles from the foothills. Strassburg is a little lower down the Rhine than the level of the Donon. Colmar lies about the centre of the plain, midway between the level of the Col du Bonhomme and the Col de Schlucht, and nearly all the towns which have so far played a part in the war are in or on a level with the third section—Munster, Guebweiler, Soulty, St. Amarin, and Thann in the Vosges valleys between the Schlucht and the Ballon d'Alsace, and the rest—Cernay, Dannemarie, Altkirch, Mulhouse, and Pfetterhausen—south of the Ballon in the plain opposite to the Trouée of Belfort, which is called the Sundgau.

It was intended that the French offensive should be carried out along the whole of this frontier line south of Metz, but especially in the plains north and east of the Vosges. The Belfort army was to advance into Alsace, occupy Mulhouse, cut the bridges of the Rhine below Basle (at Huningue, Neuenburg, and Vieux Brisach) and flank the main advance of the first and second armies in Lorraine.

In spite of their various acts of trespass on French territory before the declaration of war, the Germans at first showed little activity. Beyond the abortive attempt to recapture Montreux-Vieux, in the Belfort district, practically all they did was to shell and occupy Blamont, Cirey, Badonviller, and Baccarat, four small towns close to the frontier and almost midway between the Donon and Lunéville, on August 5th, 6th, and 8th, and to bombard Pont-à-Mousson, an unfortunate town on the Moselle fifteen miles below Nancy and the same distance above Metz, which since then has been shelled more than two hundred times, but, except for one short period, has always remained in the hands of the French.

Our Allies were much more energetic, and the advance in Lorraine, the Vosges, and Alsace was begun with wonderfully little delay. Of these three theatres of war in the east the third, the country between Strassburg and the Swiss frontier, cut off from the rest of Germany by the Rhine and the Black Forest, is strategically of great importance. Its western boundary, the chain of the Vosges, is the pivot of the long line of the French defence stretching from Dunkerque to Belfort, and on its stability depends the security of the whole of the rest of the front. In order to make that stability absolutely sure the French had to hold, besides the chain itself, at least a part of the plain of Alsace, including especially its natural bastion, the Sundgau.

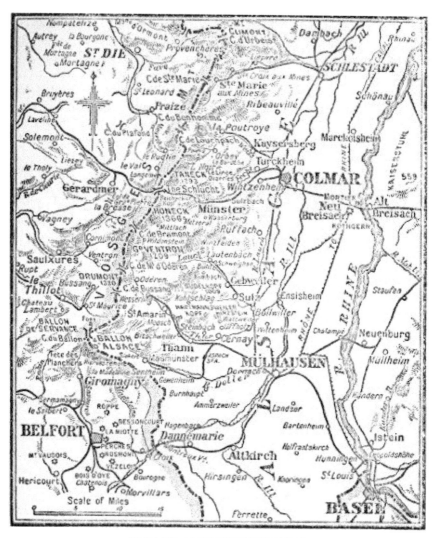

ALSACE AND THE VOSGES.
(By kind permission of *The Times*.)

The Sundgau, which is the part of Alsace to the south of Cernay, is divided by the Rhone-Rhine canal into two regions, the physical aspects, geological structure, and tactical value of which are essentially different. The country to the south of the canal, known as the Alsatian Jura, is thickly studded with rounded mammelons, like a nest of giant molehills, intersected by a series of irrigation canals, some of which are two or three yards wide and useful as lines of defence. The country, as a rule, is thinly populated, there are few isolated houses, and the villages are some distance apart. It is watered by three rivers, the Thalbach, the Ill, which flows northward from the Swiss frontier past Altkirch, Mulhouse, Colmar, and Strassburg to the Rhine, and the Largue. On the right bank of the Ill there is a light railway, constructed shortly before the war, running from Ferette to Altkirch, and on the left bank of the Largue an ordinary-gauge line, running from Porrentruy, just across the Swiss frontier, to Dannemarie. There would be a formidable risk of a German flanking movement by this approach on the fort of Lomont, to the south of Belfort, if it were not for the careful watch kept by the Swiss army on their frontier. The general character of the country is suitable for guerilla warfare, but not for operations on an extended scale. It has two main defensive positions against a French attack based on Belfort along the line Petit-Croix, Dannemarie, Altkirch, at Altkirch itself, and at Britzy-Berg. The first of these consists of a series of heights on the south of the spur of the Schweighof (Hill 381), and on the north of a ridge running in the direction of Heidwiller and the junction of the Ill and the Largue. The value of this position is especially great on the south-west side where it commands the important point at which the lines of communication converging on Altkirch meet and the defile in which lie the railway, the river Ill, and the main roads from Mulhouse and Basle. The Britzy-Berg position, three or four miles further north, near Illfurth, commands the whole of the surrounding country to a considerable distance nearly as far as Mulhouse, and also sweeps with its fire all the roads that meet at Altkirch. Both these positions had been strongly fortified by the Germans.

The part of the Sundgau north of the Rhine-Rhone canal is quite different from the Alsatian Jura. It is a rolling tableland, with gentler slopes and wider valleys, and the crests of the rises less wooded than to the south of the canal. The open country is more thickly populated and better suited for the movements of large bodies of troops. The main road from Belfort to Cernay and thence to Colmar runs across the middle of it, and at right angles to the road, west of Mulhouse, runs the Doller, a quick-flowing tributary of the Ill. Between this river and the Rhine-Rhone canal there is a wide, moderately-wooded plateau, in which the chief military position is at Galfingen, commanding the approach to Aspach, Mulhouse, and Altkirch on the Colmar road, to the south of the bridge of Aspach, where on some heights round the twin villages of Burnhaupt, the Germans had prepared a strong position overlooking the wide bare plain called the Ochsenfeld, between them and Cernay. East of the Ochsenfeld they had a second line of defence in the valley of the Thur (another tributary of the Ill, rising in the Vosges on the Rheinkopf and flowing down the valley of St. Amarin, past Thann and Cernay, a deep river with marshy banks, from fifteen to twenty yards wide). This line extended from the heights of Steinbach to the forest of Nonenbruck. It was in this country, on both sides of the Rhine-Rhone canal, that the French began their main advance into Alsace.

On Friday, August 7th, a French brigade arrived about eight o'clock in the evening in front of Altkirch, ten miles from the frontier, coming by Petit-Croix and Dannemarie. On the same day another detachment of French troops came down the valley of the Thur as far as Thann. The smallness of the combined force was perhaps accounted for (though it was not excused) by the fact that the French airmen had reported that the bulk of the German troops were on the other side of the Rhine, and that little opposition was to be expected between Mulhouse and the French frontier. Altkirch was at the time occupied by a German brigade of about equal strength, with their chief entrenchments south of the town, on the precipitous spurs of the Schweighof. A little higher up, towards the top of the hill, they had a battery of eight 77's and a number of mitrailleuses. These were quickly silenced by the French 75's, and the trenches were then carried by a surprise infantry attack which drove the Germans at the point of the bayonet off the Schweighof in disorderly flight. They were chased well past their second line of entrenchments on the Britzy-Berg, five miles further north in the direction of Illfurth and Mulhouse, by a dragoon regiment supporting the infantry, and a number of prisoners were taken before night put an end to the pursuit. Thus, three days after the declaration of war, at a total loss in killed and wounded of less than 150, Altkirch, after forty years in the wilderness of German domination, was once more in the hands of the French. The inhabitants received their long-hoped-for deliverance with every sign of frantic delight. The uprooted frontier-posts were carried in triumph through the flag-decked streets, flowers were rained on the heads of the triumphant troops, every one was cheering or in tears, and in the general tumult of joy and excitement no one apparently stopped to consider the remarkable ease with which the victory had been won or the extent of the guile which the retreat might possibly conceal.

CHAPTER VIII
OCCUPATIONS OF MULHOUSE

Encouraged by their success at Altkirch, the French set out early next morning for Mulhouse, ten miles further down the valley of the Ill. The troops which had descended the previous day on Thann also advanced by way of Cernay, and along the twelve-mile front between Thann and Altkirch the whole way to Mulhouse no trace of the Germans was seen except their deserted entrenchments. At one o'clock a small patrol of dragoons trotted up to the Hotel de Ville, and after a momentary halt clattered away again to report that not a single German soldier was left in the town. As a matter of fact, they were not, however, very far off, and the dragoons had hardly disappeared when a squad of Bavarian infantry marched into the principal square, seized a tramway car which was standing in front of the town-hall, and forced the driver to follow the dragoons, breaking the windows of the car as they went to make convenient rests for their rifles. By chance, however, they took the Brunstatt or south road out of the town, whereas the dragoons had gone west along the Dornach road, so that after a short and fruitless journey, they thought it wiser to turn back and join the main body on the further side of the town, once more leaving it empty of all but the civilian inhabitants, who by this time were in a state of the wildest excitement. After that there was another long wait till after six o'clock, and then, at last, a couple of platoons of dragoons and Chasseurs-à-cheval came riding in along the Dornach road, and the whole population turned out to greet them and the main body, which followed a quarter of an hour behind them, with the same extravagant manifestations of delight and enthusiasm as at Altkirch on the previous day.

That was on the Saturday evening, during which the French took up their position on the heights at Rixheim, about two miles east of the town, their front protected by the road and railway which curve down southwards to Basle, the Germans being a few miles north of them along the Rhone-Rhine canal towards Neu-Brisach and also in the Hardt (a big forest about twenty miles long between Mulhouse and the Rhine) on their right.

Next day, though some of the wiser of the townspeople were shaking their heads over the smallness of the French force, the rejoicings continued until the middle of the afternoon, when suddenly, between three and four o'clock, the guns on each side began firing, covering and resisting the advance of the XIVth German Army Corps, which was directed on Mulhouse through the Hardt Forest by the road from Mulheim and two other roads further north. The battle continued through the evening and all night till six o'clock on Monday morning. The artillery duel was at its height at about two a.m., and before that time a number of shells had fallen in the town, across which the batteries posted on the left flank of the French were firing. For the Germans the disadvantage of the position was that after leaving the shelter of the forest they had to advance for about two miles over an open plain, where they were exposed to the fire not only of the 75's on the heights of Rixheim, but of the French infantry on the slopes below them, and here they lost heavily. Their numbers were, however, so superior that they were able to press on without paying any attention to their losses, whereas the French, for the opposite reason, ran a great chance of being surrounded and cut off from their line of retreat on Belfort. They fought on, however, with much determination (at one time only the embankment of the railway to Basle separated the front lines of the two forces) till six o'clock in the morning, when, after a series of skirmishes in the streets of Mulhouse, they were finally withdrawn in good order and most fortunately were able to fall back on Belfort. They probably owed their escape to the fact that the German plans had not been carried out exactly as had been intended. Besides the XIVth Army Corps, the XVth were also to have joined in the attack, coming by train from Strassburg to Colmar, and from there down to Cernay, where they hoped to catch the French after they had been driven westwards by the XIVth. The only flaw in the execution of this scheme was that the XIVth started too soon and had finished their part of the work before the XVth arrived on the scene. At seven o'clock on the morning of Monday, August 10th, they marched into the town, and the French occupation—a dream the realization of which lasted for just thirty-six hours—was over.

Exactly what the intention of the French *haut-commandement* was I do not pretend to know, though it is improbable that they could have seriously contemplated the permanent occupation of an open town like Mulhouse, and any attempt at a further advance through the Hardt Forest on the strongly entrenched positions on each side of the Rhine with the inadequate forces at their disposal would have been madness. The probability is that the enemy, fully informed by some of the German-born Alsatians with whom the district swarmed of the pitiful smallness of the French army, deliberately fell back in the hopes of luring it on to destruction, while the French, on the other hand, intoxicated by the welcome which they had received and the ease with which they had marched twenty-five miles into the enemy's country in two days, thought of nothing but the moral triumph of the recapture of Mulhouse. They made their advance with far too small a force and much too quickly, and they neglected the vital precaution, all the more necessary because they were so few, of entrenching step by step the ground which they had won. At all events, we have it on the authority of the French Commander-in-Chief that the Alsace part of the offensive was badly carried out by the General Officer in charge of it, and that he was at once relieved of his command.

For the French, therefore, the net result of the first occupation of the town, beyond the temporary moral effect which it produced in France, was nil. For the loyalist inhabitants of Alsace it was the beginning of an organized system of terrorism by which the Germans, after burning the food and forage storehouses of Mulhouse when they left it on August 8th, endeavoured to create through the length and breadth of the country a paralyzing dread of the cruel weight of the mailed fist.

In Mulhouse itself the time that followed was also one of great hardship for many of the inhabitants. The enemy were furious at the welcome given to the French troops by the Alsatians (after forty-four years of the beneficent sway of the Fatherland), and they punished what they chose to consider their base and inexplicable ingratitude by treating all whom they suspected of French leanings in the true Savernian manner. To discover them was an easy matter. The two elements of the true Alsatians and the German colonists (whom the natives of the old French stock still persist in calling *immigrés*) have never really amalgamated, and the town was therefore thickly peopled with German sympathisers, only too eager to act as informers against their fellow-citizens.

But it was the foreigners resident in Mulhouse who at that time suffered the worst treatment at the hands of the enemy. Directly after the retreat of the French, several scores of them, men of all ages (from boys of fourteen to old men of over eighty) were peremptorily rounded up in the town barracks, and carried off to Germany as prisoners, leaving behind them practically all their possessions except the clothes in which they stood up. Before their departure, after they had been left for many anxious hours herded together without any food, they were suddenly told to form themselves into ranks, and the first batch were lined up, in front of some soldiers with loaded rifles, with their backs to the wall. Not unnaturally they concluded that they were to be shot, and some of them even gripped the hands of those standing near them in a last farewell. But it was only the torture of the anticipation of death, not death itself, that they were to suffer, though I suppose none of them will ever forget the time of agonized suspense that they went through before they were brusquely ordered by the officer in command to fall out, with the explanation that he had meant to show them exactly what would happen to them if they gave any trouble, and that now they knew. Afterwards, when they were on their way to their first prison-camp, one young fellow who had just married a girl-wife, who was forcibly torn away from his side, driven half crazy by his sufferings, made a feeble attempt at an assault on the guard, and was at once shot. The rest of them, after a long journey in cattle trucks, were kept in prison-camps in the interior of Germany for periods of varying length up to about six months, in many cases insufficiently fed and clothed, and as a rule it was the Englishmen among them who were the most harshly treated and set to do the most ignominious and disagreeable tasks. All of them during their journey east and on their arrival at Rastadt were constantly jeered at and insulted, not only by the populace, but by their guards.

Five days were enough to effect the reorganization of the force which had been forced to retire from Mulhouse, and on August 14th, this time under the command of General Pau, and strongly supported by the field army of the territory of Belfort, the French resumed the offensive. On that day Thann was taken for the second time, and with this place and Dannemarie and Guebwiller, a few miles further north, as his base, General Pau once more drove the enemy back on Mulhouse. But whereas on the previous occasion the main attack had been made from the south, by Altkirch, this time the advance was rather from west to east, with the left flank gradually swinging round from the north, with the object of cutting the Germans off from their line of retreat on the bridges of the Rhine and forcing them southwards towards the Swiss frontier. The French left was directed on Colmar (about twenty miles due north of Mulhouse) and Neu-Brisach, and the right wing on Altkirch, and advancing from west to east they quickly swept the enemy back on Mulhouse for the second time.

On the morning of August 19th the town was once more in a seething state of unrest and suppressed excitement. The loyalist inhabitants knew nothing of what was happening, except that the German soldiery were obviously ill at ease. Most of the crowd were collected in front of the chief hotel, where the soldiers kept pushing them back with their rifles in order to keep a clear passage for the strings of throbbing motor-cars which were ready waiting for the swarm of military and civil officials who kept hurrying backwards and forwards carrying the papers and valuables which were to accompany them in their flight to the Rhine. No policemen were to be seen. They were changing from their uniforms into mufti. Transformed into innocent-looking civilians, their service to the Fatherland was to stay behind in Mulhouse and keep their eyes open for such information as might be useful to the military chiefs, supposing that during the coming occupation the French succeeded in making good their footing in the town. An hour after the procession of cars had at last started, with intervals of a few yards between them, the barracks were clear and not a soldier was left in the town. Then there was a further long wait. The German agents and spies kept quiet and bided their time. The real Alsatians, the overwhelming majority of the townsfolk, were so wrought up with the feeling that they were rid of the Germans—this time as they hoped for ever—and so rapturously looking forward to the entry of the French troops, that nearly all of them went on standing about in the streets for hour after hour right through the day. They did not even go into their houses to eat their lunch, but bought what they could from enterprising street-merchants who went about with baskets of food, and ate it where they stood.

At last, at five o'clock, the first Frenchmen appeared, a handful of Chasseurs-à-cheval, who rode in not from the west, from which quarter they were expected, but by the Basle road at the other side of the town, where they must have passed dangerously close to the enemy. Like the patrol which had been the heralds of the first occupation, they were merely a scouting party, and, having established the fact that the Germans had retired, quickly rode off again to make their report to the Staff. The people, who had followed them in a body, then split up into two main detachments, and streamed out to Dornach and Brunstatt, on the Thann and Altkirch roads, the Germans having meanwhile massed their forces two or three miles to the east and south-east of the town, from which they were in full view, at Rixheim, Habsheim, and Zimmersheim close to the Basle railway, just about where the French had taken up their position after the first occupation.

This time, however, there was to be no triumphant entry—at least not as yet. The enemy meant to make a fight for it, and so far as that day, August 18th, was concerned, the faithful population of Mulhouse had had their long wait for nothing.

During the night a big change was made in the disposition of the German troops. From their lines on the Basle railway they advanced above and below the town till they occupied a position of considerably more than a semicircle round it from Pfastatt and Lutterbach on the north to Brubach, Brunstatt, and Hochstatt on the south, and some of them were even at Dornach, to the west of the town. The French line, which was much straighter, extended from Illfurth on the south, by Zillisheim and Morschweiler to Reichweiler on the north, where it slightly outflanked the German right at Pfastatt.

Early on the morning of the 19th the greater part of the German force in Dornach advanced to Lutterbach, and there was a general flight of the villagers, carrying their household goods and driving in front of them as much as they could of their cattle and even poultry. At ten o'clock the French batteries on the rising ground at Morschweiler opened fire, and the battle soon became general all along the line. All day long the artillery duel continued, and after a time the French gunners became so confident of their own superiority, and so indifferent to the bad shooting of the enemy, that they advanced into the open and worked their guns as calmly and with as little regard for cover as if they were engaged in ordinary training manœuvres in time of peace. All day long, too—for the fighting was at very close quarters—one hand-to-hand infantry engagement after another between two sets of men who fought with desperate dash and tenacity, resolved on the one hand to advance, on the other to stand firm, for the honour of their respective countries, caused a vast amount of bloodshed. On the left, near the big engineering works, commonly known as "The Red Sea," a body of French skirmishers advanced early in the engagement to within forty yards of a German company which was posted on the road in front, and killed and wounded half of them almost before they could reply. The rest fled to the shelter of the neighbouring houses, and there was a helter-skelter fight along the street, and in and out of doors and windows and gates and outhouses. Half of a battalion which was sent to support the routed men was wiped out by the artillery, and the other half refused to advance. A little further south, at Hochstatt, the 35th and 42nd French regiments suffered severely in the same way at the hands of the German gunners. In the afternoon, however, the 75's altogether dominated the guns opposed to them, their fire ceased, and except for stray rifle shots here and there, the battle seemed to be over, large numbers of the enemy having been driven to take refuge in Mulhouse.

One more effort was made, but it was their last. A strong body of reinforcements were sent out of the town, and, by using a large building which till then had been sacred to the Red Cross as a redoubt, managed to keep the fighting going on for some time longer. But driven out of this refuge by infantry and artillery fire, they were once more compelled to retire to Mulhouse. Soon afterwards Dornach, where the bulk of the fighting took place, was captured, and by five o'clock the French, having surrounded and captured twenty-four guns and a large number of prisoners in the outlying suburbs, entered the town for the second time in less than a fortnight. This time there was no question of the enemy having retired of their own free will in order to entice them to advance further than was prudent. They had been beaten fairly and squarely in one of the few pitched battles of the war, and were flying in confusion to the shelter of the Hardt Forest and the Rhine. It was a great moment for General Pau's army and for France, even though the engagement, compared with the events which were to take place in Lorraine and Belgium, was a comparatively small one. But unfortunately it was a moment that did not last. Twenty-four hours after France knew that the tricolour was once more floating in Mulhouse, it learnt also of the defeat at Morhange, and although there was no immediate connexion between Morhange and the evacuation of Mulhouse (only five days after its recapture), the gravity of the crisis on the more important fields further north completely out-shadowed the really considerable triumph in Alsace.

CHAPTER IX
MORHANGE

On the map the main ridge of the Hautes and Basses Vosges (and the boundary line of that part of the frontier) follows almost exactly the shape and position of a small manuscript "q." At the head of the curl of the "q" is the Donon, and at its lower curve the Col de Saales, with the town of St. Dié a trifle to the west of it.

Through the valley represented by the curl the river Bruche flows north-east past St. Blaise and Schirmeck, and then turns nearly due east past the fort of Mutzig, to Strassburg.

Following down the stroke of the "q," the principal passes, from north to south, crossed by roads which even the snows of winter do not often make impassable, are the Col de Sainte Marie aux Mines, the Col de Bonhomme, the Col de Schlucht (from near which the north branch of the river Fecht flows past Stossweiler to Munster), the Col de Bramont (from which the valley of the Thur descends past Wesserling and St. Amarin to Thann and Cernay), and the Col de Bussang, and at the southern extremity of the stroke is the Ballon d'Alsace.

Since the beginning of the war there has been a continuous series of violent struggles for the possession of nearly the whole of this string of important positions on the crests of the range. Some of them the French have gained and kept; some they have taken and lost, and then regained; some they have taken and lost, and not succeeded in recovering up to the present moment. They have always kept their footing secure on the summits of the southern part of the range from the Ballon d'Alsace to the Col de Schlucht. From the Col de Bonhomme and the Col de Sainte Marie aux Mines, which they captured at the beginning of the campaign, they were compelled to retire in the fourth week of August, 1914, but they recaptured these passes after the Battle of the Marne. The whole of the curl of the "q," from the Donon to the Col de Saales, and also the valley of the Bruche, which the French won and held for the first fortnight of the offensive, were then evacuated and have remained ever since in the hands of the enemy. All efforts to dislodge them from that sixteen-mile stretch of the frontier have failed, and their continued presence there has been and is a distinct nuisance to our Allies.

For the present, however, we are concerned only with the events which took place in this region during the successful opening of the French offensive, up to the Battle of Morhange, and the second retirement from Mulhouse. By August 7th, largely thanks to the effective fire of the Fort of Servance, on the north-west of the Ballon d'Alsace, our Allies were complete masters of the Ballon itself and of the Col de Bussang, five miles further north, and, as we have already seen, had sent a force down the valley of the Thur to Thann. By the evening of the 8th, they were astride the Bonhomme and Sainte Marie aux Mines passes, and by twelve o'clock next day, after a violent struggle which lasted all night, the town of Sainte Marie aux Mines was commanded by the fire of their guns. Almost at the same time another French column began a resolute attack on the Col de Saales. On August 12th, supported by a well-directed artillery fire which swept the rear of the German position, the infantry advanced impetuously to the attack, and the enemy retired from Saales in disorder, leaving behind them in the hands of the French four guns, a large amount of equipment, and eight hundred prisoners, most of them belonging to the 99th regiment of the line, which formed part of the garrison of Saverne and was brought into public notice shortly before the war by the exploits of the notorious Lieutenant Forstner.

Early the next morning the French followed up their attack by advancing in the valley of the Bruche in the direction of St. Blaise, where they were opposed by a strong German force consisting of the 99th and its sister corps the 132nd, two batteries of 77's, and one of field-howitzers, and a company of machine-guns. The engagement began with a brisk artillery combat, which resulted in the complete silencing of the enemy batteries by the shrapnel of the 75's. Most of the horses of the gun-teams and a large proportion of the artillerymen were killed, and the guns, deserted by the survivors, were taken by the French, practically undamaged. During the early part of the action some German machine-guns placed in the tower of the St. Blaise Church did a considerable amount of damage, but as soon as their position was discovered the 75's made short work of the tower and all it contained. Just before nightfall a battalion of French chasseurs—the 1st, I believe—charged the German positions with fixed bayonets and in half an hour had driven the enemy out and settled themselves down for the night in the captured trenches. Besides eight guns, four mortars, six mitrailleuses, ninety horses, and over five hundred men, the spoil included the colours of the 132nd Regiment, which were taken by a private of the 5th company of the Chasseurs battalion—the first trophy of the kind that was secured during the war. Among the many Germans killed was a general of division.

So far, with the exception of this last engagement, the fighting in the Vosges had mainly consisted of affairs of outposts, though the occupation of the passes was obviously a strategical gain of great importance. From August 15th onwards, though only for a few days, the offensive was pushed steadily forward in stronger force and a good slice of German territory was occupied. The possession of the Donon and the Col de Saales, commanding the valley of the Bruche, enabled the French to occupy Schirmeck, seven or eight miles north of Saales, while another column branched off to the right and took Villé on the road to Schlestadt. There was, in fact, a general advance along the valley of Bruche and the other valleys running down into the plain of Alsace. Prisoners and war material were captured in considerable numbers, in some places the plain itself was reached, and the chief difficulty of the officers was in restraining their men, who were quite unaffected by the losses which they had suffered, from going too far ahead.

I have already spoken of the voluntary evacuation by the French of the neutral zone along the frontier before the declaration of war. If it had not been for that political and pacific act of military self-abnegation, which, once hostilities began, carried with it the disadvantage that the enemy had to be dislodged from the passes before any advance was possible, the progress made would have been much greater. As it was, General Dubail's forces had got far enough forward (coupled with the second occupation of Mulhouse by General Pau) to become a possible menace to Strassburg, and the Germans, seriously alarmed by the prospect, hurriedly began to push forward reinforcements for their armies in Alsace. The first of these reinforcements advanced in the direction of Sainte Marie aux Mines, and the French advanced posts in Villé, confronted by greatly superior numbers, were obliged to fall back on the main body. Otherwise the positions remained practically unchanged—till after Morhange—though in face of the arrival of these fresh troops the situation was not as promising for the French as it had been.

FRENCH ADVANCE AT SAINTE-BARBE, VOSGES.
From "En Plein Feu." By kind permission of M. Vermot, Rue Duguay-Trouin, Paris.

Meanwhile, to the north of the Basses Vosges, in Lorraine, on the level ground between the Donon and Metz, de Castelnau's army during this same fortnight had been even more successful. Beginning with the occupation by the French cavalry on August 6th of Vic and Moyen Vic, two small towns on the German side of the frontier, close to Château Salins and sixteen miles slightly north of east of Nancy, they had gone on from triumph to triumph. Except for the temporary occupation of Domèvre, Cirey, and Badonviller, between the Donon and Lunéville, and a quickly suppressed attempt at a German counter-offensive on August 10th and 11th, all the gains were on the French side. Their most considerable success was on August 15th, in the Blamont-Cirey-Avricourt district, where they routed a Bavarian Army Corps and part of the Strassburg garrison army, under the command of the Crown Prince of Bavaria. Four German field batteries were destroyed before they had time to open fire, and the enemy finally retired in confusion, leaving behind them eight mitrailleuses, twelve ammunition waggons, and a large number of guns badly damaged by the French shells.

The remaining triumphs were not, as a matter of fact, of great importance. Still there is no denying that they were triumphs, and, as a result of them, they pressed steadily forward, day after day, from one victory to another, till finally, on August 20th, they found themselves in front of Morhange, about fifteen miles on the further side of the frontier, with a line extending from the Seille well past Dieuse across the Marne-Rhine canal to a point south of Saarburg.

But that was the end. In front of Morhange and Saarburg a formidable series of entrenchments had been prepared, largely by the genius of the veteran general, von Haeseler, and behind them and in them the coming of the French was eagerly awaited by a greatly superior force of the enemy. The result was inevitable. It fell to the army of Lorraine, first of all the armies of France, to learn by bitter experience the great strategical lesson of the war—that no troops can stand up against modern weapons in the hands of soldiers properly disciplined and properly entrenched. The French were fighting in the open. They were taken unawares. They were unsupported by their artillery. In the splendid offensive movement in Champagne, on September 25, 1915, it is true that the Second and Fourth Armies advanced across the open exposed to the full fire of the German trenches for distances varying from one hundred to eight hundred yards, and then drove them back over a belt of country averaging a mile and a half in depth. But then they started from their own trenches, which, except in one or two places, were not more than two hundred yards from those of the enemy, they were supported by a very heavy artillery fire from their rear, and for three days and nights before they made their heroic dash the enemy's trenches and wire entanglements had been heavily pounded and destroyed by an incessant deluge of explosive shells. The army that was defeated at Morhange had none of these advantages. They attempted the impossible. Their attack was extraordinarily brave, but it was foredoomed to failure, and their losses, considering the number of men engaged, were very severe. It is not surprising that after a time some of the troops exposed to the hottest fire flinched. They would have been superhuman if they had not. Possibly even some of their sternest critics would have done the same.

At all events, there the thing was, and I see no reason for slurring it over. On the contrary, the Battle of Morhange, which the Germans and Mr. Hilaire Belloc prefer to call the Battle of Metz, is, because of what came after it, as worthy of our attention as the retreat to the Marne, though it is not, as a rule, a popular subject of conversation with the French. They are, as it seems to me, unduly susceptible about it. The actual result of the engagement and the want of forethought which was its primary cause were certainly not subjects for congratulation. During the previous fortnight the army had been led on by one success after another, gained without very much difficulty, till they had come to imagine that their *élan* was irresistible and the opposition in front of them as unimportant as it seemed. Both the spirit of their advance and the cause of its abrupt and decided check were typically characteristic of the French and German methods of making war—as they were, or as most people thought they were, before the great war began. The French were like Mr. Gladstone. They were intoxicated with the exuberance of their own pugnacity. They were engaged in a holy cause, the recovery of the beloved province ravished from them in 1870. At each forward step they found themselves amongst their own people, and were *fêted* as deliverers, until they completely forgot the dangerous leaven of German-born Lorrainers among them, and the value of the information which they were able to carry back to the enemy's lines. Without doubt the composition of their force was fully known to the Germans long before they suddenly found themselves confronted by the far superior numbers based on the carefully prepared positions at Morhange and Saarburg. The trap had been set and the path up to it baited with true German thoroughness, and the French romped into it with their eyes dazzled by the glare of their previous successes, exactly as they had been meant to do. When the fatal moment came the XVth Army Corps in the centre were too far in advance of the XXth on their left and the XVIth on their right. They had plenty of dash, these men of the south, too much, in fact, for in the ardour of their advance they had outrun the artillery which should have supported them. But when they came up against the solid barrier of the Bavarian Army Corps from Strassburg and Saarburg their bolt was shot. Even if they had been strong enough to break through the impossible odds and positions before them, they had not, in any case, the same compelling sentimental interest in the reconquest of Lorraine as the mass of men forming the armies of the east. They were far from their homes on the shores of the Mediterranean. Comparatively speaking, they were strangers in a strange land, and on some of them the feeling may have had a depressing effect. At first they fought as bravely as could be wished, but the odds and the slaughter (far heavier than any that had so far been seen in the war) and the general impossibility of the situation were too much for them, and at last they broke and fled. The French estimate of their total losses was something less than 10,000: the Germans (who certainly exaggerated) claimed to have taken that number of prisoners alone, besides over fifty guns.

That, as far as I can gather from men who took part in the battle and the subsequent retreat, is a fair general account of what happened at Morhange. If that is so, then shame is certainly not the feeling with which the disaster should be regarded. Both it and its causes belong essentially to the pre-war period. At some moment during the war the French army, as well as the French people, was born again. For the XVth Army Corps, and perhaps for other units in the armies of the east, the blood-drenched battlefield of Morhange was the agony-chamber of that new birth. On August 20th they were flying in confusion towards Lunéville and Nancy. But even while they fell back, almost as soon as they found themselves under the steadying influence of the 75's of the XXth Corps and General Dubail's left wing, the change began. Two or three days later, when they had been rested and reformed behind the curtain of the divisions with which they afterwards shared the defence of Nancy, they were different men. They were no longer the happy-go-lucky children of the south, brilliant in deed but deficient in the power of resistance. One battle had made them seasoned, stern, resolute men of war, ready to take their place by the side of the finest soldiers of France, because they were themselves, as they afterwards proved over and over again, in front of Nancy, and in the Argonne, an army of heroes. And that is why France should think of Morhange with pride.

The triumph of the armies that defended Nancy was preceded, like the victory of the Marne, by an overwhelming defeat and a painful retreat. Before the war every one was prepared to find the French brilliant in attack. But the whole world, themselves included, was almost equally sure that once their attack had been stemmed, the effect of enforced retreat would be to dash their spirits to the ground, and impair, perhaps irretrievably, their *morale* as fighters. As for the Germans, they had apparently calculated on a whole series of Morhange victories, leading right up to the gates of Nancy and of Paris. Like the rest of the world, they were wrong. Out of the fiery whirlwind of the two retreats came a still small voice, the voice of the New France, or rather the reincarnation of the undying spirit of the Old France, cleaner and saner and more vigorous than ever it had been in all its glorious history, because the nation knew that the task before it was the highest and most vital that it had ever been given to France to perform.

For the moment, however, whatever the future might have in store, the position of affairs could hardly have been more serious and alarming. In the north, Charleroi and the retreat to the Marne were still to come. But in the east of France the effect of Morhange was felt at once. Along the Château-Salins route, by Vic and Moyen Vic, by Avricourt and Cirey, by the Donon, the Saales and all the northern passes of the Vosges, past the scenes of their late successes, the beaten troops and the troops which had not been beaten came pouring back into France, closely followed by the pursuing Germans. And then, four days later, to fill the cup of disappointment to the brim, came the order from General Joffre that Mulhouse was to be evacuated. The crisis in Belgium and in France had become too acute. It was no longer possible to spare enough men to continue the occupation of Alsace on a line so far removed from the base at Belfort. They were wanted elsewhere. There seemed to be every chance that the enemy might even strike at Paris. It was necessary to shield the heart of the nation, and beyond a covering force large enough to screen Belfort all the troops in Alsace had to be withdrawn. For the time being all hopes of the offensive for the recovery of the two ravished provinces, which had begun with such fair promise, had to be given up, and, three weeks after the war had begun, France, on French soil, had to fight for her very existence.

CHAPTER X
GENERAL DUBAIL'S STAND

The days that followed—I may be more precise and say the three weeks that followed—were the most critical that France had ever known. Crowded together between August 20th and September 2nd came the capitulation of Namur, the defeats at Morhange, Charleroi, and Mons, the evacuation of Mulhouse, the retreats on Nancy and the Marne, the menace of von Kluck's advance on Paris, and the migration of the President and Government of the Republic to Bordeaux. The war had begun in earnest. All along the line the soldiers of France were either making a desperate stand against superior numbers or, worse still, were retiring as fast as they could go. It was the hour of the supreme test. Except along the twenty miles between Thann and the Swiss frontier the whole line of the front had been drawn in a position chosen, not by the French, but by the Germans. Every day it was being pushed further on, and no one could say where the limit would be reached. Even the arrival of the English Expeditionary Force had made very little apparent difference. We know now how great was the part that they played in the work of saving Paris, in spite of their small numbers. But at the time all that they could do was to share in the general retreat, and make the pursuit as costly as possible for the triumphant Germans.

That was how the position in the north presented itself to the armies in the east, when they had time to look beyond their own share in the common defence, though as a matter of fact they were much too fully occupied to take the calm and dispassionate view of the situation which is now possible.

A soldier during a modern battle can see and understand nothing of what is going on except on his own immediate front. He is in a state of complete ignorance as to what may be happening to the other half of his own battalion in the next village. But these men were hundreds of miles from the events in Flanders. Even their chiefs can have known very little of what was going on. Only one thing was certain. All the news there was was bad news. Everywhere France and her armies were getting the worst of it, and all that the individual soldier could do was to obey his orders and do his own bit of fighting with all the courage and endurance he could command.

I suppose that if we could see into the minds of the rank and file of the first and second armies in those black days of disaster and doubt, we should find that the one thing that sustained them, next to their proud love of France, was the thought that they had Belfort and Epinal and Toul and Verdun behind them. They had been brought up in the belief that the four famous fortresses were to be the main defence against the invading Germans, they knew nothing of the crushing effects of mammoth siege guns, and believed that the forts of Liége were still holding out, and possibly, if they had been left to their own devices, they would have fallen back at once, as soon as they realized that the offensive was over, on the solid protection of these bulwarks of the frontier. Fortunately their generals knew better, and the series of battles that saved the entire line, and therefore France, was fought in the open country, well in advance of the fortresses. But the fine strategy and inspiring leadership of de Castelnau and Dubail and Pau and Foch, magnificent as they were, could have done nothing without the marvellous spirit of the officers and men under their command. And that spirit, after nearly a year and a half of the war, is more alive and vigorous than ever. The point is worth dwelling upon, because of its bearing on the future. The French in all probability have had their worst time and the Germans their best. But even if that is not the case, even if our Allies and we have to go through deeper waters still, we have this to depend upon, that those armies of the east, like their brother soldiers who fought at Charleroi and on the Marne, never once despaired, even when they might well have thought that their cause was hopelessly lost. Instead they first set their backs to the wall, and organized victory out of defeat, and then contentedly settled down to a method of fighting entirely foreign to the genius of their race. The fourth stage is yet to come, but as to the results of it we need have no fears.

Exactly, as it happens, a year ago, from the day on which this chapter is being written, I ended an article on a visit to the front trenches at Celles in the Vosges with these words: "The best of it all was just the one thing that it is most difficult to describe—the wonderful temper of the French troops that we passed, and sometimes talked to, on the road. In spite of cold and hardships and wounds and the constant nearness of death, these men at the front had a spirit of cheerful endurance and fearlessness that I believe nothing can conquer. If it comes to sitting in the trenches for a year looking at the German trenches fifty yards away they will sit the Germans out." The year I spoke of has gone, and they have not sat the Germans out—yet. But they are still sitting, and before November 21st comes again—well, we shall see.

Three months before that visit to the Vosges, on August 21st, 1914, there were no trenches to sit in, except the pathetic kind of enlarged rabbit-scrapes that the men used to scoop out how and when they could. But they had not much time for digging. The enemy were hard on their heels. As soon as they knew that the French troops which had fought at Morhange were retreating, followed inevitably by those which lined the frontier of the Vosges, from the Donon down to the Ballon d'Alsace, they hurried additional regiments across the Rhine as quickly as they could, and very soon the force available for the attack amounted, it is believed, to seven army corps, or something over 300,000 men. General Dubail's army, already reduced in size by the numerous levies made on it for the commands in the north, had also been obliged to extend its left wing in the direction of Nancy, and its centre, doubly weakened by these two causes, gave way to a certain extent, under the heavy pressure brought to bear upon it, and allowed the Germans to pour into France by Saales, Sainte Marie aux Mines, and the Bonhomme. Those who crossed the Col de Saales drove the French back as far as Ramberviller, twenty-five miles due west of the pass, and occupied Provenchères, Senones, Raon l'Etape, and St. Dié, while those who advanced by the two southern passes occupied St. Léonard, a few miles south of St. Dié, and threatened an attack on Epinal by the valley of Rouges-Eaux and the Col de la Chipotte.

That was the position—the very alarming position—a day or two after the battle of Morhange. The Col de Donon had been abandoned on the 21st, and other German troops had advanced by Badonviller and Baccarat as far as Gerbéviller and Lunéville, while a still larger army had crossed the Seille and the frontier by the Château-Salins road, and arrived nearly within striking distance of Nancy. The German front extended almost in a straight line north-west and south-east from Etain past Pont-à-Mousson, Champenoux, Lunéville, Gerbéviller, St. Benoit, (close to Ramberviller) and the valley of the Rouges-Eaux (just west of St. Dié) to the Col de Bonhomme.

The best way to arrive at a fairly clear idea of the operations that followed is, I think, to leave for the present everything that happened north of the Bayon-Lunéville road, culminating in the Battle of the Grand Couronné of Nancy, and to follow first the German advance south of the line between Lunéville and the Donon, in the department of the Vosges.

Record Press phot.

GENERAL DUBAIL.

Nothing had happened so far to cause any alteration in the grand plan of campaign conceived by the general staff at Berlin before the war. Its execution had only been delayed (for about a fortnight) first by the unexpected resistance of Liége and the Belgian army, and secondly by the Alsace-Lorraine offensive. Now that these two obstacles had been disposed of the German armies were able to set themselves once again to the task of rounding up the French and English in the neighbourhood of Châlons-sur-Marne, to be operated by a simultaneous "hook" or encircling movement from the north and from the south, and so to leave open the way to Paris. From the beginning Metz was meant to be the pivot of the double advance through Belgium and through Lorraine. It was, so to speak, to represent the hinge of a pair of compasses. The left or lower leg of the compasses was composed of the armies of von Strantz, von Heeringen, and the Crown Prince of Bavaria, those which acted against Alsace and Lorraine. The right or upper leg consisted of the remaining armies, from the Crown Prince of Prussia's to von Kluck's. The two legs were to be gradually squeezed together till they crushed the French and English armies between them, and then—and not till then, in my opinion—Paris was to be invested. As the war went on the left leg of the compasses, which was at first meant to stretch as far as Belfort, was gradually shortened, bit by bit, under stress of circumstances. At the date at which we have arrived it only reached as far as Epinal, a little later still as far as Nancy, and when it was found that here too the resistance to the squeezing in process could not be overcome, the original left leg was discarded, or at least left where it was, and a fresh and still shorter one forged in Metz, and thrust out to St. Mihiel. But that was not till later. In the fourth week of August the original plan had not yet been modified. The part allotted to the armies commanded by the Crown Prince of Bavaria in the east was still to break through the line of frontier fortresses, and join hands with the other Crown Prince's army somewhere near Bar le Duc, in order to carry out the encircling movement from the south.

In front of the left wing of his forces, which was now established to the west of the Vosges south of the Lunéville-Donon line, there was nothing but the open and unfortified Trouée de Charmes (the wide plain south of Nancy between Epinal and Toul), and the attenuated army of General Dubail. If they had succeeded in breaking through that human barrier, and if their companion Army Corps north of Lunéville had been equally successful in disposing of General de Castelnau's army (two rather large suppositions) it is possible that they may have intended to bring up fresh forces and heavier siege guns for the investment of Epinal and Toul, and that the main army, without waiting for their reduction, would have been pressed forward to effect the contemplated junction with the armies operating from the north, just as von Kluck and von Hausen advanced to Namur and Charleroi while at least one of the forts of Liége was still holding out. But at any rate General Dubail's army had to be dealt with first, and to this work they turned their immediate attention. As for Epinal, which was directly in front of their left flank, they found that it, like Belfort, was protected for some miles in front of its forts by a formidable network of trenches and wire entanglements, against which they decided not to run their heads, though the salient just north of Bruyères in the line of their furthest advance on this sector seems to show that they meant to make the attempt at first. That was the second stage in the process of shortening the lower leg of the compasses.

The position defended by Dubail's army after the retreat from the Vosges extended from a point a few miles south of Lunéville to the Bonhomme, along the line forming the diagonal of an approximate square, (with a side twenty miles long) of which Lunéville, the Donon, the Col de Bonhomme and Epinal (nearly due south of Lunéville) were the four angles. This tract of land is watered by three smallish rivers, the Vesouze, the Meurthe, and the Mortagne, all rising in the Vosges, and flowing through shallow valleys towards Lunéville. Along the banks of each of them there is a good road and a railway. The Vesouze follows very nearly the north side of the square, and the chief towns on it are Cirey and Blamont. The Meurthe and the Mortagne flow close together, from south-east to north-west, one on each side of the diagonal. On the Meurthe the chief towns are St. Dié, Raon l'Etape, and Baccarat, and on the Mortagne, to the west of it, Rambervillers and Gerbéviller. The three rivers, after meeting in Lunéville or just below it, continue their joint course through Nancy to Frouard, five miles further north, where they join the Moselle, which rises near Belfort and flows to the west of the three other rivers through Epinal, Charmes, and Bayon, to Toul, from which it makes a steep bend to the east to Frouard, where it is joined by the Meurthe, and then flows nearly due north past Pont-à-Mousson to Metz.

It stands to reason that the position and direction of each of these rivers has had a most important bearing on the course of the campaign in this sector. Along the valleys of the Vesouze, the Meurthe, and the Mortagne, and over every yard of the Lunéville-Donon-Bonhomme triangle which they traverse, the fighting from August 21st onwards was of the most furious description, and in the top right hand corner of the triangle, towards the Donon, it still continues in the less murderous form of trench warfare. To follow it in detail through all its ups and downs and advances and retreats in that first period before the battle of the Marne is as yet practically impossible. But the general tendency of the engagements is, I think, fairly clear, though as yet very little has been written about them. The main point is that the enemy, though in some of the fights they outnumbered the French by ten to one, never succeeded in getting within twenty miles of Epinal, or (except near Gerbéviller) to the west of the line of the Mortagne, and were obliged to give up any hopes they may have had at the beginning of marching straight across the Trouée de Charmes and so getting round behind Toul. Instead of advancing due west in this way they were forced (or possibly they may have chosen) to incline north-west along the course of the Mortagne and the Meurthe towards Lunéville. Both before and after St. Dié was occupied on the 25th, after an attack that lasted for four days, there were fierce engagements at practically every town and village on and between the two rivers. Besides the bigger places which I have already mentioned there were many others, starting from the Col de Bonhomme and working up towards Lunéville, which one by one, and sometimes more than once, were the scene of furious and bloody encounters.

At la Croix aux Mines, Mandray, Entre-Deux-Eaux, Sauley-sur-Meurthe, Taintrux, Le Bois de Champ, Brouvelieures, Mortagne, la Vallée des Rouges-Eaux, le Haut Jacques, Autrey, La Bourgonce, La Salle, Nompatelize, St. Rémy, Etivalle, St. Michel, Col de la Chipotte, St. Benoit, Bru, Menille, Doncières, Xaffévillers, St. Piermont and Le Plateau de Moyen thousands of French and Germans fought and died in those few August and September days. The fighting was particularly violent at La Bourgonce, La Salle, Nompatelize, St. Rémy, Etivalle, the Col de la Chipotte and St. Dié. At the two last the number of the German dead alone was probably over 20,000. There was no question then of off-times in leafy cantonments between the spells of duty in the trenches. The men ate and slept where they could on the ground where they had fought. Day after day and hour after hour the fighting went on. Brilliant bayonet charges and desperate struggles hand-to-hand and body-to-body followed each other with hardly a moment's break. The same positions were lost and taken over and over again, and the firing of the guns and the explosions of the shells kept up a ceaseless hurricane of noise, as the storm of shells ploughed up the green fields along those valley roads and mangled the bodies of the two armies that had been set to butcher each other to suit the purposes of the Prussian Junkers and the Kaiser's militarist advisers. But the French soldiers never flinched, outnumbered and outweighed as they were. Above all the Chasseurs-à-pied and Chasseurs Alpins, whom the Germans feared and respected more than any other troops in General Dubail's army, covered themselves with glory—glory that is none the less immortal, though very few individual acts of bravery will ever be recorded because most of the officers who saw them are silent in their graves. But that hardly matters. They were fighting not for glory and for recognition but for France and the freedom of the world. And they did their work. If they had failed, if the Teuton hordes had broken through between Epinal and Toul and the grand German plan had been carried out in all its completeness, then the whole defence of France would have broken down. But they did not fail. They gave their lives and France was saved.

Unhappily there was another side of all this fighting in the Vosges which was not so splendid. It is obvious that if the French soldiers quitted themselves like heroes in all this horrible strife the men they fought against were brave too. But not gallant, but not gentlemen, which the French are to a man. They had as a body imbibed too deeply the teaching of certain of their own philosophers. They had learnt or been drilled to substitute in time of war the religion of force for every other. Their *Credo* was the antithesis of all the recognized beliefs which civilized men must inevitably hold or pretend to hold in time of peace. "I believe in the God of Battles, Maker of the rulers of the earth, who giveth the victory to those who shrink from nothing and no means in order to attain it. I believe in terrorism and pillage and destruction and death. I believe in stifling all my softer feelings, and in making the life of the people in whose country I fight a hell."

Is that too severe a judgment? I am afraid not. No creed is consistently held or acted upon by all those who are supposedly its adherents. There are of course thousands and thousands of gallant gentlemen among the officers and the rank and file of the German armies. Innumerable letters found on their dead bodies show how the frightfulness of their fellow-soldiers shamed and angered them, and how they abominated German "Kultur" as deeply as Nietsche himself. But unhappily for Belgium and France, and more unhappily still for Germany, their opinions and example, even if they were in the majority, were powerless to control the acts of the thorough-going believers in the German war-creed. When the war is over, if not before, their voice will prevail. They will tear that creed, and perhaps the men who made it, to pieces as their Government did the treaty by which they bound themselves to respect the rights of Belgium. No nation can possibly consent to go on living under the shadow of such a disgrace as these men have brought on Germany. But for the present they must be judged by their present deeds, and it is impossible to write about the war in Alsace and Lorraine and the Vosges and the Woevre without saying something about the crimes which have been committed in the name of Germany by German soldiers. I will not weaken the case against them by repeating second-hand fairy-tales of "atrocities" which have not come under my own notice. There is enough material in the more carefully attested official reports, in what my colleague and I have been told by the victims and reputable eyewitnesses of these cruelties, and in what we have ourselves seen and heard, to prove beyond doubt that a very large number of soldiers in the German army have for some reason or other behaved during the war as brute-beasts. In this chapter I will quote only one case of "frightfulness" taken from a volume published officially by the French Foreign Office. The Foreign Office report, properly attested by the military authorities, is that at the end of August, 1914, thirty soldiers of the French 99th Regiment, having exhausted all their ammunition, were surrounded in a suburb of St. Dié by a company of Bavarian soldiers, and were shot down at close range at the moment when they were surrendering as prisoners. There is, I believe, no doubt that the butchery was deliberate, though possibly a special pleader might argue that the executioners did not know that their victims had no ammunition left and killed them either from motives of precaution or in self-defence. That line of defence cannot be adopted with regard to the numbers of instances of wilful incendiarism which cry for justice all over the invaded provinces. Many of the ruined villages which we saw in the Vosges were destroyed by shot and shell in fair fight. They are the eggs without which the omelette of war cannot be made. But that is not the case with Gerbéviller, Baccarat, Badonviller, a whole group of villages south of Raon l'Etape, and several other towns and villages in the same district, all of which have been wholly or partially destroyed by fire wantonly applied to them without a shadow of excuse on military grounds. I will reserve for another chapter the case of Gerbéviller, which, although it was perhaps the most cruel and wholesale of them all, may be fairly taken as typical of the rest. In every instance it is practically certain and generally proven that these acts of incendiarism (more common in the smaller villages where public opinion had not the same restrictive weight as in more important places) were accompanied by the murder of innocent and unoffending civilians. For the only excuse ever urged in their defence was that they were a painful necessity forced upon the Germans by the people themselves because they had fired upon them as franc-tireurs. And in practically every instance the more responsible of the inhabitants declare that that statement was a pretext and a lie.

CHAPTER XI
THE MARTYRED TOWN

It was certainly a lie with regard to Gerbéviller. That unhappy place was twice bombarded, first by the Germans and afterwards by the French, and at the first time of asking there was also a running fight through its streets. But it was not the shells of the 75's and the 77's that left roofless all but about six of its 463 houses. They were burnt by fire deliberately applied by the Bavarian soldiery by means chiefly of sulphur sticks and gunpowder pastilles, little black discs about the size of a florin, which apparently all the German soldiers carried with them. I have specimens of both taken from their cow-skin haversacks. The first time that we saw the town, about ten days after they had been driven out, we drove there with M. Mirman, the Prefect of Meurthe et Moselle, who had paid it his first official visit about a week earlier, and had at once carefully examined all the available evidence as to what had happened on the spot. That is a way M. Mirman has. He is not a collector of second-hand rumours. He deals with facts, and the mass of duly authenticated details about the doings of the Germans in his Department which he is putting together will form a damning indictment against them at the end of the war.

We drove to Gerbéviller by the road which, after crossing the Meurthe at Dombasle, skirts the river and the lower edge of the forest of Vitrimont for some miles and then cuts through the southern part of the battlefield on which for three weeks the defenders of Nancy made their memorable stand. We had therefore many chances of seeing the ruin caused by the battle at Blainville, Mont, and other villages on the way. But in none of them was there anything comparable to the wanton and wholesale destruction at Gerbéviller. In Lorraine they speak of it as Gerbéviller-la-Martyre. That is just what one feels about it. The town is like the dead body of a woman whom some inhuman monster has violated and kicked to death and then thrown into a bonfire.

When we got there some of the ruins were still smoking. We did not go inside what was left of the walls of the church. They were not in a very safe condition. In many places in the fields on the edge of the road just outside the town, and behind some of the tottering fragments of masonry that had once been the walls of houses, were lying the twisted carcases of horses; every here and there there was a horrible smell of burnt and putrefying flesh. There were also some pigs, routing about among the ruins for what they might devour. At first they were the only living things we saw. Everything else was dead, everything was burnt and smashed except the stone figure of the dead Christ on the Cross that stands at the corner where the principal street branches in two directions, fully exposed to the shattering volleys that were poured along it. By some miracle it had escaped destruction. Neither fire nor shells had touched it. From the church the street winds down the slope past the Christ on the Cross across the bridges that span the three streams into which the Mortagne divides as it flows through the town, then past what was once the private chapel of the family that owns the old chateau on the opposite side of the road, up the hill on the other side of the valley where there are half a dozen houses—at last—with roofs and walls and even windows, from one of which a Red Cross flag is floating, and then on to the wreck of the railway station. Some people have likened the remains of the town to the ruins of Pompeii. There is no need for that. They are the ruins of Gerbéviller. That will be description enough as long as the stones that are left hang together. The ruin is monstrous and unholy, especially in the part of the town on the right bank of the river, where it is, like Jerusalem of old, a city laid on an heap. We climbed at one place over the piles of stones and rubbish that had formed the front walls of one of the houses, and in a sort of ruined vault open to the air, which had been the cellar, saw lying on its back the blackened skeleton of a woman. She was one of several of the inhabitants who were burnt in the cellars in which they took refuge from the German shells and the German brutality. They could hardly be called hiding-places, because in some cases they were shot if they tried to come out of them. Others were shot in the streets like rabbits, as spies, or *franc-tireurs* or what not. Any pretext or none was good enough. I have seen a photograph which is in the possession of the French Government, taken by a responsible official, of fifteen white-haired old men whose dead bodies were found after the German withdrawal lying in a field near the town. Their hands were bound together, their trousers had been unbuttoned and were clinging round their knees, either as a brutal insult, or else—the irony of it—to prevent them from running away. They were shot in batches of five. The signal for their "execution" was given by the senior officer of the troops which had occupied the town. He sat at a table placed close to the scene of their murder drinking with some other officers. Three times he lifted his glass to his lips, and each time that he did so a volley was fired and five old men fell dead on the ground.

Photograph by Libert-Fernand, Nancy.

GERBEVILLER—MEURTHE ET MOSELLE.

By fire and by bullet probably a hundred and certainly not less than forty people were assassinated and the whole population rendered homeless, because, as the Germans said—the usual lying excuse—some of them had fired on their troops. The truth of what happened is apparently this. When they attacked the town it was defended only by a body of Chasseurs, sixty or seventy strong. These men held out all day against the Bavarian regiments engaged in the attack, that is to say about 4000 men. Till the enemy entered the town in the afternoon the defenders were subjected to a bombardment as well as to the fire of rifle bullets. After they entered it the fight was continued along the street till late in the evening, when the men were driven back to their last stand behind a barrier which they constructed on one of the bridges. From here during the night they escaped—they had fought like heroes and nothing was to be gained by staying any longer—all except two or three who had got separated from the rest and had hidden in a cellar. Before morning these others also got away safely, but in order to do so they had first to kill a sentinel who was posted at the fork of the roads, near the stone Cross. When his dead body was discovered by the Germans, who were furious at the resistance they had met with, they decided that he had been killed by one of the inhabitants, and by way of punishment the acts of incendiarism were begun and were continued at intervals till the final general bonfire was lit on the day when they were driven out by the French soldiers.

Through the two bombardments, and the fight in the streets, and the burnings and the executions, the horrible story of human blood-lust and brutality was redeemed by the womanly courage and pity and devotion to duty which was shown by a little band of Sisters of Mercy, who, with the now famous Sœur Julie at their head, nursed the wounded all through those dreadful three weeks, with no thought of their own danger. The cross of the Legion of Honour was pinned on Sœur Julie's serge robe by the President of the Republic, in front of the house where the Red Cross flag is still floating from the window, and where she and her fellow-Sisters gave such a splendid proof of the faith that was in them. Of the many deeds of heroism which they performed there is one little story which belonged entirely to herself. When the German soldiery were first let loose in the town, sacking and pillaging, they sacked and pillaged amongst other places the church (or perhaps it was the chapel, which is much nearer her house), and tried in vain to break open the sanctuary above the altar, by firing bullets at the lock. After they had gone Sœur Julie came to the place and with a bayonet which they had left on the stones wrenched open the door of the sanctuary, for fear that the sacred elements might fall into their sacrilegious hand if they came again. Though no one but a priest had the right to touch the wafers which were scattered on the floor of the sanctuary, she took them and the chalice, pierced by the Bavarian bullets, to her own house, and then, still with the same fear, herself consumed them, as David did the Shewbread, though with a rather higher object. And then, I am told, she felt rather uncomfortable in her mind—till she had made her confession to an ambulancier priest and received absolution for her "sin."

Gerbéviller differed only in degree from what happened in scores of other towns and villages all over Lorraine and the Woevre and Alsace and the Vosges. It was not an isolated case. At Baccarat, at St. Benoit, at Badonviller, and many other places south of the Meurthe, as at Nomeny, Réméréville and many other places north of it, there were the same burnings, and the same shootings of innocent civilians. At Badonviller, where, besides eleven other victims, the wife of the singularly brave mayor, Monsieur Benoit, was shot in the street before his eyes, much more damage was done by incendiarism than by the fights that went on for the possession of the town. On the French side of the town there are few signs that it has often, since the beginning of the war, been the centre of furious fighting. A few French and German graves, distinguished by *képis*, or spiked helmets, one or two houses damaged by shells—and that is all. Then, as the road drops down into the town you see on the crest of the opposite ridge the ruins of the church, which, with the cemetery behind it was the part of the town that suffered most from the bombardment. Dome and roof have both been entirely shot away; shattered fragments of the pillars in front of the church and the shapeless remains of the four walls are all that is left, except for one thing—a statue of Joan of Arc, with one arm broken off short at the shoulder, standing erect and serene on its pedestal, surrounded by the piles of stone and mortar and timber and glass that litter the floor of the roofless nave. Outside in the cemetery, at the time of our first visit, coffins stripped of their covering of earth, broken tombstones, and shattered crosses completed the dreary scene of desolation, another proof that the church was the chief target of the German artillery. But of that there is no doubt. In the rest of the town, away from the church, comparatively little damage had been done by the shells, and there is this further curious fact to note, that the bombardment which did the mischief took place while the place was actually occupied by German troops. They were simply ordered to keep out of the range of the fire—which meant away from the actual neighbourhood of the church.

These troops—they were Bavarians—completed the work of destruction by burning the quarter of the town nearest to the German frontier, some thirty houses in all, besides pillaging many others. They also shot twelve of the inhabitants, including a woman and the child she was holding in her arms, and an old man of seventy-eight, who was sitting peacefully by his window.

These were the chief events of the first occupation, which took place early in August. The second—there have been three in all—began on August 23rd. At eight in the morning the French hurriedly evacuated Badonviller and took up a position at Pexonnes, about two miles to the rear, and the Germans, after a desultory bombardment, which went on all day, marched in at six in the evening. For the next few hours there was furious fighting in and around the town between the Chasseurs Alpins and the Chasseurs d'Afrique on the one side and the Landwehr, the 162nd Regiment of Strassburg, and the regiment of Lieutenant von Forstner (since reported killed), the 99th of Saverne, on the other. During the night a stronger German force approached the town, and as soon as they entered it, began ordering the terrified inhabitants to come out of the cellars in which they had taken refuge, when suddenly they were interrupted by a furious counter-attack of the Chasseurs, and driven out of the town at the point of the bayonet. Once more the natives shut themselves up in the cellars and listened panic-stricken to the noise and confusion of the struggle overhead. One comfort they had in their alarm. All the time, above the din of the fighting, they heard the stirring notes of the French bugles sounding the charge, and all the time the voices of the French soldiers singing, as they charged, the famous Sidi-'Brahim bugle-march:—

"Pan! Pan! L'Arbi!

Les chacals sont par ici!

Mais plus haut c'est les Turcos!"

Little by little the Germans retreated, and the sounds died away in the distance, and then suddenly they began again, as the Chasseurs, still chanting the Sidi-'Brahim, marched back through the town and retired to their position at Pexonnes. Then once more the Germans, and at last the silence of the night.

St. Benoit, near Raon l'Etape, is another of these murdered towns. It has been destroyed, that is to say, burnt by the Germans, about as effectually as Gerbéviller. The church has only its four walls left. The Germans, during their occupation, placed mitrailleuses in the tower, which stands high up and commands the main road. A body of French troops passing along this road, which skirts the village to the north, came under the fire of the mitrailleuses and suffered severely, without being able to see where the attack came from. A second detachment was more fortunate in finding out the position of the machine guns. A battery of 75's was trained on the church. Shortly afterwards the French retired on Rambervillers, and when the Germans reached St. Benoit they set fire to the village to avenge the death of their comrades who belonged to the same corps. They did not, however, the Mayor told us, kill any of the inhabitants, of whom only 12 out of about 250 were missing.

In the little schoolhouse there are no doors, the blackboards are riddled with bullets, and there is not a pane of glass in the windows. But in this skeleton of a house we found the schoolmaster teaching a class of twelve little boys who had their fathers' coats and old sacks hung on their shoulders to keep out the cold, and when we came in they stood up like one man and sang a verse of the "Marseillaise."

A little further on, in the Col de la Chipotte, which both sides called the "Hole of Hell," we came to the place where for several days was fought the bloodiest battle of all this border warfare. Three or four hundred feet below the road on the left, as it rises to the top of the pass, there is a beautiful valley, with a quick little burn running at the bottom of it with fir trees growing thickly on each side. On the right the ground falls away in a more gradual slope. For some miles along each side of this road there is not a space of ten yards in which there are not the graves of French and German soldiers, marked by crosses made of branches of trees, and here and there by a battered *képi*. On the crosses are carved little flat slabs. If you read the rough inscriptions on them—"Thirteen Germans," or "Seventeen French Soldiers"—you will see that those on the German graves are written sometimes in German (in which case the number of the regiment is given), and sometimes in French, but those of the French in French only. In other words, the enemy buried only their own dead, and only some of them, and it was left to the French to finish the work for both sides, or to finish it partly. For up from the valley and the woods came the sickening smell of still unburied bodies, the last remains of this butchery of a battle.

There was fighting for about twelve or thirteen days round that stretch of valley and mountain road, German attacks from both sides that drove the

French back by weight of superior numbers, and later a counter-attack of the French in stronger force which pushed the enemy back over the crest. It was a battle of rifle fire and hand-to-hand fighting with bayonets and knives and rifle-butts and fists, a battle on one side of the road of short breathless bursts and long painful scrambles up and up to the deadly trenches cut on the bare slopes, on the other of slow aimless groping through the low branches of the dripping fir trees, so thickly planted that where they grew neither aeroplanes nor artillery could do their work, a bewildering, nerve-shaking game of blindman's-buff under a hail of whistling bullets that came from all sides at once, a hideous battue in an impenetrable covert with men for ground-game.

But, after all, it was a fair stand-up fight between gallant soldiers, with no quarter given or asked, in which each side could respect the other, not a shameful massacre of unarmed innocents among the flaming wrecks of their ruined homes, like those which in other parts of the Vosges and Lorraine covered the Bavarian butchers with undying disgrace. Gerbéviller and Nomeny were far more hellish "Holes of Hell" than the Col de la Chipotte.

CHAPTER XII
BATTLE OF THE GRAND COURONNÉ. I

By this brilliant series of hand-to-hand, town-to-town struggles, Dubail's army, operating in the Bonhomme-Donon-Gerbéviller triangle, had prevented the enemy from penetrating westwards between Epinal and Toul. At the same time, on their left, de Castelnau's men were fighting the desperate battle of the Grand Couronné of Nancy. Their line, continuing in the same direction as the valley of the Mortagne, ran from Gerbéviller across the Meurthe west of Lunéville to Crévic, and on to Amance, north of the Nancy-Château-Salins road, and some distance beyond it. It was a real pitched battle which lasted for nearly three weeks, and was one of the most important of the whole war. For on its result depended not only the fate of Nancy and of Toul but of all the other armies further north. In order to get an idea of one part of it we can hardly do better than to take our stand at the point which we have reached with the Second Army, to the west of Gerbéviller, on the Bayon-Lunéville road. From there, through the eyes of a French officer of dragoons who found time after he was wounded at Héraménil to publish an excellent little book on *La Victoire de Lorraine* (Berger-Levrault: Nancy), we shall be able to follow in some detail the part of the battle which was fought to the west of Lunéville south of the Nancy-Lunéville road. That was where the battle was fiercest in its early stages. The section on the other side of the Nancy road we will leave till later. It was there that the XXth Army Corps held the line northwards up to Amance, and that the victory was finally won.

At one o'clock on the morning of August 19th our dragoon officer's regiment started from near Altkirch, where they had formed part of General Pau's army, for some uncertain destination further west. The Colonel, of course, knew where they were bound, but he kept his own counsel, and the junior officers could only speculate. Clearly, however, since they were being withdrawn from one successful offensive, they were wanted to smash the Germans somewhere else, either in Lorraine over the border, which was over-run (they believed) by French cavalry, or in Belgium, where report said that the enemy had been pulled up short in front of Liége.

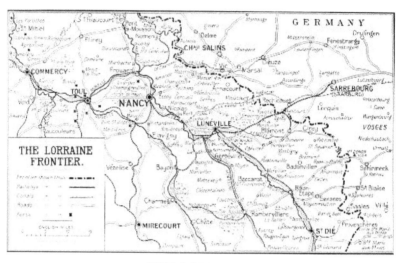

THE LORRAINE
FRONTIER.

After an interminable train journey by Belfort, Lure and Epinal, they reached Charmes in the middle of the night, rested for a few hours, and then started towards Lunéville. This time they felt there could be no doubt. They were making for the frontier, and next day would certainly see them in the annexed province. It was a long march, but the sun was shining brightly on the forest of Charmes, the valley of the Moselle on their left, and the hills of Lorraine in front of them, and everyone was in the best of spirits. Then suddenly there came an unexpected check. An orderly rode up to the Colonel with despatches, the regiment was halted at a little village on the road half way between Bayon and Lunéville, and there they spent the rest of the afternoon and the night of the 21st in ignorant inaction. Next morning everything was changed. The sunshine had gone out of the air, a steady drizzle was falling, and when the Colonel informed his officers that they were to be attached to an infantry division which was to organize a line of defence behind Lunéville they could hardly believe their ears and began to wonder anxiously why, instead of continuing the march to the frontier, they were ordered to fall back on Einvaux, on the south side of the Bayon-Lunéville road.

It was still raining when they reached the road, and they were obliged to halt to let a long convoy, which was passing along it across their front from east to west, go by. They waited five minutes, ten minutes, half an hour, and still the stream of men and horses poured on and on, an odd jumble of peasants' carts, farm-carts, tradesmen's carts, and every imaginable kind of country vehicle, plodding along drearily through the rain, the soldiers who were driving them huddled under the awnings, and all the ammunition and provision carts piled high with wounded. It must at least, they thought, be the convoy of a whole Army Corps. But why was all this mass of men and vehicles hurrying along in the mud, away from Lunéville, towards Bayon? Their hearts began to misgive them. They asked some of the drivers what it all meant, but no one seemed to understand and no one answered, until at last they stopped a non-commissioned officer and from him learnt part of the incredible truth—that the triumphant army which had invaded Lorraine was in full retreat.

After that they waited no longer. The melancholy string of carts which stretched along the road in both directions as far as they could see was halted to let them through, and they continued their march to their cantonments at Einvaux, five or six miles south of the road. There the young dragoon officer was at once given his marching orders. He was to take with him half a dozen troopers, cross the Meurthe and the forest of Vitrimont as far as the Lunéville-Nancy road, and try and get in touch with the enemy, who were pressing hard on the heels of the retreating troops.

When he reached the Bayon-Lunéville road again he had on each side of him two railways running nearly due north and south and cutting the road (which to the east crosses the Mortagne at Lamath, and then turns northward past Xermaménil, Rehanviller, and Hériménil to Lunéville) at a distance of about three miles apart. The one on the right curves away behind to Gerbéviller, the one on the left to Bayon, eventually to meet some distance to the south at Epinal. In front, to the north, both of them join the railway which runs from Lunéville to St. Nicolas-du-Port round the lower edge of the forest of Vitrimont, following closely the course of the Meurthe. On the further side of the forest the road from Lunéville to Dombasle, St. Nicolas-du-Port, and Nancy stretches across from right to left, and, as you see it on the map, the whole area composed of the forest and the ground beyond, as far as the Lunéville-Nancy road, is shaped like a feeding-cup, with Lunéville for the handle and Dombasle for the spout. North-west of Lunéville, along the Dombasle road, comes first the Faubourg de Nancy, and then two miles and four miles further on the villages of Vitrimont and Hudiviller, with the farm of Léomont midway between them, standing up on much higher ground just to the north of the road. In the parallelogram between the two railways south of the forest (which is about five miles long by two and a half deep) there are two villages, first Mont (with a bridge over the Mortagne), and then a little further west Blainville, both of them on a road which runs parallel to the Meurthe and quite close to it. At the point where this road crosses the Dombasle-Bayon railway there is another small village called Dameleviéres, and, also on this railway and a mile south of it, the village of Charmois. Taking a wider view of the whole terrain, the Lunéville-Dombasle road and the railway running round the forest with the two railways south of it and the stretch of the Bayon-Lunéville road between them form a rough figure of eight. To the west of the lower half of it trenches had been dug that morning on the plateau south of the Meurthe by the troops under the command of General Bigot, one of General Dubail's brigadiers. The plateau of Saffais, midway between the Meurthe and the Moselle, was occupied by the 64th division, and on their right another division, the 74th, guarded the gap between Saffais and the Mortagne. Between them they formed a curtain of troops which was to play a very important part in the coming battle, which was fought chiefly over the ground covered by the figure of eight, but partly also further south, below the Bayon-Lunéville road, as far as the line between Bayon and Gerbéviller.

When the little party of dragoons once more reached the road, at the level crossing where it cuts the line from Epinal to Nancy, it was still covered with a dense mass of fugitives. This time it was not merely a procession of carts but of the army itself, the soldiers of the XVth and XVIth Army Corps. It was the final stage of the retreat which had begun after their defeat in front of Morhange and Saarburg by the armies of Metz, of the Crown Prince of Bavaria, and of General von Heeringen. For two days, by all the roads that cross the frontier between Vic and Réchicourt and meet on the south-east side of Lunéville, they had come crowding along to this harbour of refuge, the angle between the Mortagne and the Meurthe, where they were to find sanctuary behind the curtain of troops prepared by General Dubail and General Bigot. Infantry of the line, chasseurs, artillery, young men of the active army, territorials, troops of peasants, women and children and old men, some in carts and some on foot, all mixed up in inextricable confusion with the soldiers and regimental wagons, the drivers flogging their worn-out horses in the vain effort to make them move faster, the men on foot, almost as many of them wounded as not, too tired or too weak to get out of the way, marching anyhow without any formation or any attempt to keep to their own companies, splashing along in a slough of mud, wet to the bone by the ceaseless rain, without discipline, without courage, almost without thought, the tragic procession filed slowly by, away from the enemy, away from the frontier that they had been sent to defend.

But only for the time being, and only for two days. That was the marvel of it. By their failure—in face of the impossible task by which they were confronted—they had thrown the whole scheme of the eastern campaign out of gear. The XXth Army Corps under General Foch, which had the position on their left at Morhange, was forced to retire with them, and worse still would have befallen the corps from the Midi and the Pyrenees if it had not been for the steadying influence of the men of Lorraine and the magnificent rearguard action which they fought as they retreated steadily and in perfect order to their position in front of Nancy, marching by the roads to the north of Lunéville and the Meurthe. Much the same thing had happened on the right, as we have already seen. The advanced regiments of Dubail's army, finding their left uncovered, were also obliged to give up their successful offensive and fall back on Baccarat, Raon l'Etape, and St. Dié, leaving to the enemy the strategical advantage of the positions on the crests of the Vosges, and at the same time prolonging their line westwards to the angle between the Mortagne and the Meurthe, so as to stand between the fugitives and the pursuing Germans and join in the one object that now mattered—the defence of Nancy.

That, then, was how the scene was staged for the first act of the Battle of the Grand Couronné on August 23rd. There was no question of the defence of Lunéville. It might possibly have been attempted, and successfully attempted, by the men whom we have just seen straggling along the road to Bayon. But they were not ready for so great a task yet. So the town was abandoned. The enemy marched into it without any resistance on the 23rd, and the line was drawn further back, behind Lunéville and behind the Mortagne instead of in front of them. On the left, from the Meurthe to Amance, were Foch and his men, the XXth Army Corps with its heart of gold—the famous 11th Division de Fer. Of them we need have no fear. What man can do they will do. But those others, who have retired in confusion behind Bigot's covering troops, prolonging, between the Meurthe and the Mortagne, the line occupied by the XXth—what of them? This of them, not in my own words, but as they were seen by the young lieutenant of dragoons whom we left on his way to the Meurthe to look for the enemy—

"Ils se sont reformés avec une souplesse meridionale étonnante. Et ce fut un sujet d'admiration sans pareil, que de voir ces soldats hier encore battus, découragés, revenir ardents à la bataille deux jours après, leurs regiments reformés, les brigades dans la main du chef—lutter en héros—et vaincre!" And again: "Ce sont ces mêmes troupes qui, dans trois jours, reformées, vont contribuer à l'héroïque défense de la trouée, et ne laisseront pas un seul instant branler la muraille vivante dressée contre l'envahisseur: chaque soldat deviendra un rampart infranchissable. *Miles murus erit.*"

On the right, too, then, as well as on the left, France had an army of heroes, all the more invincible because they were thirsting to blot out the memory of Morhange. They were to have the chance they wanted. From all directions through the forest of Vitrimont and along the roads south of Lunéville the enemy's vanguard was converging on the angle between the two rivers. The rain of heavy shells which all day long had been speeding up the French retreat was continued now to cover the German advance. Far off across the forest, from the plateau where the farm of Léomont crowns the ridge that runs along the north side of the Nancy road, the 75's of the XXth corps were firing at the big German batteries behind Lunéville. Suddenly, as the dragoons advanced towards the Meurthe, the farm burst into flames, which shot up like a huge bonfire into the crimson evening sky, streaked with the screaming shells and specked with the white puffs of the shrapnel which littered farm and road and plateau with wounded and dying men. At Mont, the little village where the two rivers meet, a battalion of Chasseurs Alpins, who had just come through the forest, were engaged in blowing up the bridge over the Meurthe. They told them that not a Frenchman was left on the other side, and warned them not to go on, as the forest was full of German scouts. The lieutenant's orders, however, were to see, and not only to hear, where the enemy were, so, as his men were ready for anything, they crossed the river by a ford five hundred yards lower down, and advanced along one of the numerous rides through the forest till a brisk fusillade put the matter beyond a doubt. Then they rode back, without a scratch, to make their report, first to the Colonel, and then to the General at Bayon. The night and the next day passed without any vigorous action on the part of the enemy, though some of their patrols crossed the Meurthe. They were probably themselves not too fresh after their long forced march from beyond the frontier, and wanted to collect their strength and their forces for the grand attack.

On August 24th the storm burst at last. From Damelevières and Mont on the near side of the forest of Vitrimont, from Lunéville along the Bayon road, and out of the two smaller forests of Vacquenat and Clairlieu, which, from Lamath on the Mortagne, stretch along each side of it up to the most western of the two railways, the enemy came pouring on, battalion after battalion, regiment after regiment, till they had nearly got up to the concave sweep of the French defensive position, extending from the Sappais plateau eastwards across the road and railway in the direction of Gerbéviller. At the same time the German guns began to speak, and along the whole French front a hurricane of explosive shells and shrapnel ploughed and tore up a belt of ground over a mile deep. An hour after midday, in brilliant sunshine this time, no longer under the depressing rain, the French batteries opened fire and went on firing all through the afternoon and night, after a time without any sustained reply from the enemy except for one general cannonade before sundown.

Photograph by Libert-Fernand, Nancy.

FARM OF LEOMONT—MEURTHE ET MOSELLE

If you are standing on the outskirts of a modern battle—say at a distance of a mile from the nearest battery, for a civilian is not likely to get much closer in these days—you hear what I may call the symphony of it far better than those who are actually taking part in the fighting, who are deafened to all other sounds but the guns that fire and the shells that burst near them, and the rifles of their own company. To the spectator, when heavy guns, field guns, rifles, and machine guns are all booming and banging and rattling at the same time, the noise is so tremendous that it seems that it must be beyond the limits of human endurance to face the storm of steel and fire. At the hottest moments it keeps changing curiously and horribly in character, volume, and tempo, rising and falling with alternating diminuendo and crescendo and hurrying and slackening pace. It is all extraordinarily relentless. Sometimes the deafening volleys of reports sound like the clattering of a clumsy, lumbering wagon, jolting heavily over the frozen ruts of a rough country lane; sometimes like the brisk hammering of thousands of carpenters and rivetters at work on thousands of wooden joists and steel plates; sometimes like the rumbling of hundreds of heavy goods-trains thundering and bumping over uneven points and meeting every now and then in hideous collision. Against the changing undercurrent and background of sound and confusion the different kinds of reports are always distinguishable—the heavy slow boom of the big guns, the sharp vicious bang of the field pieces, with their lightning-like velocity and shattering irresistible force, the shrieks of the shells, the whistle of the bullets, the crackling and spitting and spluttering snap of the lebels and mannlichers, the rapid pitiless tapping and rattling of the machine guns, and most awful of all, I think, the sudden unexpected silences, which make you hold your breath and wait—like a condemned murderer with the noose round his neck must wait on the scaffold—for the dreadful moment which you know will come when the storm will all begin over again *da capo*, and in the twinkling of an eye hundreds and hundreds of living vigorous men will be struck down dead. Mercifully few things are so false as the saying that every bullet has its billet. Otherwise not a man of the armies that fought in front of Nancy would be left.

Soon after the great battle, long before nature had begun to heal the gaping wounds that French and German had made in the bosom of the brown old earth, I or my French colleague or both of us visited most of the roads north and south of the Meurthe and north and west of the Mortagne which cross the ground on which it was fought. The whole country—the once happy villages, the wooded hills and wide rolling plains of grass and stubble fields with never a hedge and hardly a ditch—is one vast field of battle and one huge cemetery. From part of it the German flood of invasion was just beginning to recede. What was left of the towns and villages and farms, which had first withstood its advance like massive breakwaters and then been submerged as the tide of battle ebbed and flowed, looked much more like piles of rugged and weather-beaten rocks than human habitations. Everywhere the fields had been drenched with the blood of French and Germans. Everywhere they were scarred with deep shell-holes surrounded by great clods of brown earth scattered in all directions. It is a characteristic feature of the Lorraine country that in many places the roads, when they run between two belts of woodland, are bordered on each side by level stretches of grass, fifty or sixty yards wide. In these roadside glades—because roads lead to towns and villages, and because armies move more easily along them than over the soft fields—the shell-holes were so close together that often they were almost touching. In other places, where only a single line of trees marked the two sides of the road, trunk after trunk had been cut straight through by the shells, or whole rows of them ruthlessly felled to open up the line of fire. And everywhere there were blown-up bridges, broken telegraph poles, hanging wires, hop-gardens scorched and withered by sheets of fire, blackened corn-stooks rotting where they stood, ploughs and farm-carts twisted and smashed, festering bodies of dead horses in hideously ungainly attitudes, rifles, bayonets, caps, helmets, coats, saddles, haversacks, socks, shirts, boots, water-bottles, all kinds of things that men have made and used and worn, all manner of rubbish that once had form and beauty—a horrible unsightly jumble and litter of wreckage and decay, a tragedy of untellable noise and fury and suffering and death. And then there were the dead themselves—the pitiable little heaps of clothes, red or blue or grey, that once were men, that helped to make this tragedy and fell its victims. Most of them had been buried and hidden away in the shelter of the earth. But here and there they were still lying, sometimes prone on their faces as they fell, more often carefully laid on their backs, staring up at the sky with unseeing eyes. Some looked peaceful and at rest. Others had suffered horribly before they died, and their coal-black faces were twisted and drawn, and their outstretched arms and hands clutched at emptiness in an agony of intolerable pain.

The three weeks' battle was now well under way. On the first day the opening rush of the German attack had spent itself in vain against the French right wing south of the Meurthe. The fire of Morhange had done its work. It had forged a tough line of Ironsides, which the Bavarian corps could neither bend nor break, and during the night they began to fall back toward the Mortagne leaving masses of dead behind them. A French cavalry patrol, sent out early on the morning of the 15th along the Bayon-Lunéville road to reconnoitre, got as far as Lamath, on the left bank of the river, before they found the enemy. During the day the village was gallantly carried by a battalion of Chasseurs-Alpins. Further south, in the triangle beyond the road and the forest of Vacquenat, the enemy held on more persistently to the ground which they had gained, and on the 25th and 26th at Einvaux, Clayeures, Réménoville, Rozelieures and other villages between the two rivers they were only driven back step by step as the result of most determined and gallant efforts on the part of the French. The loss of life on both sides was very great. A little stream which flows through Réménoville into the Mortagne was so choked with dead that the cavalry found it impossible to water their horses in it. All over the field of battle, especially in the woods, the air was tainted with the smell of putrefying bodies. But death and wounds had no effect on the morale of the two French Army Corps. Now that they had made their stand they were irresistible. They were constantly attacking instead of being attacked, and retreat was everywhere turned into advance. At the same time the chief weight of the German counter-attack—for though they were retiring they were always trying to make ground—was gradually shifted southwards away from the Bayon road towards Gerbéviller and Moyen, higher up the river, probably in the hope of breaking through between the XVth corps and the First Army on their right. But no breach was made. On the 27th a Colonial Regiment was fighting a little to the west of the martyred town. They had suffered severely and had lost two colonels since the 24th. A third came to join them, reported himself to the brigadier, rode forward towards his men and was knocked over and killed by a shell before he had been ten minutes in command. But still his men and all the other regiments fought on, the batteries continually shifted their positions from one place to another with wonderful mobility, some of the villages where the fighting was hottest were taken and retaken two or three times over, and step by step the long line of French bayonets forced the enemy back towards and at some points beyond the two rivers.

At last, on September 4th, though the battle was still far from won, the great attack had been so effectively checked that it was found possible to move the XVth corps across to the Argonne, to help General Sarrail and the Third Army in their struggle against the Crown Prince. From the moment when they had assumed the offensive on August 25th, they had fought with extraordinary courage. In two days one regiment alone, the 112th of the line, had forty-eight officers killed and wounded out of sixty-one. But losses had no effect on them now. The past was wiped out, and both during the defence of Nancy, and later on in the Heights of the Meuse and the Argonne, especially at Vassincourt, they took a prominent share in the victories by which General Sarrail relieved the pressure on Verdun. From every point of view the story of what they did and suffered and the way in which—like a ship on her maiden voyage—they found themselves after their first defeat, was and is one of the most significant features of the war. For it means that France cannot and will not be beaten. The steadying support and fellowship which they received in the hour of crisis from the sorely pressed corps on either side of them, their own heroic recovery, and the confident and confidence-inspiring leadership of the generals under whose command they redeemed themselves from the reproach of their momentary failure, all point to the same conclusion—the invincible solidarity of the whole of the French armies. On August 20th the chain of the eastern armies snapped at its weakest point. By the 25th the jagged ends of the broken link had been welded together and it was firmly joined up, stronger than it had ever been, with those on each side of it. Morhange might have been the beginning of another Sedan. Instead it was the prelude to the glorious triumph of the Battle of the Grand Couronné of Nancy.

CHAPTER XIII
BATTLE OF THE GRAND COURONNÉ. II

All towns are feminine by rights, but Nancy, I think, more than any that I have ever known. In its municipal arms the chief feature is a Scotch thistle. The emblem should belong rather to the gallant armies of the east, and especially to the famous XXth Army Corps, which was the backbone of General de Castelnau's army. During all that long three weeks, while the XVth and XVIth with part of General Dubail's army were checking the attack south of the Meurthe, along a front of about fifteen miles, the XXth held a still longer line on the north side of the river, from Dombasle nearly as far as Pont-à-Mousson. To all of them, but particularly to the men of the 26th, or Nancy Regiment, and the 11th Division, long and proudly known as the Division de Fer, the town appealed as a beloved and graceful and beautiful woman. She was their mother and their sister and their bride. She was in deadly danger from the covetous assaults of the Germans and the German Emperor, and they alone stood between her and ruin. For, woman-like, she had no defences of her own—fortunately for her and for France. When Bismarck interfered in 1874 to prevent the construction of fortifications round the town by threatening to renew the war of 1870, he was unconsciously working against the interest of his country instead of for it. If Nancy had been encircled by a ring of stereotyped forts, like Toul and Verdun, it is highly probable that after the rapid retreat from Morhange the French would have fallen back on the protection of their guns, and that Nancy would have been overtaken by the same fate as Liége. It was because her defenders did not, because they could not, put their trust in forts, that the town was saved. For the success of the Allies, for their delivery in the hour of their deadliest peril from almost certain disaster, that meant everything. To the south, as we have seen, the enemy had swept across the difficult barrier of the Vosges and continued their triumphant advance right up to the moment when the battle for the defence of the town began. To the north the whole of the rest of their line swung across Belgium and part of France as far as Compiègne, and even far south of Verdun on each side of it, like a bar (though never a straight nor a rigid bar) hinged to a fixed point. And, with the not quite parallel exception of Verdun, the only part of the line that remained firm, the immovable pivot which those three weeks of persistent and frenzied sapping on three sides was powerless to undermine, was the open and unprotected town of Nancy. Its defenders, or, at all events, the rank and file of them, knew almost nothing of what was happening elsewhere. They were fighting in the dark with their backs to the wall. But they knew what their own job was, and they did it, always, it seems to me, from the way they talk about it, with that feeling that they were standing in front of a helpless woman, whose honour they must defend at any and every cost. And when finally they had saved the town, when the fear of a barbarous assault like those which had wrecked and ravished one after the other of the towns and villages of Lorraine was at an end, they called it—still from that personal objective point of view—*Nancy l'Inviolée*.

The German conception of its importance was more strictly military. The Kaiser himself appears to have cherished some imperially sentimental notions on the subject of its capture. No doubt if he could have ridden in triumph into the beautiful Place Stanislas at the head of the White Cuirassiers of the Guard (who were on the spot in readiness), like a Cæsar or a Roman general swaggering along the Via Sacra, he would have felt extremely pleased with himself, and the moral effect on the people of both countries would have been immense. But it was also obvious that through Nancy lay the way to the barrier of the frontier fortresses. Until General de Castelnau's army had been disposed of the project of smashing the forts of Toul was only an idle dream. To that end the whole force of the German left wing, except the troops (chiefly Landwehr) which were held up in Alsace, was concentrated on this one point. The march of von Heeringen's men from the south-west along the valleys of the Mortagne, the Meurthe, and the Vesouze, we have already followed, up to the time of their check by de Castelnau's right. At the same time an even fiercer attack was made on his left, from the east, north-east, and north by the Crown Prince of Bavaria's army and some additional troops of the Metz garrison army.

Before the Germans spread out into battle formation the four main lines of the whole of their advance on Nancy were from Pont-à-Mousson, Château-Salins, Cirey, and St. Dié. If we substitute London for Nancy, the relative positions and distances of these places will be approximately represented by Waltham Cross, Brentford, Sittingbourne, and the village of Sandhurst (half-way between Tunbridge Wells and Rye). Or, to put the matter still more simply, the enemy advanced in directions which coincide almost exactly with those of the Great Northern, the Great Eastern, the London, Chatham, and Dover, and the South-Eastern Railways; and they were not finally checked till they had reached a point nearer to Nancy than Walthamstow is to Charing Cross.

For the people of Nancy the prospect was sufficiently alarming. It is not surprising that at that time some of them, though not many, migrated to what they thought were safer quarters. But they need have had no fears. To the north-east and east of the town, in the quadrant of the circle between Pont-à-Mousson and Lunéville, the legionaries of the XXth corps were to prove an impenetrable barrier. Once they had crossed the boundary river, the Seille, in the general retreat, there was no favourable position in which to make a stand until they came to the ring-fence of wooded heights which long before the war was christened by some French strategist the Grand Couronné of

Nancy. The term is, as a matter of fact, rather a stretch of the imagination. If you stand at the top of any high building in the town and look eastwards towards the frontier (which is as near to Nancy as Wimbledon to Hyde Park Corner) you see, with one or two unimportant exceptions, no hills at all. The ground for the most part is flat and unbroken, rising in a gentle slope to the horizon five miles away. (Once and once only a body of German cavalry came over the rise, and, till they were driven back, were visible for a short time from the town.) On that side the Couronné consists only of the Forests of Champenoux and St. Paul, about seven miles north-east of the town, north and south of the Château-Salins road, the woods of Crévic and Einville north of the Marne-Rhone canal, a low ridge beyond Léomont on the north side of the last two or three miles of the road to Lunéville, and the Forest of Vitrimont south of the road. To the west of the town, and to the north in the direction of Metz, the Couronné is, however, well marked, and a semicircle of hills, about one thousand feet high, broken only by the valley of the Meurthe, stands high up above it, and sweeps round to the north-east, where the wooded Plateau of Amance carries on the curve almost as far as the forest of Champenoux.

The position defended by the left wing of General de Castelnau's army extended from Ste. Géneviève, a few miles south-east of Pont-à-Mousson, past the heights of Mont St. Jean, La Rochette, and Amance (the rock on which the attack broke), and then by Laneuvelotte and Cerceuil across the plain to Dombasle, just east of St. Nicholas-du-Port and west of the forest of Vitrimont, in a line which is almost parallel to the course of the Meurthe below Nancy, and about five miles in front of it. From Dombasle, south of the river, it was continued in a slightly concave curve, as we saw in the last chapter, through Saffais, across the Bayon-Lunéville road, to Gerbéviller on the Mortagne.

In the prolonged battle which was fought along that front—of course very many times as large as the field of Waterloo—the losses of the enemy in killed alone probably amounted to nearly 50,000. Every scrap of the ground between it and the frontier, that is to say, a length of about thirty miles and a depth varying from five or six to well over twenty, was fought over at least twice and in many places still oftener. Everywhere there are long wide stretches of ground so torn and ploughed by shells that it seems impossible that any single soul could have gone through that awful fire and come out alive. On the heights of Frescati above the Lunéville road as far west as the farm of Léomont (in the last chapter we saw it flaming against the evening sky from the other side of the forest of Vitrimont), all round the forest itself, particularly near the now ruined building called the Faisanderie, and from there right away up the line past Crévic and Maixe and Courbesseau and Réméréville, the ghastly ruin of the battlefield south of the river was repeated over and over again. In some places it was not so bad as in others. But that is all you can say. In the worst it is beyond belief. Trenches in the modern sense of the word hardly existed; what there were were comparatively rare and shallow. The slaughter was therefore much greater than it ever is in these later times, except when an offensive movement is being carried out. The villages and churches and scattered cottages and farms were battered and pounded by the shells of both sides till nothing of them was left but heaped-up ruins. Here, as elsewhere, many of them were burnt, and always for the same miserable and lying excuse. At Réméréville, near the forest of Champenoux, the epitaph of the murdered village, composed and signed by "Un Allemand," was still chalked up on the blackboard in the little schoolhouse when we first saw it: *"Réméréville n'existe plus, parce qu'on a tiré sur les troupes Allemandes. Ainsi soit il fait sur toutes les endroits pareilles."* His French was not, perhaps, of the best, but his conclusion was correct enough. *Réméréville n'existe plus.* In some of the villages, where incendiarism had not done its destructive work, there is hardly a square inch of house-wall, except where gaping holes were torn by the shells, that is not pitted with bullet marks. There is hardly a wall enclosing a yard or a compound or a farm that was not loopholed for purposes of defence, and when the wall ran all round an enclosure it was loopholed on all four sides. That shows exactly what the fighting in a large number of cases was like. Both French and Germans held the farms and the other isolated buildings like block-houses, and resisted attack sometimes from all four quarters at once. There was no getting away from them. Death, surrender, or victory were the only alternatives. Both sides showed extraordinary bravery, but it was the French, because of what depended on their success, and because they were being attacked, who put most fire into their fighting. They knew that they could not afford to give way. They were fighting in their own country, in the homes of their own kith and kin. Day after day and night after night long convoys of wounded jolted slowly and painfully past them, back to the hospitals of Nancy, where for all the preparations that had been made there was sometimes not room for them all to be admitted at once, and for a long time they lay on their stretchers in the corridors, and once or twice even in streets and squares of the town under the open sky, before they could be cared for. Almost more melancholy still were the troops of homeless refugees who were forced to turn their faces in the same direction, carrying with them in their hands, or piled in confusion on their ricketty carts, the poor little household gods that they wanted to save from the clutch of the marauding German or his cruel fires. But not all of them escaped. Some were too dazed by the suddenness of the invasion, or too old, or too young, or too feeble. Of these many were remorselessly butchered by the German soldiery, drunk or sober. Yet their deaths were not in vain. Wretched, uncounted, unconsidered victims of the war, they, too, had a hand in the victory. For if any one thing had still been needed to nerve the armies of Lorraine to do all that armed men can do for the defence of their country, it was the sight of the blighted homes and murdered bodies of these unfortunates. That was why France, and especially France's soldiers in the field, realized long before England the deadly importance of putting every ounce of their strength into the war. They had no need of newspaper reports and blue books and recruiting appeals to awake them. They saw with their own eyes. "In Nomeny," one of them wrote in a letter home, "the dead bodies of the inhabitants are more or less everywhere; on the staircases, in the cellars, on the piles of rubbish, in the open street. In one heap there were five corpses, two of which were children, and a little farther on were lying three young girls. Our impression was that these unfortunates had been shot down, and not killed by shells. In what were once the streets there are pigs wandering about and feeding on human flesh. Whenever we catch one we shoot it and bury it at once. Nothing is left of this charming little town but dangerous panels of walls, which every now and then tumble down. You can still make out the lines of the streets. The few houses that are left have been stripped and pillaged. You walk about on linen undergarments. The furniture has been disembowelled"—the word exactly describes what one sees in one house after another—"the doors torn off their hinges. On the floors there is a litter of clothes, letters, burst mattresses and eiderdowns, fragments of furniture, shattered pottery, broken food, dung, and other rubbish, so that you cannot set foot on the boards of the floor."

In letters, by word of mouth, with our own eyes, M. Lamure and I heard and saw over and over again similar stories and similar sights. I did not see the scene which was described to a French officer by an old maidservant in a house near Lunéville, where a party of German officers, some of them stark-naked except for their helmets, some of them dressed in the nightgowns and undergarments of the ladies of the house, danced with one another in a drunken carouse, and defiled the beds and the other linen which they left in the drawers of the clothes-chests; I quote it because the French officer who had it from the heart-broken old family servant who saw it happen seems to me to be an absolutely reliable witness. But there is a deeper reason than that for repeating it. It is typical of the extraordinary vein of bestiality which even before the war was known to run through certain strata—and certain of the higher strata—of German society. We are always asking and wondering who is going to win the war—even, in some of our darker hours, the most optimistic of us. The answer is written in these ravaged villages and towns of Lorraine and other parts of France. When to the mere wanton destructiveness of war is added the particular form of bestiality of which disgusting traces have been found by the French in many houses which had escaped the flames, it is practically certain that the roots of it must lie deep down in a bed of rottenness digged and prepared long before the war began. A nation, the cultivated circles of which are to any serious extent tainted with the unnatural vice of which this filthiness is a sure sign—even if its existence and its toleration had not already been notorious in Germany—is intrinsically corrupt and has in its organization the seeds of death, no matter how highly it may have developed its Kultur and commerce and physical and military science. Germany has grown with extraordinary rapidity and to extraordinary proportions in an extraordinarily short period of time, like a rank weed, forced in an ultra-scientific hothouse. Outwardly her structure is in many respects a marvel and even a thing of beauty. But with this canker at the core she cannot be a healthy organization. You cannot gather figs of thistles. The war has brought the canker (which is in the whole body, though it does not poison the whole of it) to the surface. Perhaps the war, which Germany has brought on herself, is the surgeon's knife that will finally eradicate it, as it must without doubt excise other tumours from the bodies of all the nations engaged in it. But the difference between Germany and the others is that they have entered upon the war with cleaner hands and cleaner minds, and that cleanness, because the world is continually being purified, is going to win in the long run. For even if it were the other way, if Germany were going to win this particular war, which is, after all, only a moment in the history of time, that could make no difference in the final result. Right must triumph and the world must progress, and the Allies, since they have right on their side, are fighting not only in its defence and the defence of their countries, but to give Germany a chance after the war of redeeming herself. For it is as certain that only her own people can purify her and make her what she is meant to be as it is that not the united powers of the whole world can wipe her as a nation off the map of Europe. Of course, individual soldiers and individual politicians think and speak differently. There are many people in France and England with whom the last sentence of the following paragraph, which was written by a French soldier in the armies of the east on August 26th, 1914, is a fixed creed. "We will make these barbarians pay dear," he wrote, "for their robberies and their proud folly. In front of us there is nothing but miles of ruins, burnt villages, and corpses of old men and children. Truly this race is not worthy to have produced Goethe, Schiller, and Wagner. *This time she must disappear from the map of the civilized world.*"

That she should disappear from the map of the civilized world is obviously a wild impossibility. You cannot, even if you wished, wipe out a nation of 65,000,000 people, nor even reduce them to a state of unarmed defencelessness. Inevitably they would again become in course of time a powerful menace to the peace and freedom of the rest of the world. What we can do, and what, please God, we will do, is to beat them thoroughly now, and then to believe that the German people themselves will rise up and insist that in their own country an end shall be made of the mad folly and the mad fools whose pride and selfishness and moral uncleanness have brought this vile war on Germany and the suffering world.

But that is to look far ahead, much further than was possible or desirable for the defenders of Nancy. All that they had to think of was the town and the country and the cause for which they were fighting. All that they had to inspire them was the love of Lorraine and France, and the detestation of what they saw in front of them in the track of the Huns, which filled their hearts with rage and the burning desire for vengeance. In that they were united with the whole people of Lorraine, and because they were united they won. They had their mothers and their wives and their sisters and their sweethearts at their backs. A great deal has been said—but not nearly enough—of the part which the women of France have played in the war. I will not try now to add my personal tribute to the marvellous courage and unremitting self-sacrifice of the section of the French people upon whom the war has borne most cruelly. I will, instead, let one of them speak for herself, and for all the rest. She was writing at the beginning of September, 1914, from Moyen Vic, on the German side of the Lorraine frontier, to her brother at the front, and this is what she said for herself and for another sister:—

"MY DEAR EDOUARD,—

"I hear the news that Charles and Lucien died on the 28th of August. Eugène is dead too. Rose has disappeared.

"Mamma is crying. She says that you must be strong, and wishes you to go and avenge them.

"I hope that your officers will not refuse you that. Jean has won the Legion of Honour: you must follow his example.

"They have taken everything from us. Out of eleven who were fighting eight are dead. My dear brother, do your duty, that is all we ask.

"God gave you your life: He has the right to take it back from you. It is Mamma who says so.

"We embrace you with all our heart, though we should long to see you first. The Prussians are here. The young Jandon is dead. They have pillaged everything. I have just come back from Gerbéviller, which is destroyed. The cowards!

"Go, my dear brother, make the sacrifice of your life. We have the hope that we shall see you again, for some kind of a presentiment makes us hope.

"We embrace you with all our heart. Adieu, and au revoir, if God allows it.

"YOUR SISTERS.

"It is for us and for France. Think of your brothers and of grandpapa in 1870."

With women like that to encourage and inspire them, with those other women, outraged and murdered, to avenge, with their woman-city of Nancy and their mother-country France to defend, is it any wonder that the men of Lorraine fought as they did, and won? "Thy love to me was wonderful, passing the love of women." Yes, but the courage of women—is there anything in the world that passes that, or even equals it? I wonder.

CHAPTER XIV
BATTLE OF THE GRAND COURONNÉ. III

The attempt to reach Nancy from the north was to be carried out by a detachment of the Metz army. In the earlier stages of the campaign, that army, or a part of it, had marched westwards towards Verdun, probably with the idea of joining up with the Crown Prince of Prussia's command—that fatal illusory missing-link on which hinged so much of the German plan—or else of filling up the gap which at that time broke the continuity of the lines across what has since become the base of the St. Mihiel triangle, from Pont-à-Mousson to Fresnes in the direction of Verdun. After General de Castelnau's army had retired to its position on the Grand Couronné, a considerable portion of the Metz force wheeled round facing south, with Pont-à-Mousson as their base. The opportunity certainly seemed a good one. Whatever was the precise object which the troops from Metz originally had in view, it was well worth while to sacrifice it for the moment, in order to take the extreme left of the French force from the flank and in the rear almost before they had taken up their new position after their exhausting retreat. Instead of being able to strengthen the main line of General de Castelnau's defence against the Crown Prince of Bavaria, the French on their exposed flank had to turn their attention to a new enemy coming up behind them from the north. Fortunately, that part of the line was under the command of General Foch, a leader whose reputation has gone on steadily increasing since the war began. The Germans were full of confidence. To them, no doubt, and perhaps also to the much smaller body of French troops whose business it was to check them, there seemed to be excellent grounds for the boastful cries of "Sainte Génévieve to-night: to-morrow Nancy," with which, on the morning of the 22nd, they set off on their march up the valley of the Moselle.

Ste. Génévieve is a village that lies about five miles south-east of Pont-à-Mousson, and rather less south-west of Nomeny, on the line of hills that runs from Nancy along the valley down to Metz, rising a little way back from the right bank of the river. As soon as the Germans turned off the road to their left to climb up to the French outpost at Ste. Génévieve, which they were obliged to reduce before they could march further south, they began to find trouble. A thick belt of wire entanglements which the French had prepared to the left of their trenches and about half a mile in front of them obliged the attacking force to make the final advance from their own left front up a steep and exposed pitch. They did not, however, move forward at once. There was no need to take unnecessary risks, or they thought there was not, and for two whole days, with field artillery and a few heavier guns, which fired in all some four thousand shells on the village, they prepared the way with the now fashionable preliminary bombardment. The French had only one infantry regiment in Ste. Généviève, but they were well sheltered in their trenches, and in the two days they lost no more than three men killed and about twenty wounded. The batteries in support were also well-concealed—too well for the German aeroplanes, which failed to locate them—and they allowed the enemy to waste their ammunition without firing a shot in return. That must have been a severe test of their powers of self-restraint, but they knew that the crisis was extremely serious, and that in all probability the fate of Nancy depended on their standing firm.

Pierre Petit phot.

GENERAL FOCH.

On the evening of the 24th the German commander, possibly deceived by their silence and imagining that the infantry had been crushed by the bombardment, gave the order for the attack. In massed columns his formidable little army of 12,000 men, four German soldiers for every Frenchman in front of them, advanced up the hill, still supported by the fire of their artillery. Then at last, when they had come to a convenient range, the 75's opened on their closely formed ranks. Most of the work fell on one particular battery from Toul, as the others were so placed that they could not fire effectively without endangering their own infantry. For three hours they pounded the Germans, cutting them up badly, and then, when he had fired the last shell, the commandant of the battery ordered his men to join the infantry in a last resolute effort to check the assault.

Crouching low as they came up the slope, the Germans now advanced in earnest. The infantry had been ordered to let them get within three hundred yards. When they reached that distance the French officers shouted at the top of their voices the command which, at that period of the war, always seemed to inspire the Germans with terror, "*En avant à la baïonette!*" But the command was a ruse. The regiment had been warned that, when it was given, they were not to charge but to fire a succession of volleys from the trenches. As soon as the Germans heard the order snapping along the ranks and the bugles sounding the charge, the front ranks hurriedly rose from their crouching positions and with fixed bayonets advanced to meet the attack. That was their undoing. The first volley caught them just as they reached the wire entanglements two hundred yards in front of the trenches and mowed them down in hundreds. They fell in such dense masses that the men coming on from behind climbed and jumped over their bodies and the first line of entanglements at the same time. But they could get no further. Four separate times they came on to the assault over the open with fine courage, and each time they were checked by the withering fire from the Lebels, till at last, almost at nightfall, they gave up the attempt, and fell back on Pont-à-Mousson, leaving four thousand dead in front of those murderous trenches. For the moment their demoralization was complete. In the darkness some of them lost their way, and stumbling over the wire entanglements in front of Loisy-sur-Moselle, fell into the river and were drowned. This time, when the survivors reached Atton, the village south of Pont-à-Mousson, which they had passed through so confidently two days before, there were no longer shouts of "*Nancy demain!*" They had made their attack in overwhelming force and they had failed, and for Ste. Geneviève they had coined a new and more expressive name. They called it, in bitter memory of the losses which they had suffered there, "The Hole of Death."

On the same day that the force from Metz started on their disastrous expedition, the battle was raging fiercely all along the line which was being attacked by the German Sixth Army under the Crown Prince of Bavaria, from Mont St. Jean, a little south and east of Ste. Geneviève, to Dombasle on the Meurthe. In that twenty-mile stretch there were many Holes of Death, many desperate encounters, and many uncounted acts of corporate and individual gallantry on both sides. But for coolness and forethought and disciplined restraint as well as for mere courage in what might have seemed to officers and men an almost hopeless position, the defence of Ste. Geneviève must rank with the very first achievements of the army of heroes that fought and won in front of Nancy.

At first on this section of the line the most furious fighting was on the right, along the Marne-Rhine canal, round Haraucourt and Dombasle, which, on the 22nd, was actually occupied for a time by the enemy, though they were quickly driven out and forced to retire on the heights and woods of Crévic. The next day there was the same kind of give-and-take struggle along the ridge north of the Dombasle-Lunéville road, round the farm of Léomont, and along a front north and south of it, from Crévic to the forest of Vitrimont. On the 25th, still a little further north, between Drouville and Courbesseau, a strong German position was attacked by five French regiments. For some reason, however, they were not properly supported by their artillery, and suffered severely, one regiment losing sixty-five per cent. in killed and wounded. But, although for the time being that particular attack failed and had to be given up, the general run of the battle, all through the last week of August and the first few days of September, was slightly but surely in favour of the French. That, always bearing in mind the disastrous retreat which it followed, was the amazing wonder of it. It is true that the final retreat of the Germans to the frontier did not take place till September 12th, when the Battle of the Marne had been won, and that the movement to their rear of the Crown Prince of Bavaria's and von Heeringen's armies was therefore in a sense part of the general retirement of the whole German line with which it coincided. But it is also true that on the day when the Battle of the Marne began, at the end of that first fortnight of fierce charge and counter-charge, in the forests and hedgeless fields and ruined and smoking villages of Lorraine, the enemy, though they were still there, had been beaten almost to a standstill. That, at least, was the case on September 5th along the whole right half of the front, north and south of the Meurthe, from Gerbéviller through the forest of Vitrimont, past Crévic as far as Haraucourt. Further north it was a few days later before the attack was finally rolled back. The batteries of Amance drew the German battalions like a magnet, and it was here and in the forest of Champenoux that the final fury of the assault spent itself.

Before that, at Drouville, Courbesseau, Cerceuil, Réméréville, Hoéville, Erbéviller, Champenoux (into which the guns on Amance poured shells at the rate of between 2500 and 3000 rounds a day for a fortnight), and other small hamlets round the forest, most of which, like Réméréville, *n'existent plus*, there had been a long series of hand-to-hand struggles and trench warfare, during which day and night the roar of the guns and the rattle of the mitrailleuses and rifles, was almost continuous. In the trenches the men got so used to the turmoil that though they slept through it peacefully in their off-moments, they missed it when it stopped. It was the sudden lulls and not the noise that they found startling. As a young officer who was wounded at Réméréville said to me one day when he was talking of the night on which he was knocked over, "The silence woke me." "The shells," wrote another, "keep falling all round, but there are so many that one takes no notice of them. Even the horses don't move, which pretty well proves that there is nothing heroic in keeping cool." In a way, of course, that is true enough. It is all, as he said, a matter of luck, and the less one thinks about getting hit the better, though the fact remains that men have imagination and horses have not, which does make a difference. But, imagination or no imagination, men who are used to fire certainly do become extraordinarily fearless and even contemptuous about its effect. I was talking one day—not in Lorraine, but on the Champagne front—to the commandant of a battery of 75's, which were trying to put out of action a German machine gun about three miles off which was worrying the infantry in a particular trench in front. He pointed to the corner of a wood two or three hundred yards behind us round which were coming about twenty men, mounted and on foot. "They don't seem to mind a bit," he said, "about getting hit. They all know that the German gunners can see the rise at that corner and that they have got the range of it to a yard, and yet—now look," he added quickly. A shell, three shells together, whistled over our heads. There was a roar, a column of brown smoke thirty feet high shot up into the air at the exposed corner, apparently right in the middle of the group. The horses bucked a little, and one of them screamed, but a second or two later the men on foot, who had thrown themselves flat on their faces when they heard the shells coming, got up and came slowly sauntering past us quietly smoking their pipes, and the commandant went on with his conversation—which was interrupted twice again in the next few minutes by exactly the same abrupt interlude. "Nothing can teach them," he said. "They know that these big German shells have a way of bursting straight up and down instead of laterally, the corner is a short cut, and they prefer to take the risk. After all, the Boches may not shoot—and they don't care."

In Lorraine, at the moment of which I was talking, the men were not so used to fire as they are by this time; they were exposed, not to occasional shells like those nine which between them only wounded one horse and spoilt one helmet, but to a constant rain of them, and they were fighting a great and all-important battle, without the sense of security conveyed by an elaborate system of deep trenches and shell-proof *abris*. Also they were wearing the old *képis* and the conspicious dark blue coats and red trousers in which France has won or lost all her battles since the days of Napoleon. The famous new cloth of *tricolor* blue was still on the looms of England, and steel helmets were undreamt of, or many lives that were lost in front of Nancy would have been saved. Compared with the German corps in their uniforms of invisible grey, the French soldiers were in those days at a distinct disadvantage.

But neither did they care. Death had no terrors for them, and as for their wounds, there would be time enough to think about them afterwards, and then only because they fretted and fretted until they were healed so that they might go out and meet the hated Boche again. Now they had their work cut out for them. Very largely it was individual work, for in these scattered fights in the woods and village streets and the shallow concealing hollows which in many places furrow the rolling plain small bodies of infantry as well as cavalry patrols were often thrown on their own resources. Young lieutenants and sergeants and corporals and even privates constantly had to assume responsibility and think and act for themselves in sudden emergencies—a style of fighting which, when it came, was much better suited to the temper and genius of the French soldier than that of the more strictly disciplined German—and no one will ever know the number of unrecorded acts of gallantry and quick-witted coolness which helped to swell the general tide of the French success.

But one more combined effort was wanted before the victory was complete. There was still that one part of the line round Champenoux where the French were acting purely on the defensive. Erbéviller, Réméréviller, and most of the villages round the forest where so much blood had been spilt, are on the east and south of it, and Amance, in front of which the final struggle took place, on the west. Here, where the main and probably the most seasoned body of the German troops were concentrated, our Allies had been slowly driven back. But they had behind them the plateau of Amance—barely six miles, remember, from the outskirts of Nancy. It was the key to the position. The whole of the battle was in reality and in the end directed to the defending or the gaining of this particular point. At all costs it had to be taken. At all hazards it had to be held. The violent struggles in the villages on the other side of the forest had been only a preliminary to the grand general attack which was to come, first from the south and then from the north and east. Up till then the splendid batteries from Toul, by which it was manned, had taken only a comparatively distant part in the battle, in support of the infantry in front of them. Now they were to defend the hill itself at close quarters. The last two days of August were a time of trying suspense for them. The hill and the men on it were surrounded by a thick mist. Instinctively they felt that the enemy were drawing nearer, that the attack was coming. But they could see nothing. All the practical work they could do was to put the finishing touches to the entrenchments which they had been constructing since their arrival, and occasionally to shell at a venture the roads along which the enemy might be approaching. The Germans, meanwhile, had been getting their heavy guns into position, and on September 1st the bombardment, which lasted for a week, began. On the 4th enemy airmen flew over the plateau, and though they kept very high they were able more or less to make out the positions of the batteries. The fire then became more severe than ever, and at one time most of the men serving the French guns were ordered to take cover in the village behind the hill. But there as well they were quickly detected by the enemy airplanes and captive balloons, and were followed by a volley of shells which sent the villagers scuttling to their cellars or flying over the plains towards Nancy. As for the troops, they made a dash back to the plateau, through a very hot fire, and once more got into their trenches, managing to take their wounded with them. Fortunately the guns had been well concealed, and were undamaged, so that when at last there was a lull in the storm, presumably because the Germans concluded that they were silenced for good, they were able to come out into the open again and soon had them once more in full action.

The rest of the engagement was very much a repetition of the affair at Ste. Geneviève on a larger scale. But there was one big difference. In spite of the gravity of the situation on the Marne the Kaiser had journeyed to the eastern front to give to his armies there the encouragement of his presence and authority—or for another reason. Exactly when he arrived no one seems to know, but he was certainly in Lorraine on September 8th, that is to say, the day before his first five armies began their retreat from the Marne. That seems to me to be a fact of some significance. On the 8th and even on the 9th the line of the first five German armies still stretched from near Paris south of Compiègne across the Marne, well south of Epernay and Châlons, to a point not so very far north of Bar le Duc, before it curved north of Verdun on its left and came down again on the other side of the Meuse almost to the Rupt de Mad, which flows north-east from near Commercy, to fall into the Moselle at Metz. Then there was a gap of some miles where neither French nor Germans had any considerable force, and after the gap, on the east side of Rupt de Mad, the German line began again with the Sixth and Seventh Armies.

On September 8th it was still possible that the first five German armies might hold their ground against the French and English attack. On September 8th it was still possible that the Sixth Army under the Crown Prince of Bavaria might break through the opposition of General de Castelnau's army, and open up the way to Nancy and Toul. Nothing could have been better timed. The Germans were a little late (say about three weeks) in carrying out their original programme, but the correspondence between the two parts of it was exact, almost to a minute. Only two things were necessary to carry out the famous "hook" and begin the encirclement of the main armies of the Allies: the first five armies from von Kluck to the Crown Prince had to stand firm; the other two, under von Heeringen and the Crown Prince of Bavaria (and the Kaiser) to advance. It is not surprising that the Great War Lord chose to place himself with the two armies which were to advance. It was (or it should have been) even leaving out of account the possible triumphant entry into Nancy, incomparably the more interesting and picturesque position. Any soldier, let alone any War Lord, would have given all that he most prized to lead the armies that were to carry out the actual work of completing the circle by taking the French and English armies from Bar le Duc to Paris in the rear. It is at least highly probable that that was what was in the Kaiser's mind. He went to Lorraine, not to encourage the Bavarian armies in a forlorn hope, but to secure the front seat for the display of the final tableau.

How nearly exact his calculations were will probably never be known. It was certainly a case of touch and go whether they came off or not. In my opinion what upset them more than almost anything else was the final stand at Amance, in which guns and infantry both bore their full share. For consider what they did, and above all when they did it. They were put to the supreme test on September 8th, the day, let me recall, before the retreat from the Marne began. The Kaiser himself gave the order for the final assault. From the woods a mile away, headed by their fifes and drums, wave upon wave of Germans advanced as steadily and as pompously as if they were on parade, to the attack of the French infantry positions on the side of the hill. The French guns were silent. There was nothing to show whether they had been put out of action by the preliminary bombardment or were only biding their time. Except the music of the bands there was not a sound, for the infantry also reserved their fire till the enemy were within two hundred yards. Then their time had come. With their bayonets fixed and with shouts of "*Vive la France!*" they sprang suddenly from the trenches and charged. The two lines met with a desperate shock, and after a violent hand-to-hand struggle it was the German ranks which broke. As they fled to the shelter of the forest the 75's came into action, and firing at short range mowed them down rank by rank. But they were splendidly gallant. They fought like knights, not like the savages who had sacked and burnt the villages of Lorraine and the Vosges. There were always others ready to take the places of the men who fell. Six times they advanced towards that deadly hill, and six times they were driven back to the sheltering woods. At some places at its base the bodies were piled up five or six feet high, and when the survivors took cover behind the heaps of dead and wounded the 75's still raked them through and through, smothering dead and living in a horrible mire of flesh and blood, while the 155's, firing over the heads of the front ranks, finished off the work further back. The losses were enormous. Thousands of German dead were left lying on the plain, and in the evening they asked and were granted a few hours' truce to bury them. The victory was complete. There was no longer any risk of a German advance. Nancy was inviolate. The Grand Plan had broken down.

But supposing the defeat had been a victory? Then, I think, after the preliminary walk-over into Nancy, an army could have been sent forward to Bar-le-Duc, large enough, even if it could not bring about the rounding up of the Allies, to form a serious menace to Sarrail and Langle de Cary, and perhaps even to have altered the whole course of the Battle of the Marne. It is true that Toul and the Meuse stood in the way. But the garrison of Toul had been seriously weakened by the withdrawal of the guns and troops that had taken part in the defence of Nancy, and in any case the Germans might have walked round it, as they did round Verdun, supposing that they had not the guns to blow it to pieces as they had the forts of Liége.

But after all these are unprofitable speculations. What has been has been, and the operations in front of Nancy, though comparatively little attention has been drawn to them, were obviously of such vital importance in the huge general battle which saved France that there is no need of "if's" and "an's" to prove it. At the same time it is well worth while to notice how the two great victories of the Marne and the Grand Couronné reacted on each other. Each was an indispensable part of the homogeneous plans of German invasion and French defence. If the armies of the east, by their stand in front of Nancy, helped to make the victory of the Marne possible, the victory of the Marne certainly helped them to finish off the work they had begun so well. Even after their repulse at Amance, when a sadder if not a wiser Kaiser had motored back to Germany, the enemy were still uncomfortably close to Nancy. The French believe that they took advantage of the four hours' truce which was granted them on the evening of the 8th to place two heavy guns in position at Cerceuil. At all events, the next day, there the guns were, and between eleven and twelve that night seventy of their shells crashed into the streets of Nancy, damaging a few houses and killing six or seven harmless civilians. People went to bed very early in those days, and most of the inhabitants had been in bed and asleep for an hour or two before the shelling began. A violent thunderstorm was raging at the time, and it was not till the 75's began to reply that the town woke up and realized what was happening, and then, almost before there was time to wonder seriously whether the bombardment was to be the prelude to a German entry, the whole thing was over. The smart little 75's had done their work and silenced the heavier pieces from Essen, or the men who were serving them, in less than an hour. The town heaved a sigh of relief, not unmixed with indignation and contempt—and went to sleep again.

The whole affair was singularly futile and pettish. It was like a little boy throwing stones from a safe distance at an opponent whom he has failed to beat in a fair stand-up fight, before he runs away. Possibly the object was to damage the Cathedral, which was exactly in the line in which most of the shells fell, as a parting message to the Nanceiens of what they might expect another time. Or they may have hoped to start a conflagration or an explosion by hitting the gasworks or the huge boilers of some big works close beside them. That was a thought which occurred to the young Yorkshire engineer in charge of the works (about the only Englishman in the town at the moment), who at once went down through the streets where the shells were falling and emptied the boilers himself. But anyhow there was no military object in the pyrotechnic display, since there were no soldiers sleeping in the town, and the chief inconvenience it caused—a very real one—was that in some of the hospitals the wounded had to be carried down from the upper wards to the ground-floor or the basement.

Whatever the meaning or no-meaning of the bombardment, it was the beginning of the end, and a sign that the Germans were going. It was a habit of theirs always to destroy before they retired. Many of the acts of incendiarism were, so to speak, parting shots, or exhibitions of temper on a large scale. But they fought, too, with desperate if sullen courage. The retirement had now become almost general and once more the unfortunate villages in the path of the receding Army Corps were deluged by the double baptism of fire. Before the enemy were finally driven out of the forest of Champenoux the French had to charge them again and again, and whole regiments were decimated on both sides. But step by step, all along the line from Pont-à-Mousson, which was evacuated on September 10th, to the Vosges, they were forced steadily eastwards—from Champenoux along the Château-Salins road, and through the group of villages on the edge of the forest past Arracourt; from Velaine and Creceuil past Courbesseau and Serres; from Harraucourt and Dombasle along the canal, past Crévic and Maixe and Einville, from which some of them went north along the road to Vic and others kept along the banks of the canal to the forest of Parroy; and south of the canal and south of the Meurthe, through Lunéville and on each side of it, past Gerbéviller and Baccarat and Raon l'Etape and St. Dié—in all cases back towards the frontier which they had crossed in triumph three long weeks before. Except for a narrow strip on the edge of Lorraine and a rather larger tract in the Department of the Vosges west of the Donon, the occupation was at an end. The attack on the Epinal-Verdun line by way of Nancy had completely failed. The Kaiser and his men had looked at the promised land and turned their backs on it, leaving misery and disaster—and perhaps 50,000 dead—behind them, but carrying with them in their hearts the greatest disappointment of the first part of the war. The Germans are rather fond of mixing metaphors; for once let me imitate them. They had nibbled greedily at the Thistle of Nancy, but the Mailed Fist was not quite long enough to reach it.

But the French troops, the men who had turned defeat into victory, had suffered horribly. In one division, 22,000 strong on August 23rd, only 8000 men capable of fighting were left on September 10th. Still, dead and living, they had done their work: de Castelnau and Pau, Foch and the XXth Army Corps, Dubail and Bigot, the men and guns of the Toul garrison and the whole of the armies that stood in that deadly breach, had covered themselves with undying glory and had written in letters of blood on the plains of Lorraine and in the spurs of the Vosges one of the most splendid chapters in the history of France and the world.

The whole of the country over which they fought is now one vast cemetery. There are graves everywhere, by the roadside, in the woods, in the middle of exposed plateaux, in remote corners of fields, in the steep passes of the Vosges, in the trenches and village gardens where the dead men fought each other and died—long green mounds, carefully fenced and tended, where hundreds of broken bodies lie side by side in the last sleep of life, lonely little neglected heaps of earth, marked only by a rough cross of sticks and a tattered and weather-beaten *képi*. You cannot get away from them and their silence.

While the battle was still raging the life of the countryside never seemed to come to an end altogether. Somewhere near, sometimes in the very places over which the shells were screaming, there were always—when they were not hiding in the cellars—old men and boys at work in the fields, children playing on the doorsteps, and dazed and anxious women occupied in household tasks. On the day of judgment, up to the very moment when the last trump sounds, I believe there will still be women washing clothes in the Meuse and the Moselle and the Mortagne and the Meurthe and all the other rivers of Lorraine and France which through all these terrible months have run red with the blood of France and Germany and their Allies—British and Belgians, Australians and Canadians, Sikhs and Ghurkas, Algerians and Moroccans.

Now, where the battle has rolled back, it is the turn of the dead. They lie in the midst of life, and the living can never forget them. The last time that I stood by one of these resting-places, covered already with green grass, it was an autumn evening, cold and dreary. We were on ground from which the enemy had been driven back with huge slaughter on both sides. Almost as far as one could see the face of nature was hideously scarred with an intricate network of saps and trenches. What had once been happy homes were piles of brown rubble and gaping walls and spires. What had once been green woods were stiff rows of shattered leafless stumps. It was a flat country, but in front, a little further on, there was a ragged man-made dune, thirty or forty feet high and ten times as long, enclosing a deep crater in which were lying hundreds of mangled bodies, some of them with their limbs sticking through the surface, killed and buried or half buried by the same appalling explosion in one dreadful moment of eternity. Far beyond, but not so far that it was out of range of the guns, the horizon, where the enemy lay concealed, loomed up grim and threatening against the evening sky. To me the horizon on the Lorraine frontier, seen from far off, always had that dark and ominous look. The vague and dreamlike mystery of what lay beyond that silent line of low dark hills, the thought of the preparations that might be going on behind it, the feeling that no Frenchman or Englishman could go up to it and live, and most of all, I think, the knowledge that across the road on which one stood, and all the other roads and railways that once were thoroughfares between the two countries for all the world to use, a line was now drawn which no man might pass, always seemed to make of the frontier a dreadful symbol of the war and its menace of evil to come. Close at hand it is different. When you reach the impassable line of the furthest trench or the tall barrier of sandbags on the other side of which the enemy, in the same trench, is lying behind a similar barrier twenty yards away, the sense of mystery and foreboding melts away. There is no cure for a fit of the blues like a visit to the front. For after all, the line is not impassable. It has been crossed and pushed back before, and it will be crossed and pushed back again. All along it, where you had let yourself think there was only the foe, there is an underground world swarming with French soldiers, watching and fighting, or ready to fight, day and night, up to any move that the enemy may attempt to make, and sworn and resolved for France and freedom to push on to the end. And that is the view that all of us have got to take when the horror of the war and its limitless and frowning horizon is upon us. We must get right up to our difficulties and meet them face to face. We must work and watch and pray, like the men in the trenches—for they do pray in the trenches—and leave the rest to God.

But that day I was four or five miles back from the front, and the weight of that horror of the horizon was heavy upon me. Man goeth forth to his work and to his labour until the evening. It was evening now, and getting dark, yet still the cruel unending work went on. Behind me quick red flashes of flame showed the position of the nearer French batteries, which till then one could only guess at from the sound of the guns. Far off in front brilliant flares shot up into the darkness over the trenches, that the men on both sides might be able to go on watching and killing all through the night. After all, was God in His heaven? Was all right with the world? I thought of General de Castelnau, the winner of that great victory in Lorraine, and his three dead sons. I thought of all those French and German lying there dead behind me, and the husbandless wives, and fatherless children, and brotherless sisters, and friendless friends, and sonless mothers, whose agonized prayers for their young lives had been answered by those silent graves. I thought of the killing that was going on through the night, and the killing that was still to come for weary months and perhaps for weary years. And then I thought of something else, of the splendid heroism and self-sacrifice of the women who prayed and suffered and the men who fought and fell, and of some words that I had seen before the light faded, written over one of the graves that I had passed—it makes no difference that the man buried there was a German, for surely German soldiers as well as French believe that they are fighting for the right—"Be thou faithful unto death, and I will give thee a crown of life." And that, it seems to me, when you get right up face to face with death, instead of standing and looking at it afar off, is the only possible meaning of the Battle of the Grand Couronné, and all the battles and all the horrors and all the suffering of the whole war. For all of us, even for the enemy, even for those who do not fight, it is a war of redemption, and the greatest and most hopeful war of redemption that the world has ever seen, and it will be won by those whose faith in what is right lasts up to death and beyond it.

CHAPTER XV
LUNÉVILLE

One of the immediate and most satisfactory results of the victory in front of Nancy was the hasty withdrawal of the Germans from Lunéville, after an occupation which lasted for just three weeks. For four or five days before the evacuation the Bavarian troops in front of the town had been gradually falling back on the protection of the batteries in and beyond it. Only one of these batteries, I believe, was in Lunéville itself. It was placed, in obedience to the maxim that war and what the Professors call sentimentality are poles asunder, close to one of the hospitals, under the shadow and protection of the Red Cross. During the bombardment one of the French nurses, a girl of eighteen, was unfortunately killed by a chance shell. But the battery was perfectly safe. For naturally, seeing where it was, the French gunners did not choose to fire on it. They could not play the game except as gentlemen, and the other side consequently scored, as has been known to happen in our own country in the kindred game of football, also rather apt to suffer from the disease of "Professoritis." In any case, when the French got near enough to bring an effective fire to bear upon the town, their bombardment was bound to be half-hearted. They knew that there were German soldiers quartered in the barracks and in many of the houses. But they knew also that a large proportion of its inhabitants were still there and they naturally shrank from the chance of spilling French blood and the certainty of destroying French property, beyond what was absolutely necessary. As a matter of fact, the amount of damage done by shells was surprisingly small. The chief monument to the power of the 75's was the melancholy wreck of the official residence of M. Minier, the Sous-Préfet, which a couple of shells completely gutted. Not far off, near the station, one or two other houses were about as badly wrecked, but except for a certain kind of destruction which was due, not to French shells, but to German fire-lighters a short-sighted man might have walked through nearly all the streets a day or two after the evacuation without once noticing that there had been a bombardment. Inside some of the houses there was more to be seen. One of the inhabitants, for instance, showed me with quaint pride the mess which a 75 shrapnel shell had made of his comfortable home. It had first drilled a neat little round hole through the wall of his dressing-room, and then burst and sent bullets and jagged fragments of the case flying through the walls into his study and the kitchen and every room on the first floor. Amongst other things, it had riddled his bath-tub like a sieve. Fortunately, he was not in it at the time. He was out on one of the heights west of Lunéville talking to the commander of the very battery which broke up his happy home, and actually saw the shot fired. Like every one else who suffered at all from the bombardment (including M. Minier, who lost practically everything he had), he took it quite cheerfully because the shell which did the mischief and the cause in which it was fired were both French.

But the bombardment, which was mainly cautionary, was not yet. It came at a later stage in the occupation, when there began to be a chance of turning the enemy out. The first Germans entered the town on the evening of August 22nd, after a stiff fight which had lasted all day and resulted in the orderly retreat of the garrison, too few in numbers to hold them back indefinitely, in the direction of Gerbéviller. They marched in slowly, with marked caution, as if, the inhabitants said, they were afraid of a surprise attack. However, there was no further opposition, and on the 23rd, with drums beating and bands playing triumphal music, a much larger body of troops made a parade entry into the town and spread over it like a flock of locusts. Here, as elsewhere, they seem to have had a particularly keen appetite for wine and women's underclothing and anything in the shape of a clock. They were not all strangers to Lunéville. As commercial travellers, and in other capacities connected with the peaceful pursuit of trade, several of them had been well known to the inhabitants for years before their arrival in the guise of warriors, and, for their own purposes, made good use of their local knowledge. But on the whole, the behaviour of the Germans, considering that they were Germans, was not particularly outrageous. A military governor was appointed and some effort was made to preserve order and even justice. The pillage was not wholesale, the incendiarism only extended to one part of the town, the Faubourg d'Einville, and one or two single buildings in other quarters, including the Jewish synagogue, and the cases of cold-blooded murder of civilians were not very numerous. Lunéville is not an obscure village, and it is not unfair to say that, as a general rule, the larger the place which the fortune of war had placed at the mercy of the German troops, the more careful they were in the way in which they treated it. Still, even in Lunéville, in spite of the restraining influence on their actions of such important witnesses as M. Minier, the Sous-Préfet, M. Mequillet, the local Député, and M. Keller, the Mayor, all of whom behaved in very trying circumstances with great judgment and courage, the German record was pretty bad. Most of the cases of shooting at sight seem to have been due not so much to wanton lust for blood as to the nervous haste of sentinels in the streets who imagined when they heard a window suddenly opened that their own lives were in danger. But the burning of the Faubourg d'Einville, a row of about forty houses which were set on fire two or three at a time for days till the whole street was destroyed, was an unwarrantable and unpardonable crime. For the Military Governor, from the moment of his entry into the town, had taken every precaution to prevent the acts of franctireurism which were usually made the excuse for this kind of outrage. In the first place rules of extraordinary severity were made and published and rigorously enforced as to what the civilian inhabitants must or must not do while the Germans were in the town. One of these *affiches* is, I think, worth quoting as a historical document:—

"AVIS À LA POPULATION

"Le 25 Aout 1914, des habitants de Lunéville ont fait une attaque par embuscade contre des colonnes et trains allemands. Le même jour, des habitants ont tiré sur des formations sanitaires marquées pas la Croix Rouge. De plus on a tiré sur des blessés allemands et sur l'hôpital militaire contenant une ambulance allemande.

"A cause de ces actes d'hostilité, une contribution de guerre de 650.000 francs est imposée à la commune de Lunéville. Ordre est donné à M. le Maire de verser cette somme en or et en argent jusqu' à 50.000 francs, le 6 septembre 1914, à 9 heures du matin, entre les mains du représentant de l'autorité allemande. Toute réclamation sera considerée comme nulle et non arrivée. On n'accordera pas de délai.

"Si la commune n'exécute pas ponctuellement l'ordre de payer la somme de 650.000 francs, on saisira tous les biens exigibles.

"En cas de non paiement, des perquisitions domiciliaires auront lieu et tous les habitants seront fouillés. Quiconque aura dissimulé sciemment de l'argent ou essayé de soustraire des biens à la saisie de l'autorité militaire, ou qui cherche a quitter la ville, sera fusillé.

"Le Maire et les otages, pris par l'autorité militaire, seront rendus responsables d'exécuter exactement les ordres sus-indiqés.

"Ordre est donné à M. le Maire de publier tout de suite ces dispositions à la commune.

"HERAMENIL le 3 septembre 1914.

"Le Général en chef,

"VON FASBENDER."

In addition to the stringent regulations and threats contained in this and other proclamations of the same kind (the statements in which were unproved and false) the German authorities in command of Lunéville took a further precaution to guard themselves against any kind of reprisal on the part of the French population. Every day six prominent residents of the town had to present themselves before the Governor and remain at his disposal for twenty-four hours as hostages responsible for the orderly behaviour of their fellow-citizens. Their position was not enviable. Exposed, like every one else in Lunéville, to the danger of being killed by the shells of their friends outside the town, they were guarded day and night by sentries with loaded rifles, knowing (because they had been warned) that at any moment they were liable to be shot if one of the inhabitants in a fit of desperation lifted a finger against the sacred body of a German soldier. The fact that they were not shot is proof positive that no acts of the kind were attempted, and that therefore there was no sort of excuse for the burning of the Faubourg d'Einville.

As the occupation continued, as the fortune of the battle between Lunéville and Nancy turned more and more against the Germans, and the French troops and the French shells came nearer and nearer, the Germans in the town day by day became more nervous and irritable and their attitude to the hostages and the rest of the townsfolk more and more harsh and capricious, and it was with something more than a sigh of relief that at last, on September 12th, M. Minier, M. Mequillet, and M. Keller realized that for the town and themselves the time of trial was at an end. M. Keller I only knew slightly; the other two I met often while I was in Lorraine. All three make light of the difficult part which they played when the Germans were in the town and while they were waiting at their posts for their coming. But I know from others that the courage and quiet dignity and practical wisdom with which they stood between their fellow-citizens and the invader were beyond all praise. They were all three fine types of the scores of Frenchmen in official positions all over the occupied provinces who stuck to their posts in the hour of danger. During those three weeks, when it was cut off from the rest of the world, life in Lunéville, under its twofold tribulation of occupation and siege, was not exactly gay for any one. The stern application of martial law, the regulations about open doors and lights, the growing shortness of food, the restrictions on personal liberty, the noise and risks of the bombardment, the glare of the burning houses, the fear for every one of possible death by a bullet fired by some drunken soldier, and, for the women, of something worse than death, and the constant presence of the hated and domineering invader, all combined to keep the inhabitants in a continual state of anxiety and alarm and general wretchedness. But it was on the shoulders of those three men that the burden of it pressed most heavily, and the debt which Lunéville owes them is real and great.

While they were doing their best inside the town to save it for France, or, at all events, to save it from being sacked and burnt, they were in a state of complete ignorance as to what was happening outside it. Rumours, of course, there were, but nothing was certain. They were surrounded on every side, left stranded on a lonely island in a German ocean of invasion. They could only guess vaguely from the nearing or receding sound of the guns and the temper of the German men and officers round them how the battle was going. Yet all the time they kept up their spirits and the spirits of all the French within the reach of their influence. At the worst they never allowed themselves to doubt—think what that meant—that the turn of the tide would come and

Lunéville be joined to the mainland of France again. And they were right. Their splendid confidence in their own men and the destinies of France was justified. All the time the rush of the tide was slackening and the hour of their deliverance coming nearer.

The ebb began in earnest on September 8th. On that day the young dragoon officer in whose company we began the great battle, crossed the Mortagne at Mont by a temporary bridge erected by the engineers, and after a brush with half a dozen Uhlans on the Lunéville side of it, rode with his men along the Meurthe to Rehainviller, a village only two miles from the south-west corner of the town, and found that not a German was left in it. That news he sent back by one of his men to the general, and then walked on alone, as the sun was rising, along the wall of the cemetery on the right of the road just beyond the village. "I reached," he says, "the corner, where I stopped dead. I found myself face to face with a German captain, like me alone and on foot. He was as thunderstruck to see me as I was to meet him. Like me he had his map-case in his hand. He had been examining the country.... We looked at each other, with our eyes wide open. He felt for his revolver. Feverishly I tried to open my case. Both of us knew that this contest of speed would decide our fate, and we looked straight into each other's eyes. Then I smiled, my revolver came out of its case, the butt tight in my hand. My arm stretched out. Then the officer no longer felt for his weapon: he knew that he was beaten. My revolver flashed. He fell, with one bullet full in his heart. The whole thing only lasted a second. It hurt me to see him lying there; he had large blue eyes, open in death."

To me that young French dragoon is only a name, or not even that, since he has none, but a type of all the gallant soldiers of France who fought in the gap between those blood-stained rivers. Still more, after that contest of speed, that duel to the death at sunrise by the corner of the cemetery wall, he becomes for me a symbol of France—France facing Germany, both knowing that one or the other must fall, both clutching at their weapons and staring into each others' faces with wide open eyes. I think we will not leave him now till he in his turn rides in triumph into the streets of Lunéville.

The sound of the shot brought his men running up to him, and also drew the fire of the company of the dead German officer, who were hidden in a ravine a quarter of a mile further on. Luckily for the handful of dragoons, whom presumably they took for the advance-guard of a larger body of men, they did not, however, advance, but retired to the corner of the buildings of a big manufactory, almost in Lunéville itself.

The German position was now on the road just in front of the town, the first houses of which were within easy range of the rifles of the French, who had by this time occupied Rehainviller and were gradually closing in all round.

But they still had three days of stiff fighting in front of them before the end was reached, during which they were heavily handicapped, as they had been all through the early part of the war, by the fact that even their 155's were outranged by a large number of the German pieces, whose average effective range was at that time about six miles, while the French could barely reach four. Supported by these heavier guns from behind Lunéville the enemy advanced again in force to within a mile of Rehainviller, up to a line between Hériménil and the wood of Fréhaut, and it was not till the evening of the 11th that they were finally driven back and that the French were able to look forward with confidence to the prospect of being able to enter Lunéville on the next day.

On one of the three days our lieutenant with some of his men was riding through a village which had been occupied by the enemy a few hours before. Not a single inhabitant was left in it. All the houses were sacked. The flight of the Bavarians had been so hurried that they had not had time to burn them. The rest of his story, which it seems to me ought to be told to English readers, I give—because English readers have English ways of looking at life and talking about it—in the original French:—

"Par la fenêtre brisée, je voyais la salle à manger d'une demeure confortable. Le buffet eventré, renversé, écrasant la table. La vaisselle s'amoncelait sur le parquet, avec les bouteilles vides et cassées, jusqu'à la hauteur des chaises. Une suspension, tombée du plafond, s'était abîmée sur le buffet, et son globe vert, sans une félure, par un prodige d'équilibre, se maintenait sur ce meuble penché, comme allongé sur la table.

"Une voix m'appela par mon nom.

"C'était un officier du bataillon de chasseurs qui avait pris le village. Il était à la fenêtre, au premier étage de la maison dévastée.

"Monte un peu, me dit-il.

"Je repondis: 'Je suis fatigué et pressé de rentrer cantonner.'

"Il reprit. 'Cela en vaut la peine. C'est un de ces cochons qui est crevé au sein de son fumier.'

"Je descends de cheval. Sur la porte de la maison une plaque de cuivre brillante: 'Etude de M. X. Notaire'. Je monte. Mon camarade rit aux éclats, entouré d'un groupe d'officiers. Il y a de quoi.

"La chambre est saccagée, comme le reste de la maison; le linge sorti des armoires, piétiné, les meubles démolis. Le lit est défait et sale. Un lieutenant allemand a passé là la nuit précédente, et s'est couché dans les draps sans retirer ses bottes. Une odeur écoeurante règne dans la piece. Mais pourquoi S ... m' a-t-il fait monter?

"Regarde, dit-il.

"Je n'avais pas vu! Un lieutenant bavarois est assis, mort, entouré d'ordures, d'excréments humains, dans le tiroir ouvert d'une commode ancienne. Ses culottes sont abaissées sur ses bottes. Sa tête et ses épaules penchées tombent sur la poitrine vers les jambes. Il est dans une posture ignoble, grotesque, malgré la mort.

"'Nous sommes entrés brusquement dans le village,—me fit S..., sans crier gare. De cette maison on nous tire un coup de feu. Je monte. C'était un soldat qui nous visait de cette fenêtre. Je l'abats. Je me retourne; et je vois ce cochon de gaillard en train de faire ses insanités dans le tiroir de ce beau meuble, sur les dentelles de famille! Il était si ahuri de me voir qu'il ne s'est même pas levé, restant dans sa position ignoble et relevant sa chemise à deux mains. Je lui ai tiré un coup de revolver. Il s'est abattu sur son fumier....'

"Et je pense à la fiancée allemande, dans ce village de Bavière, qui apprendra la mort de ce lieutenant et se représentera cette mort héroique et chevaleresque ..."

It is not a very pleasant story, as we say in England, but then the seamy side of the war is not pleasant, especially war as it is made in France by some Germans. And the more people in England realize that fact the better for the cause and hopes of us and our Allies.

On the night of the 11th, or rather at two o'clock in the morning of the 12th, the lieutenant assisted at a rather different scene, as dramatic and glorious for all the sons of France as the other was vile and ignoble for all Germans. He was roused from his sleep by an orderly with the news that the General wished to see all the officers at once. With all the others he hurried to the General's quarters, and there—it was in the police station—the brigadier handed them the famous telegram of General Joffre, announcing that the Germans were retreating, the Battle of the Marne won, Paris freed from the menace of the enemy, and France saved.

There was no more sleep for those men that night. They embraced each other, as Frenchmen do, they cried, as all men may sometimes in hours of great joy after times of exhausting strain and anxiety, they congratulated each other as though each man was the victorious Commander-in-Chief himself, and at four o'clock the order was given "To horse! To Lunéville!" On the Marne the enemy were beaten and in full retreat. From the Grand Couronné they had been driven back to the Seille. Only one thing remained to be done here, on de Castelnau's right—to hunt them out of Lunéville and chase them back to the frontier without a moment's delay.

INFANTRY ATTACK ON FARM OF SAINT EPVRE, ON THE HEIGHTS ABOVE LUNÉVILLE.
From "En Plein Feu." By kind permission of M. Vermot, Rue Duguay-Trouin, Paris.

The way was across the Meurthe, through the forest of Vitrimont, out past the ruined Faisanderie with its loop-holed crumbling walls, over the shell-pitted slope below it and the shell-pitted dip beyond, and up the slope again and down to the Nancy road to the right of the ruins of the farm of Léomont, ragged and blackened against the sky, always past rows of deserted German trenches, littered with rifles and ammunition and haversacks and empty bottles—especially bottles—and then right-handed along the broad road to the Faubourg of Nancy, the north-west entrance to the town. Till they reached the road not a sign of the enemy. Only near the ruined farm-buildings of St. Epvre on the ridge of Frescati beyond it, covering the retreat, a company of Bavarian Chasseurs, dislodged with some difficulty, for they fought bravely, and then the road to Lunéville, clear at last. They entered it, these dragoons of the advance-guard, at a gallop, galloping over the cobbles and pavements of the streets in an ecstasy of triumph, dashing across the river somehow (for the Germans had blown up the bridges), active little Chasseurs-à-pied running beside them and easily keeping up with their thundering chargers, women scattering flowers on them, waving handkerchiefs from the doors and windows, and cheering and crying, and every one shouting "La France! Vive la France! La France!" up to the wide square in front of the grave old Palace of Stanislas, up to the line of sweating horses of another squadron of dragoons which had galloped into the town just as madly by the shorter road from the south. It was Mulhouse over again, without the Mulhouse mistakes. It was utterly different from the measured entry of the Germans three weeks before, with their massed bands and formal triumph. If the men were a trifle excited they had excuse enough. For that frenzied headlong entry into Lunéville put the finishing touch to the victory of the Grand Couronné, and set the seal on all the sacrifice and all the heroism of those splendid three weeks. That night Lunéville was free and French once more; not a German was left within some miles of it. That night, for the first time for more than a month, our lieutenant of dragoons was able to take a bath and sleep between sheets. And on that night, September 12th, 1914, thousands and thousands of French men and women all over France slept more soundly and more calmly than on any night since the war began because from Paris and Nancy and little Lunéville the abominable menace of German occupation was gone, never to return again.

CHAPTER XVI
NEWSPAPER CORRESPONDENTS

As soon as not only the menace but the cruel reality of the occupation was lifted from the smaller towns and villages, some of which had suffered so far more terribly than Lunéville, M. Mirman and M. Linarés, the Prefects of Meurthe et Moselle and Vosges, and M. Minier, the Sous-Préfet of Lunéville, were engaged almost every day in visiting different parts of their Departments in the track of the ruthless invader, partly to take stock of the crimes and destruction of which he had been guilty, but chiefly with the object of doing what could be done to relieve the bitter distress of what was left of the population. It was principally owing to the courtesy, and, if I may say so, the wise tolerance of these gentlemen and of M. Simon, the Mayor of Nancy, that M. Lamure and I were able to see with our own eyes some of the handiwork of the Teuton Kulturists in that part of France. I say wise tolerance because, although I know from personal experience that newspaper correspondents are as a rule a despised race, I still believe that they have their uses. The newspapers which they help to supply with news and comments on news are read by every one, and not only, as is commonly supposed in some quarters, by the enemy. They are even read by the high authorities who to all appearances are minded to thwart them and throttle their vitality, partly, perhaps, because they think that they may catch them tripping (in spite of the watchful supervision of the censorship), but partly and still more because they have the natural and human craving for news and like to be interested and well-informed. When, therefore, ministers and other high officials try to suppress and do suppress as effectually as they have in this war the liberty of newspaper correspondents, they inevitably put themselves in a false position and even do harm to their country. No sensible man in such serious times as those in which we are now living objects to a thorough supervision of news published in the newspapers by men who are supposed to know more of the wider issues of the war than the editors who control them. That is what the censorship on the despatch and receipt of telegrams and all the calculated delay of the postal service exists for. But these well-meaning but autocratic gentlemen are not satisfied with that. They go a long step further and not only say to the newspapers (and their readers), "Everything in the shape of news about the war shall be censored"—which is right—but "As far as is possible we will prevent you from getting any real news about the war at all"—which is wrong. For truth, unfortunately for their theory, will out, and if it is violently suppressed it has a way of finding its way out like lava from a volcano, which will certainly do a great deal of harm before, as it must, because it is truth, it does good in the end. My own belief is that nations, like men and women, practically never gain anything by concealing the truth, because its place is certain to be taken by mistakes and doubts and lies—as has been proved over and over again during this war. It is partly because diplomacy is, perhaps necessarily, founded and built up on concealment that it is so often, as it has been more than once in the last eighteen months, a complete and dismal failure. And as for war—as my warrior friend said to me earlier in this book—"War is a serious matter: let us make it seriously." By all means let us make it and take it with the utmost seriousness possible. But also let us be sensible about it. His own complaint against the journalists whom he implicitly accused of taking it lightly was that he could not move out of his quarters without the enemy knowing it. Yet till he met me, not a journalist, French or English, had been within miles of his quarters, as he knew perfectly well. What he did not appear to know, like many other people in authority, is that the Germans have no need to go to French or English newspapers for information about the movements of generals or of troops. They know in any case that to do so would be futile, since they are already checkmated in advance by the censor. Most of the information that matters they gain in open fight in the field. They knew long before even *The Times* knew it that the English army was short of shells and especially of the right kind of shells. A soldier does not take much time to learn whether he is being fired at with shrapnel or with high explosives. They knew long before any newspaper correspondent could have informed them of the fact (supposing there had been any at the front, which, of course, there were not) that the French and English were going to attempt a strong offensive movement in Champagne and at Loos on September 25th, 1915. Their informant was a preliminary bombardment along that particular part of the front which lasted for seventy-two hours. As for other kinds of useful military information, which cannot be gathered on the field of battle, but only from behind the enemy's lines, for that they depend once again not on newspapers but on aeroplanes and spies (including, thanks to the scanty patriotism and common-sense of some soldiers, women belonging to the profession of Rahab). From each of these sources alone they probably get as much news in a week as all the correspondents of all the newspapers "behind the front" could gather in a year.

But there is another side to the question. Under an enlightened censorship there is practically no fear of newspapers and newspaper correspondents doing harm. Under enlightened editors there is every chance of their doing a great amount of good for the cause of their country and its navy and its armies in the field. Every body knows that, even the enlightened censorship itself, whose members have had precisely the same training at the same schools and universities as the purblind editorial staffs. But most of all the enemy know it, and, because they know it, they fear the newspapers and rejoice when their freedom of speech is curtailed. They fear first of all their own newspapers; and because of that fear they forbid them not only to tell the truth, but urge them, if they do not command them, to tell lies. That is the sort of thing, I suppose, which is meant when one is asked to take war seriously: as in most things, even in their follies, the Germans are more thorough than England and France. But even more than their own newspapers they fear those of London and Paris, for two reasons. They dread them first of all for the effect which they have on public opinion in the neutral countries, and secondly because they know that to them and their pressure are due practically all the political and military changes, useful to the Allies and detrimental to Germany, which have been brought about during the course of the war.

The second of these two points I will not labour to support by instances. They are written large in the leading articles and military articles of *The Times* and other newspapers. All the world knows what they are, though all the world does not as yet acknowledge them.

About the other point, the question of the effect which English and French newspapers have and might have (and might have had) on the opinions of neutrals, I have a word or two to say. I said just now that nations practically never gain anything by concealing the truth. There is an important exception to that rule. They gain, or at least they seem to gain, and do gain for the time being, when they conceal their own misdoings. That is exactly what happened in Belgium and in the invaded provinces of France. For a considerable time the horrible wrong-doings of Germany in those two countries were concealed from the world, and are even now not fully believed by those who do not wish to believe them, because they were not seen and recorded at the time by credible eye-witnesses, that is to say, by competent newspaper correspondents. A few days before those atrocities began to be committed in Belgium all the foreign newspaper correspondents were ordered by their own governments to leave the country. As a consequence practically every account of them which we have is second-hand, taken, that is to say, from the lips of the victims who escaped death some little time after they occurred, and therefore not made known to the public of the allied countries and to the rest of the world, except in general terms, till a further time still had elapsed. What England and France gained by this suppression of newspaper correspondents, and therefore of the truth, it is difficult to see. What Germany gained is obvious. I will take only one instance the evolution of which I happen to have watched on the spot.

At the beginning of the war most of the public opinion in Switzerland was strongly in favour of Germany. That this was only partly due to natural racial tendencies (for seven out of every ten Swiss are of German origin and speak or read the German language) is obvious from the way in which, after about six months of the war, a large proportion of the German-Swiss majority began to lose their pro-German proclivities and to come round to the side of the Allies. Naturally we all wish to have the neutral nations on our side, not only because it is our side, but for the higher reason that we believe it to be the side of right. But besides this there were and are particularly strong economic military reasons which made it desirable for us to secure the support, or at least the really benevolent neutrality, of the Swiss. While any considerable part of them, especially before Italy joined the alliance, were for the Germans and against us, secret contraband was bound to run riot, with disastrous consequences for our projected blockade of German war-material. And that is exactly what happened, chiefly owing to our policy with regard to the Press. At the beginning of the war, Switzerland, like America, could only form her views of the rights and wrongs of the conflict and the course which it was pursuing, from the newspapers. In German-Switzerland numbers of the newspapers are financed by German money and even written by German writers. Quite naturally the readers of these papers believed what they told them. In other words, they were convinced that the atrocities in Belgium were either imaginary or grossly exaggerated, that Germany would at the end of the war make good her promise to make up to Belgium for the violation of her neutrality, and that meanwhile she was winning all along the line.

That was the positive side of the newspaper evil in Switzerland, over which France and England had, of course, no control. The negative side, which they might have controlled, which was indeed of their own making, was that the true news, which should have acted as a corrective to the false, hardly existed at all on the question of the atrocities in Belgium, because there were no correspondents in Belgium to give it. If the Swiss had known then, as they know now, though many of them still do not choose to believe it, the real truth about Belgium, there is no doubt at all that the greater part of the old pro-German feeling would have perished at the beginning. It throve only on lies and the concealment and ignorance of the truth. That is a fact which can be very simply proved. As soon as the Swiss knew, because they saw it for themselves with their own eyes, something of the way in which Germany has made war, the revulsion against her and therefore in our favour began. It happened in this way. From the ruined villages of Lorraine and the other occupied provinces the Germans carried away to Germany at the beginning of the war a large number of what they called "hostages" and the French *"internés,"* old men and women and children, mainly of the poorest classes. They had committed no military or political crime, they had only lost their homes and their possessions and most of their relatives, and they could under no conceivable circumstances affect one way or the other Germany's chances of winning or losing the war. For months, wretchedly clad and fed, they were kept in prison-camps in the fatherland. Then by the good offices of the compassionate Swiss and partly probably because the Germans were beginning to find them a nuisance and to wonder why they had ever taken them away from France, they were sent back in relays of three or four hundred at a time to their own country by way of Switzerland. At the same time the far smaller number of *internés* whom the French had detained in France or taken from Alsace in retaliation were sent back in exchange. I never myself saw any of the *internés* from France on their way back to Germany. But the Swiss, who worked untiringly day after day and month after month to show practical sympathy to all these unfortunates on their way through their country, constantly saw both the French and the Germans, and the effect on their judgment of the German nation, even against their own natural inclinations, showed very decidedly which nation had treated worst these innocent victims of the war. I never met a Swiss man or woman, German-Swiss, or French-Swiss, who had seen the French *internés* on their way back to France—not to their homes, for their homes in most cases no longer exist—who was not intensely shocked and indignant at the state in which they were and the sufferings which they had undergone, and from the date at which they first began to see them and act the good Samaritan to them, at Schaffhausen, at Basle, at Zurich, at Berne, at Lausanne, and at Geneva, from that moment the marked revulsion of a large part of the Swiss people against Germany and Prussian militarism took its rise. It is my firm opinion that it would have begun long before if only the correspondents of French and English newspapers had been allowed from the beginning to see for themselves, as nearly as they could, what happened in Belgium, and to publish it to Switzerland and the world.

All this is only a parenthesis—I am afraid rather a long one—to what I was saying some pages back about the large-minded tolerance as well as the great personal kindness which the Prefects and Sous-Préfets of the eastern provinces of France, from Belfort to Commercy, showed to M. Lamure and myself as representatives of the English Press. All of them, like every Frenchman who has talked to me on the subject, and, unfortunately, unlike some Englishmen, believed in *The Times* as a great power for good. With that feeling in their minds they took us with them, as they had, of course, an official right to do, on some of their official visits to the ravished districts, because they believed that the publication of the truth about them in *The Times* would be of service to the common cause. M. Mirman in particular held that view. He believed that the articles we sent to London, which, but for him and his fellow-Prefects and Sous-Préfets, could never have been written, were of real positive use for France and against the common enemy.

I seem, perhaps, to be getting a long way from the main purpose of this book, which is to state, as strongly as I can, the debt which I believe France and England owe to the generals and armies that have fought for the common cause in the east of France. But while I am on the subject I mean to go a little further, and to illustrate what I have said on the subject of newspaper correspondents (if the Censor will let me say it) by a reference to a personal matter, because as I see it, it is not a personal matter at all, but of real importance to the country. After we had been in Nancy for four months, during all which time we were in constant and friendly relations with many of the civil and military authorities, we were one morning politely but peremptorily ordered to leave the town within twenty-four hours. Otherwise we were told that we should be arrested and tried before a court-martial on a charge of espionage—not, of course, because we were spies, but because we were journalists exercising our *métier* within the zone of the armies (in which, up to a few days before that time, Paris was also included!). No complaint was made against us personally, because none could be. In a letter which M. Mirman wrote to me at the time, most of which is too personal to quote, though he gave me full liberty to show it to any French authorities whom I might meet, he expressly said that I had been guilty of no indiscretion during my stay, that my papers and my comings and goings had always been perfectly in order, and that he would be happy to see me come back to Nancy.

Photograph by Libert-Fernana, Nancy.

OUTSIDE THE PREFECTURE, NANCY.

M. Mirman, Mme. Mirman, M. Puech, who acted as M. Mirman's chauffeur, and some members of the staff of the Prefecture. Seated in front, the author and M. Jean Rogier of the *Petit Parisien*.

Now, a Prefect of France, and above all, one of M. Mirman's standing and record and experience and ardent patriotism, does not take upon himself the responsibility and trouble of making a direct appeal to the highest authorities on behalf of the correspondent of a foreign newspaper without very good reason. In this particular case I believe that what chiefly affected him was the conviction that in the present critical times one of the most important functions which an allied newspaper can fulfil is the promotion of a fuller understanding and still more cordial relations between England and France, and that few things could serve that purpose so well as the permanent presence of an English correspondent near the French fighting-line.

Since then, in my efforts to return to the place where I believe honestly I can be of most use to my country in this war, I have shown that letter to some of the highest authorities in France, but without practical effect. Sometimes it has nearly melted their hearts, but not quite. But I mean to go on trying. That is why I am writing this chapter. I not only believe, but I am certain, not because I am I, but because I am a responsible correspondent of *The Times*, that "somewhere in France"—somewhere in the east of France for me—I can in my small way (but *The Times* is not a small paper) help to win this war, and, with a little encouragement and help from the military authorities, do much more useful work than was possible under the restricted conditions by which M. Lamure and I were handicapped during our stay in Lorraine in 1914. And I believe firmly that that is true of the great mass of correspondents of the big English and French newspapers, and that a grave mistake is being made in not using us, and giving us real and not little snippets of pretended liberty. We are not out for scalps and "scoops," as we might be in ordinary journalism and an ordinary war. We are ready to take the war as seriously as any general or any minister. What we want to do is to tell the truth, or as much of it as the Censor and our own discretion will let us, because we know that only the truth will prevail.

CHAPTER XVII
A DAY WITH A PREFECT

Having said so much of what our friends of the various Préfectures did or tried to do for two humble newspaper correspondents, I should like, before going on to consider the next phase of the war, to try and give an idea of the work which they did for the people in their districts, and the risks which they often ran in doing it. I will begin with a description of a *Conseil de Révision* at St. Nicholas-du-Port, to which I went with M. Mirman and one of the Generals of the district. While we were in Lorraine there were a large number of special sittings of these courts, at which the young men of the nation go through their final medical inspection before entering upon their statutory term of military service. Sometimes they were presided over by the Préfet himself, sometimes by M. Slingsby, the President of the Prefectorial Council, a direct descendant of the old Yorkshire family but a Frenchman to the bone. In ordinary times the regular annual inspections take place in March, and the normal age of enlistment is twenty. Soon after the war began boys of nineteen were called up to undergo training for service with the colours, and it was to judge of their fitness to bear arms and also to revise cases that had previously been turned down or put back that these extraordinary *Conseils de Révision* were held.

There was, of course, an obvious difference between the case of these boys and the armies of volunteers which Lord Kitchener was at that time recruiting in England. This was compulsory service in being, the so-called conscription which then and for many a long day after so seriously agitated the tender bosoms of English agitators and champions of personal liberty. These young Frenchmen had got to be soldiers whether they liked it or not. But compulsory service, whatever its uninformed opponents may say, is service and not slavery. That is precisely why in France, in peace as well as in war-time, the inspections are presided over by the civil and not the military authorities. The Prefect, or his deputy, in conducting them, is fulfilling one of his chief functions, which is to represent the people as their official champion, and check any tendency to the possible evils of militarism. It is his bounden duty to see that no man is taken for service in the army who on account of physical incapacity or for any other reason ought and has the right to remain a civilian.

There was, however, little need for this kind of paternal *surveillance* in the extra *Conseils de Révision* which were held during the war, except possibly in the way of restraining some whose capacity to bear arms was not so certain as their enthusiasm. There was not a suspicion of reluctance. One and all they were itching to be up and at them. When we arrived at the Hotel de Ville a crowd of between three and four hundred of them were waiting outside in the street, talking to their friends and relations, who looked just as proud as the boys themselves that they had been called up, and just as eager that they should be passed as fit—if not *bons pour service* in the Army, at all events for some kind of auxiliary service. It was impossible to look at them and not to think of the hundreds of thousands of boys in England who, in spite of all that could be done to coax and wheedle and bribe them into the army, in spite of every kind of ignoble coercion short of compulsion, were at that time still hanging back from the honour and glory of serving their country in arms. Not even the thought of those other still more numerous hundreds of thousands who had gladly volunteered and given up everything else at the one supreme call could quite take the taste of the contrast out of my mouth.

In ordinary times I dare say some of those French boys would have been frankly annoyed at the prospect of giving up their civil employment and their personal freedom for a period of enforced military service. But now as they came pouring up the stairs after us into the big bare room—decorated only by a tricolor flag and a white bust of the République Française, crowned with a wreath of oak leaves—there was no mistaking their extraordinary enthusiasm or the reason for it. The soldiers of the Kaiser when they went to the war, believed firmly that they were going to fight because the Fatherland was in danger, because otherwise it would inevitably be crushed by the ring of jealous nations by which it was surrounded. That was the idea which had been carefully drilled into them. That was what they had been told by the ignoble and servile army of professors and sergeants. But these boys of Lorraine needed no telling. They knew. If they did not all actually come from the blackened and ruined villages and towns which marked the track of the retreating incendiaries, they lived without exception within a few miles of them. Saint Nicholas-du-Port had only just escaped occupation by the enemy. Dombasle was only two miles off. For weeks the Germans' guns had been thundering in their ears, for weeks they had heard—and known—of the murder of innocent women and children and old men; for weeks they had been familiar with the effects of pillage and incendiarism and rape. No wonder they were willing to die for *la patrie*. If the things that were done in Lorraine and the Vosges had been done in Kent and Norfolk the shirkers of England would long ago have repented in khaki and ashes. There would have been no need of lurid posters and cinematograph films and compulsion to bring them in. They would have fought because they would have known— as these French boys knew—that otherwise their country and all that they loved must die. And if they had been rejected because, though the spirit was willing, the flesh was too weak to make a fighting soldier, they would have been as bitterly disappointed as these boys of Lorraine were whenever they failed to pass the doctor's tests.

Among the boys, in one of the batches that came in a dozen at a time to be examined, there was, I remember, a man of well over fifty, long past the military age but still perfectly fit and strong, who had been called up owing to some mistake made by a clerk. It was curious and it was exhilarating to see this greybeard standing up stripped to the skin, quietly and with proud dignity explaining to the uniformed full-dressed committee in front of him that he had already served his terms as active soldier, reservist, and territorial, but that he was still able to fight and asked nothing better than to be reckoned *bon pour service* if the country had need of him.

There were other grey beards in the room besides this willing veteran's. Ranged at the upper end of it by the daïs on which M. Mirman sat with the committee, were the mayors of the various towns and cantons from which the boys came, about twenty in all, ready to answer questions on doubtful cases. Before the actual inspection began, the whole thing reminded me oddly of a Public School function at home, except that the headmaster wore the uniform of a Prefect of France, the boys were all of the same age and practically of the same height, and the assistant masters, many of them humble peasants, looked like hard-bitten farmers from the Yorkshire moors or the lowlands of Scotland. There was a great contrast between them and the boys. Mayors, as a rule, are men of peace, associated in the mind with gold chains and heavy dinners. But the mayors of Lorraine are different. They live very close to the frontier, and, as M. Mirman said in an earnest and spirited speech to the young recruits, they had lately had need not only of much patience and good humour, but of unusual physical and moral courage. All of them whose cantons lay between St. Nicholas-du-Port and the frontier had a few weeks before at least run the risk of being carried off as "hostages," to say nothing of graver perils. Still, after all, the men by the daïs, bravely as they had stuck to their posts, had escaped with their lives. But the boys—I was looking at them, and thinking of the pity and wickedness of it all, when M. Mirman began to talk to them. The war that they were going away from their homes to fight in was, he told them, a war to kill war. When he put to them the question, "Do you want not to serve?" they thundered out the kind of "No" with which in England political audiences are in the habit of declaring to the world and to each other that they are not down-hearted. Sometimes these political negatives are not as confident as they seem, and are rather efforts at self-encouragement than statements of fact. But the "No" of the boys of St. Nicholas-du-Port was absolutely genuine. There was no question of that. Their only wish was to join the ranks and fight, and fight, and fight—till the wrongs of France were avenged and the victory won.

Another day that we spent with M. Mirman almost directly after our arrival in Nancy was rather more *mouvementé*. It was a week after the Germans had finally been driven back from Amance and Champenoux, and the news had been brought in that Nomeny, a town between St. Généviève and the frontier, had just been evacuated by the enemy. So M. Mirman was going to visit it, and he offered to take us with him. Before we started we lunched at the Préfecture with a fairly large party which included, besides M. Mirman and his eldest daughter, M. Abeille, his sécrétaire général (who has since been killed fighting for France), M. Mage, the Sous-Préfet of Toul, M. Guiran Scevola and M. Royer, two well-known French artists, painters in ordinary to the Ministry of War, temporarily attached as artillery privates to the Toul garrison, M. Dominique Bonnaud, the Parisian chansonnier, attached to the staff of the Préfecture, M. Jean Rogier, of the *Petit Parisien*, the only special correspondent of a London or Paris newspaper besides ourselves who stayed more than a few days in Nancy, and M. Puech, a big ironmaster of Frouard, five miles down the Moselle, who for the first part of the war acted as M. Mirman's chauffeur, and went with him through some rather exciting scenes during his prefectorial visits. After lunch—it is a pleasant way the French have—there were a few speeches, one of which fell to the lot of the English correspondent of *The Times*, and was delivered haltingly and slowly in Public School French. As events proved afterwards, it was fortunate for us that there were speeches and that one of them took some time, for if we had started ten minutes sooner we should probably not have come back—at all events for some months.

We set off at half-past one, M. Rogier and I in the Préfet's car, an open one, with him and M. Puech, the rest in a larger and slower Limousine behind. At that time there were a large number of troops in and round Nancy—most of them the men who had fought in the Battle of the Grand Couronné—and for the first five or six miles we were constantly passing them, in the town and the villages and along the roads, marching, driving long processions of hooded country-carts, hauling down a captive balloon, lighting fires against the walls of the houses, cooking their meals, grooming their horses, furbishing up their arms and accoutrements, foraging, laughing, singing, shaving, washing, tailoring, eating, drinking, smoking, and chatting as busily and light-heartedly as if the enemy were a hundred miles away instead of only a little way beyond the horizon on the frontier.

After we had gone some way along the Château-Salins road we turned northwards, leaving Amance on the right, and began to get away from the many soldiers who were off duty to the smaller number who were fighting. The road we were now on ran parallel to the frontier at about three miles from it. On our left was the range of hills which stretches northwards to Ste. Généviève and Pont-à-Mousson, on our right an almost flat plain sloping down to the frontier and the Seille. By the side of the road a battery of 75's was banging away into the distance, and in one or two places clouds of white smoke were rising up from burning villages. We stopped to speak to the gunner commandant, who looked rather suspiciously at a car-ful of *civils*. But there is no mistaking the silver lace on the *képi* of a Préfet, and eventually he said that as far as he knew there was no reason why we should not go on to Nomeny, though he advised us not to dawdle for the next few miles, as we were rather close to the frontier and the enemy. M. Puech, who can drive as well and as fast as any one I know, consequently let her rip, and we covered the next seven or eight miles in almost as few minutes. Batteries on the hills on our left were firing over our heads at the enemy positions across the Seille, and once or twice we passed trenches manned by companies of *fantassins*, but the return fire did not come our way, and some minutes later we passed into a quieter region, by contrast curiously still and peaceful. As we drove up to a small village about a mile from Nomeny, the day, which had been beautifully sunny, suddenly clouded over, the sky in front of us became inky black, and the German horizon looked darker and more threatening than I ever saw it. In the village, not very badly damaged considering its position, we saw not a soul except one old woman who was standing at her door looking out with dazed eyes, but quickly turned in and disappeared as we dashed past. That might have warned us. We ought to have been struck by the death-like emptiness of the village street. But we were thinking of other things, of the pace we were going at, the gathering storm, of what Nomeny would be like, and especially of the slower car behind, and why we had not seen it for so long. I was just looking round for it again when suddenly the car slowed and stopped dead. Then "Cachez-vous," said M. Puech quietly, and though it did not feel very glorious, we did, without losing very much time. As I crouched down on the seat (the Préfet was in front with M. Puech) I looked ahead and on the brow of the slight slope up which we had been running, not more than a full iron shot from where we were, saw four grey figures in spiked helmets, with levelled rifles pointing straight at us, kneeling by the side of the road. It was a tight place, and it was lucky for us all that we had M. Puech to drive. Instead of trying to turn the car, as he might have done, on a convenient bit of level ground by the side of the road, he made up his mind what to do, and did it, in the same second, jamming his lever into the reverse speed directly we stopped, and the car began moving steadily backwards, though not quite as fast as we should have liked. He was sitting bolt upright in front of me, with one hand on the steering-wheel and the other on the back of his seat, looking away from the Germans along the road behind us. As soon as they saw that we were not coming on they began to fire. Still perfectly cool and French, he backed down the slope of the hill, which was as straight as a two-foot rule, counting the shots out loud as we went: "One, two, three, four...." They made a flick just like the crack of a small hunting-crop. "Another thousand yards and we're all right ... five, six—that touched us" (it had grazed the right front lamp and glanced on to the trumpet) "seven ..." and so on up to "nine, ten ... eleven," and with that we reached a side lane into which, with the same quick decision, he backed the car to turn her. And then, just when it seemed as if we had got off safely, things began to go wrong. The engine stopped dead, and the off-wheels stuck in the ditch. So out we jumped. M. Puech to the front to start the engine if he could, M. Mirman and M. Rogier and I to push behind—our very hardest, but without the slightest effect, M. Puech grinding away just as hard and just as vainly at the engine crank—and then suddenly the engine started, and we flung ourselves into the car, this time with our backs to the foe but our heads erect, and in a moment were flying back to the village as fast as our excellent M. Puech could push her along.

NOMENY.
By permission of M. Martin, Secrétaire Général, the Prefecture, Nancy.

In the village street we found M. Lamure and the others and the second car, standing in the middle of a group of excited villagers. When they had come along, a minute or two behind us, the whole population, instead of only our old woman, rushed out and barred the road in front of them, and when they had pulled up told them they could not possibly go on as sixty Uhlans had just left the village, only ten minutes before our car went through. While they were talking to them, wondering what to do, the shots fired at us, or rather at M. Puech, began to sing into the village, but over their heads, chipping the plaister off the upper walls. And that, no doubt, was the explanation of our escape. The Germans had been firing from the village, most probably at a long range, before we came into it, and when they retired towards Nomeny the four men whom they had left on the road as a rearguard had forgotten to lower their sights, till one of them saw what he was doing, corrected his mistake, and fired the shot which hit the lamp of the car.

I expect when our four friends got back to the other fifty-six, or at all events when they learnt that they had missed bagging a Prefect of France, they had a poorish time of it. But that was not our affair. Thanks to the courage and nerve of M. Puech we had got safely out of a rather awkward fix, for at the best, if they had crippled our chauffeur or the car, we should have paid a prolonged visit to Germany. And thanks to the speeches at lunch, including, I am proud to think, the one in Public School French, we had escaped by ten minutes running our head into a much larger nest of hornets in the village.

So we decided to put off our visit to Nomeny till another day. We had had enough of Germans for the present. Also we thought it more prudent to go home by a different road, at the back of the hills where the French batteries were stationed, round by Ste. Généviève and up the valley of the Moselle, especially as, before M. Lamure and the other party reached the village, when their car was panting after ours, one particular shell had fallen rather too near them to be pleasant, and there was no urgent need to repeat the experience.

When we got back to Nancy, after getting stuck in the middle of a large field flooded by the Moselle, from which the car had to be dragged out by a passing team of artillery horses, M. Mirman wrote for me a *petit mot* on one of his cards. It was dated Nancy, Dimanche 20 Septembre, 1914, and ran as follows:—

"Léon Mirman, Préfet de Meurthe et Moselle, s'excuse très humblement de n'avoir pu montrer à M. Richard Campbell"—he always would call me Richard—"la pauvre ville de Nomeny, assassinée par les Allemands, et qui garde les traces des meutres commis sur des civils et de l'incendie systématiquement et scientifiquement organisée comme il en verra un exemple demain à Gerbéviller—et il lui remet cette carte en souvenir très amicale d'une promenade … un peu mouvementée où le 'feu' et l'eau n'ont pu altérer leur commune bonne humeur.

"Et vive l'Entente Cordiale d'hier qui a préparé l'action commun de deux grands nations pour assurer le triomphe de la civilization contre la Barbarie Teutonne!"

So "now you know," as M. Rogier wrote in the vivid account of our trip which he sent to the *Petit Parisien*, "why I didn't go to Nomeny." But at least I am glad that we tried to go. For it showed me first of all the sort of chances that a Prefect in the occupied provinces had to take in carrying out his duty, and secondly what our Allies mean by *sang-froid*. It seems to me that is rather a fine quality, in a motor or outside it, and that it will yet help us to win the war.

CHAPTER XVIII
THE ATTACK ON THE RIVER FORTS

In following the course of the war in the eastern provinces up to this point we have seen first of all how the tide of it ebbed and flowed for five weeks along the line of the frontier, that is to say, the river Seille and the range of the Vosges. Broadly speaking, the net result of this five weeks of fighting was that on the left or northern section of the line, from a point a little east of Nomeny nearly as far as the Donon, the French had pushed the enemy back to the frontier; that in the centre from near the Donon to about Ste. Marie aux Mines, half way along the Vosges, the Germans still held a footing in France in the Department of the Vosges; but that on the right of the line the French were a little way across the frontier in Southern Alsace.

We have seen, secondly, that behind this first line there was another, roughly parallel to it, running from Pont-à-Mousson past Dombasle and Gerbéviller and then on to St. Dié in the direction of the channels of the Moselle, the Meurthe, and the Mortagne, along which the Battle of the Grand Couronné was fought.

Beyond this second line there was, and is, a third, which stretches from Verdun along the valley of the Meuse to Toul, from which it is continued to Epinal and Belfort—the line or barrier of the great frontier fortresses. The whole of the war so far on the part of the invaders has been a sustained and desperate attempt to get near enough to this wall—against which the French had their backs—to batter it down. On their left, on the Belfort-Epinal section, they had failed, in a military sense, to get anywhere near it. In the centre, from Epinal to Toul, they had equally failed, thanks to the resistance of Dubail and de Castelnau, to come within striking distance. On the right, from Toul to Verdun, they had for the third time failed, in so far that neither Toul, which was protected by the armies in front of Nancy, nor Verdun, which was defended twelve miles in advance by the Third Army under General Sarrail, had ever fired more than an occasional shot at the enemy even from any of their outlying forts.

On the other hand, as the result of the advance of the main German right before the Battle of the Marne, the armies commanded by the Crown Prince of Prussia and the Duke of Wurtemburg had succeeded in turning Verdun, so that although the Germans had never got up to the wall of the fortresses, much less broken through it, they had, on the Verdun-Toul section, got to the farther side of it and the Meuse. There was a time, before the point which we have now reached, and before the Battle of the Marne, when, east and west of this stretch of the Meuse, two French armies, part of General Sarrail's force and part of the left wing of the Second Army, with the Toul garrison force to help them, were actually fighting back to back, on opposite sides of the river. But the more important part of this double engagement—Sarrail against the Crown Prince of Prussia—was on the west side of the Meuse, and does not therefore belong, strictly speaking, to the scope of this book; the fighting on the right bank, except that extending a few miles south of Verdun on its east side, between part of its garrison army and part of the garrison army of Metz, was not at first very serious. There was, as I have said, at that time a gap of some miles, across the base of what afterwards became the St. Mihiel triangle, in the otherwise continuous line of the two opposing forces.

But in the period immediately following their defeat at the Grand Couronné the enemy began to attack this part of the barrier of fortresses with extraordinary vigour; on the rest of the line, the part with which we have already dealt, they confined themselves on the whole to the task of maintaining the positions to which, after their first advance, they had been driven back, and it was the fighting which resulted in the formation of the St. Mihiel wedge that became the really interesting part of the eastern campaign.

Before, however, going on to talk about the St. Mihiel business, and the attack on the northern half of the fortress line, something, I think, ought to be said about another fortified position, the only one between the great Verdun-Belfort fine and the frontier, the solitary fort of Manonviller, a few miles east of Lunéville, which stood alone between it and the enemy. The mystery of Manonviller also stands alone, or almost alone, in the history of the war. I know very little about it; no one, I fancy, knows much, except, perhaps, the high authorities and some members of the garrison, and these last are prisoners in Germany. It was supposed to be immensely strong and considerably feared by the Germans. There are many stories about its fall which may or may not be true. Some people say that the garrison only lost four or five killed and wounded, that right at the beginning of the attack it was found that the telephone communication with Toul had been cut off, and even that its guns were never fired at all. But in any case it is certain that the garrison of nine hundred men surrendered on August 28th after a two days' bombardment, probably carried out by two Austrian 305's stationed on the frontier at Avricourt, and that it was loudly whispered and widely believed that there was something queer about the matter. Since Longwy was able to hold out for three weeks there cannot, I am afraid, be much doubt that there was something curious about the surrender of its stronger sister-fort, which was swept out of the way of the German advance like a sand-castle by the waves of the sea.

After the Battle of the Grand Couronné the army of the Crown Prince of Bavaria occupied a front extending to the north-west from the frontier opposite Lunéville, past Pont-à-Mousson and Thiaucourt in the direction of Verdun, stopping some distance short of the point at which the left of the Crown Prince of Prussia's army began. The left wing, as far as Thiaucourt, was kept busy in preventing the French from advancing on Saarburg and Metz; the right, reinforced by part of the Metz army, began at this time a determined forward movement across the plain of the Woevre to the wooded Hauts de Meuse. They had two objects in view: to break through the line of the fortresses between Verdun and Toul, and to cross the river and join hands with the right wing of the Crown Prince's army so as to encircle Verdun.

The fortress of Toul is almost exactly half-way between Epinal and Verdun, about forty miles from each. In the lower stretch of country, the Trouée de Charmes, which had been so gallantly defended by the 75's and Chasseurs-à-pied of the First Army, there are no forts. Between Toul and Verdun the French position was much stronger. East of the Meuse the Hauts de Meuse slope gradually down to the river, broken at intervals by a series of deep and precipitous ravines, guarded by numerous forts, ancient and modern. On the north the district is bounded by the Verdun-Metz railway, below which is the plain of the Woevre, and on the south by the quick-flowing Rupt de Mad, which runs from near Commercy on the Meuse north-east past Thiaucourt to Arnaville, where it falls into the Moselle close to Metz. The chain of forts extends all along the Meuse, on both sides of the stream. South of the Rupt de Mad, between Commercy and the Moselle (which here takes a sharp bend north-east from Toul, almost parallel to the Rupt de Mad, till it is joined at Frouard by the Meurthe) the forts of Liouville, Gironville, Jouy, Lucey, Bruley, and St. Michel, point their guns to the east and north, towards the German frontier. Lower down, on the right bank of the river, the guns of the Camp des Romains, a little south of St. Mihiel, like those of Forts Genicourt and Troyon to the north of the town, command much of the surrounding country and are ready to dispute (or rather were ready to dispute) the passage of the river, and still further north are the southern defences of Verdun, facing up the channel of the stream, on the further or left bank of which the Fort des Paroches, close to St. Mihiel, looks across the river to the east.

Libert-Fernand, Nancy, phot.

REMEREVILLE—MEURTHE ET MOSELLE.

Libert-Fernand, Nancy, phot.

CHÂTEAU DE HARAUCOURT—MEURTHE ET MOSELLE.

The real grand attack on this formidable position began about September 19th, I suppose when there were enough forces available. But before that there was a determined assault on Fort Troyon—once again on September 8th, the date which was to have been pregnant with such glorious possibilities for the Kaiser, the day of the most furious attack in front of Nancy, the last day before the Germans began their retreat from the Marne. It is worth going back to, for the defence of Troyon during both of the two bombardments which it suffered was one of the most gallant stands of the campaign. Earlier still the Crown Prince had tried to bombard it in a feeble sort of way, but apparently without much effect, for on September 8th, after the attack from the east had begun, an officer of the garrison wrote to his wife, "Nous avons été tranquilles pendant trente-sept jours," that is to say, from the beginning of the war.

Even the day before, so peaceful was the tranquillity, this same officer had been out partridge-shooting. It looks as if it might be a fairly good partridge country, though to English eyes there is rather a lack of cover. The fort stands fairly high, and far off to the south, across the bare sweep of the down-like grass and stubbles, you can see higher still the jagged outline of the Camp des Romains, silhouetted against the sky like the sand dunes at Sandwich on a slightly larger scale. (At that time, of course, the Camp des Romains was still in the hands of the French.) Troyon itself is not very large. Outside it looks the most innocent thing in the world—a more or less quadrangular collection of rounded gravel banks, thickly covered with grass. Inside there are—or were—deep wide ramparts and ditches and vaults and walls of earth and solid masonry and iron—and the guns (155's) and the steel cupolas.

On the evening of the 7th the garrison received news that a strong column coming from the direction of Metz (through the gap between the French Second and Third and the German Fifth and Sixth Armies) had reached Mouilly and St. Remy in the Hauts de Meuse, a little way south of Les Eparges, and five miles north-east of Troyon, and the next morning they were at Seuzey, nearly due east of the fort and only three miles away. At eight o'clock the bombardment began, and by eleven the German siege-mortars of 150 millimetres, concealed in deep ravines where the French gunners could not get at them, had dropped one hundred and eighty shells into the fort, which, though they only killed one man and wounded four, had knocked out seven of the French guns. The garrison were clearly in a bad position. All the French troops which had been on that side of the Meuse had crossed the river to join the final stages of the Battle of the Marne, so that they could count on no immediate support, though they knew that a division of cavalry and a regiment of artillery had left Toul early that morning. But there was no chance of their arriving till next day. The Governor of Verdun telephoned soon after the bombardment began to tell them that the success of the big battle on the other side of the river depended on their holding out for forty-eight hours; the commandant replied that they would—and prayed that the gun cupolas might not be smashed. Then Verdun telephoned again to say that they were sending an aeroplane to spot the enemy's gun positions for them, but as they could not show themselves on the parapets that was cold comfort. At three, by which time four hundred shells had fallen, there was a short breathing space of comparative quiet, and they were able to take stock of the extensive damage done by the shells, of which, fortunately, about one in four failed to burst. Then came a third message to say that if the worst came to the worst the men were to take shelter in the ammunition cellars, but that the fall of the fort would be a grave disaster, and, in fact, that they positively must hold out for the success of the operations across the Meuse.

From half-past four in the afternoon to half-past seven there was another storm of shells, and then again a lull, and more stock-taking. Even though the vaulted shelters in the fort are immensely solid, the casualties were surprisingly light. Only eight more men had been wounded, so that the total number of deaths caused by four hundred shells was only one. There had been many hair-breadth escapes, but though the defences were crumbling to pieces before their eyes—when they could see for the blinding clouds of black smoke which hung about for two or three minutes after each explosion—so far they were not hopelessly broken in. In the bombardment of modern forts that is the principal factor—since on their standing depends the lives of the gunners—that and the resisting powers of the gun embrasures and cupolas, which cannot, however, last for ever. Their destruction is only a matter of time.

With that prospect in front of them, and also the practical certainty of a night attack, perhaps by infantry as well, the garrison were quite remarkably calm and resolute. Some of them even managed to snatch an hour or two of sleep, and all were thirsty enough to drink, though only one or two were able to eat anything.

During the night a brisk fusillade every twenty minutes or half-hour up to three o'clock was all that they had to put up with, except for several false alarms raised by the sentries of imaginary enemies trying to cross the barbed-wire protections, which kept everybody's nerves on edge. The besiegers had evidently concluded that the fort was not yet sufficiently broken up to make an infantry attack feasible. So at about five, just after the fort of Les Paroches had rung up to say that they could do nothing to help them, as their guns could not reach the German positions, the 150's began again, and one of the first shots hit an ammunition store and exploded about twenty 90-millimetre shrapnel shells. Then came another message (they must have found the telephone rather a comfort in their isolated position), this time from Commercy, to say that the 2nd Cavalry Division from Toul was well on the way to relieve them, and had reached Buxerulles on the Commercy-Fresne road, north-east of St. Mihiel, hardly more than twelve miles off. But it was not till well on in the night, nearly twenty-four hours later, that the Toul division at last arrived, and before that time the garrison had gone through a still more severe bombardment.

The day began with a white flag incident, or rather with the appearance of two German cavalrymen accompanied by a bugler, and carrying a large flag of truce. The commandant went forward to speak to them—they had stopped thirty yards the other side of the wire entanglements—and three times they summoned him to surrender the fort. To the first summons he answered simply, "Never"; to the second, "France has given me charge of the fort and I will blow it up sooner than surrender it"; and to the last, "F.... moi le camp, je vous ai assez vus ... A bientôt, à Metz!" So that was the end of them and their mission.

Up to now the guns bombarding them, as far as the garrison could make out, consisted of a battery of 150's at the edge of the wood of Lamorville, about five miles to the east of the fort, and a field battery of 77's, posted between one and two miles away on the reverse side of Hill 259, called La Gouffière. There were also some infantry engaged in digging trenches on the Signal of Troyon, close by, where the commandant had shot his partridges on the 7th. (On the 8th, in one of the lulls in the bombardment, he had two shots himself with 90 shrapnel at the men on his partridge ground, and rather spoilt their excavating work, but then the 150's began again.) On the second day, after the white flag and its bearers had taken their departure, the bombardment began again, with greatly increased severity, as the enemy had now brought up some 280's and 305's, but in spite of the extraordinary havoc which they produced the plucky garrison still continued to serve their guns as best they could without any thought of surrender. When night fell there was another alarm of an infantry attack. This time there was no doubt about it. They could make out a black mass of men advancing towards the south cupola of the fort, and some of them were already busy cutting the barbed wire in front of it. The commandant, whose diary of the siege I have followed in this account, got his men together, ordered most of them under cover, and then opened fire on the swarm of assailants with machine-guns. That was too much for the Germans, and they broke and fled, leaving the ground strewn with their dead and wounded. Still later in the night he was knocked over and wounded in several places by fragments of a 305 shell which fell only a yard behind him. But as soon as his wounds were dressed he was up again, commanding and encouraging his men, and still the fort held out through the dark night, continually lit by the explosion of the bursting shells. And then, at last, the division from Toul arrived (I presume that the cavalry had had to wait at Buxerulles for the slower troops who were following them), the enemy were forced to abandon the bombardment not a moment too soon, and the commandant was carried off to hospital at Verdun (where he received the Croix de Guerre), but not before he had left fluttering on the crumbling parapet the flag of France. On the next day, and the next, and the next, further fierce onslaughts on the fort by large numbers of Germans were driven back with great slaughter by the garrison, strongly reinforced by the cavalry division and a Toul battery of 75's, and the attack on Troyon was finally abandoned on the 13th. The German losses in front of the fort, as the result of the five days' fighting and a second unsuccessful attack which they made on it a week later, were between seven and ten thousand men.

This splendid defence of Troyon was typical of what happened in several of the Meuse forts when the enemy, on September 20th, resumed their efforts, but with many more troops, to force their way across the Hauts de Meuse to the river. Having reoccupied Thiaucourt, on the Rupt de Mad, eight miles north-west of Pont-à-Mousson, they took up a position well to the west of it, with a long front extending north and south in front of St. Mihiel, through Heudicourt (eight miles north-east of the town) along the Hauts de Meuse. The gap in the line of the German front between the Fifth and Sixth Armies was now at last permanently filled up, for the first time during the war.

From this forward position they began a systematic bombardment of Troyon, les Paroches, the Camp des Romains, Liouville, and the other river forts. Their base position behind this line reached from Thiaucourt to Fresnes, on the edge of the Hauts de Meuse, seventeen miles across the plain in the direction of Verdun, and ten miles short of it. This position it is worth while to notice with some care, because it forms the base of the triangle of which St. Mihiel (of which we shall hear something) forms the apex. Its strength lay in the fact that it had Metz, with its big supplies of stores and men, less than twenty miles behind it, with direct railway communication; its weakness in its exposure to flank attacks, on its right to the north by the garrison army of Verdun, on its left by that of Toul and the left wing of de Castelnau's army. The driving force of the Metz supplies of men and ammunition from the rear was strong enough to enable the centre of the German line to push forward like the point of a wedge to St. Mihiel in the west. But the lateral pressure of the two French forces on their right and left flanks was also strong and compelled them, as the point of the wedge advanced, to extend their forces on each side of it, facing outwards in two almost opposite directions. And that was how the original St. Mihiel triangle came to be formed, with a seventeen-mile base from Thiaucourt to Fresnes, and two equal sides, each fourteen miles long, from Fresnes to St. Mihiel on the north-west, and from St. Mihiel to Thiaucourt on the south-east. Nearly parallel to this lower side of the triangle, and five or six miles to the south of it, most of the road from Commercy to Pont-à-Mousson, a distance of twenty-five miles, was in the hands of the French. Their only railway ran along the valley of the Meuse, from Commercy past St. Mihiel to Troyon, and as a rule they were not able to use it except at night.

The Germans were better off. They commanded, to begin with, a line from Metz along the Moselle to Arnaville, from which it turned westwards along the Rupt de Mad to Thiaucourt. Half-way between these two places it was joined by another line running due south from Briey, and as their position was consolidated at least one other light railway was constructed in the direction of St. Mihiel. There was also another railway (a section of the Verdun-Commercy line) which runs south from Fresnes along the east edge of the Hauts de Meuse to Heudicourt, half-way between St. Mihiel and Thiaucourt, part of which was available for German traffic, besides a fairly large supply of level roads all through the district, and of these various facilities for transport they made excellent use.

In the plain of the Woevre behind the Fresnes-Heudicourt line everything worked with the precision of a huge machine. During and after the bombardment of the river forts the scene was more like the surroundings of an immense centre of industrial activity than the ordinary conception of a battlefield. From their emplacements between the infantry lines German and Austrian field-guns and siege artillery pounded away incessantly at the forts with 8¼-inch, 12-inch, and even 16½-inch shells. Observation balloons and occasional aeroplanes swayed and hovered over the lines, and ragged fan-shaped columns of brown or white smoke shot up into the air here and there as the charges of high explosives and shrapnel from French or German guns fell and burst. But apart from these inevitable and unconcealable signs of battle—noise and pillars of smoke by day, noise and flashes of flame by night—all the machinery of the fighting was hidden underground, and as far as eye could see the plain looked unpeopled and deserted. Only in the rear the supply trains constantly rolling up from the German base and the methodical work of the men loading and firing the guns and recording the effect of the shots, like shifts of artisans labouring round the furnaces of a gigantic mill, spoke of life and energy. But in appearance it was always the creative energy of a busy manufacturing district rather than the destructive energy of war.

Inside the forts, the direct object for the time being of all this system and activity, there were no illusions of this kind, nothing but grim reality and red ruin. Troyon was hotly bombarded for the second time till it had only four guns left capable of firing a shot, and still the plucky garrison refused either to retire or surrender. The storm of high explosives had only done part of its work. It had reduced Troyon and Les Paroches and Liouville and some of the other forts to a shapeless melancholy desolation of crumbling mounds and yawning pits, littered with tons of rusty steel and shattered blocks of scattered masonry and concrete, till they looked like discarded gravel-pits half buried under scrap-heaps of iron waste. But, though their existence as forts was at an end, the remains of them, with one exception, were still in the hands of the French, protected no longer by their bastions and the guns in their dismantled cupolas, but by the rifles of the men in the trenches, the real flesh and blood rampart of the Republic.

Unfortunately, the one fort in which the enemy did set foot—the Camp des Romains—was the most important of them all. It lies on a ridge nine hundred feet high, barely a mile to the south of St. Mihiel, and therefore at the apex of the triangular position occupied by the opposing lines of trenches, and commands the whole of the surrounding country except parts of the loops of the river immediately to the west and north of it. Its capture, after a heroic resistance on the part of the garrison, was finally brought about by the occupation of St. Mihiel by the army of Metz.

Why that occupation—a particularly disastrous blow for our Allies—was effected as easily as it was, it is not easy to understand. St. Mihiel, or at least the Camp des Romains, was the crucial point of the Meuse position. It was by this time quite obvious that the main object of the Germans was almost at any cost to break through the fortress barrier and cross the river so as to effect a junction with the Crown Prince's army, which now occupied a position in the Argonne between the Aire and the Aisne, to the west of Verdun, extending eastwards to the north of that fortress. If this scheme had succeeded it would have had the double effect of completing the investment of Verdun with a ring instead of only a horse-shoe of hostile armies, and at the same time of relieving the pressure brought to bear on the Crown Prince's army by the French troops in the Argonne between St. Ménéhould and Clermont. It might even have compelled these and the armies on their left to retire once more in the direction of the Marne. Consequently it was of vital importance for the French to concentrate every man they could spare at the point where the German thrust was likely to be most vigorous, and to hold on to St. Mihiel and the Camp des Romains like grim death.

Left to itself, the garrison could do next to nothing. It could account, and did account, for a large number of the enemy in front of its earthen ramparts. But sooner or later its doom was certain. Its fall was only a question of days, or even of hours. Like all fixed forts, ancient or modern, exposed to the fire of modern siege artillery, it was, in itself, about as impregnable as an umbrella. It lay on the extreme left of the French fine from the Meuse to Pont-à-Mousson. To the north it was protected to a certain extent by St. Mihiel, supposing that St. Mihiel contained any troops. But its real defences, on which the French had spent a considerable sum of money before the war, consisted of a large number of trenches, strengthened with concrete, some miles in advance of it on the farther side of the Hauts de Meuse, between

Les Eparges and Thiaucourt. They occupied, that is to say, practically the whole of the space which I have spoken of as the gap in the lines of the armies, and which was partly accounted for by the fact that as the German Fifth Army inclined slightly westwards, to keep in touch with the others which had Paris as their principal objective, the French Third Army was to a certain extent obliged to follow it, besides which for the time being the French Second and the German Sixth Army were too much occupied with their own affairs round Nancy to be able to extend very far in the direction of Verdun. But the carefully prepared trenches were there all the time, and, as far as it is possible to judge without knowing all the circumstances, might and should have been held almost indefinitely, instead of which the chief purpose they seem to have served was to act as a shelter for the advancing Germans. By some further mischance or miscalculation, at this particularly critical moment, two or three days after the Germans had begun the general bombardment of the river forts, St. Mihiel was suddenly left almost wholly denuded of troops, with the result that on August 24th the enemy's advance-guard walked into it practically unopposed.

There are two or three possible explanations of the way in which this regrettable mistake was brought about, in all of which there is probably a certain amount of truth. The French may have made up their minds that the enemy had for the moment given up the idea of making a determined effort to cross the river. Or they may have still clung to the mistaken belief that the fort on the height, chosen centuries ago by the Romans as the most commanding strategic position of the district, was strong enough to defend itself and look after the river as well. Or, thirdly, they may have concluded that they had no choice in the matter, and that the pressure nearer Metz, on the right flank of their line forming the south side of the St. Mihiel triangle, was for the moment more dangerous than that on their left, and that it was safe to move part of their force on the Meuse across to the Moselle.

That, at all events, is what they did, on or near September 22nd. The line in the south of the Woevre had already been considerably thinned by the despatch of a certain number of troops westwards across the Meuse to strengthen the right wing of the army in the Argonne during the Battle of the Marne and the operations which followed it. The effect of the removal of several additional battalions in the opposite direction, to the north of Nancy (where they found that their presence was urgently needed) was that St. Mihiel and the Camp des Romains were left almost isolated, with practically no soldiers at all to guard the town.

The news was quickly carried to the enemy (not by journalists, since there were none anywhere near, but by the spies who were particularly thickly planted in that district of France) and while the French troops which had moved eastwards were engaged to the north of Nancy, and the Toul force from the south was pushing back the main body of the XIVth German Army Corps in the direction of the Rupt de Mad, the extreme right of the Army of Metz, as the result of a bold flank-march along the left or north bank of the Mad, were able to advance nearly as far as St. Mihiel.

The presence of their advance-guard was first observed on the 23rd by a small patrol of French dragoons, who were attacked by a company of German infantry lying in ambush in a little wood by the side of the road about a mile from the town, and fell back on St. Mihiel after a slight skirmish. The news of the approach of the enemy created a panic in the town, and a large number of the inhabitants fled in the direction of Commercy. Next morning a squadron of Uhlans rode in and took possession of the place, cutting the telegraph and telephone wires, and carrying off as "hostages" some forty of the inhabitants, who must have bitterly regretted not having joined in the general exodus of the day before.

(Three months later M. Lamure received a letter on the subject of these hostages from a sergeant attached to the Bureau de Police of one of the eastern armies, who was anxious about some relations of his who were among them, as nothing was known up till then of their fate. He was a stranger to us, but he had heard of our existence, and had a pathetic though gratifying belief that the correspondents of *The Times* might be able to give him the information which his own intelligence office could not.)

The Uhlans were followed, some hours later, by the main body of the German army, which turned off from the Vigneulles-St. Mihiel road somewhere near Chaillon and made its appearance on the Meuse to the north of St. Mihiel at a point where by the natural lie of the ground and the intervening hills it was protected from the fire of the guns both of Les Paroches and the Camp des Romains, which were in any case busy fighting their own battles.

The Germans, or at least a part of them, had now penetrated as far as the line which it had been the object of all their forces operating on the eastern frontier to reach. Their first appearance on the Meuse, which the other armies had crossed lower down to the north of Verdun weeks before, should have been one of the dramatic moments of the war. It had, however, been brought about so tamely and with so little opposition at the last moment that it rather lost that character, and it was not till an attempt to cross the river was made that the position became really exciting. It was still about as unfavourable as it could be for the French. Only a single battalion of Territorials, with no guns and even no mitrailleuses, guarded the river at that point, against a line of probably ten times their own number. The bridges had been hastily destroyed as the enemy advanced, and from the left bank the Territorials did their best to keep them from crossing the river, and during the night of the 25th, by the light of their one searchlight, successfully dealt with the persistent efforts of the German engineers to build a pontoon-bridge. But the next morning the enemy opened fire on them with some heavy batteries which they had brought up from Thiaucourt, and, as the heights of the river prevented the guns in the Camp des Romains from giving them any help, the Territorials were forced to retire under a hot fire, picking up and carrying with them their killed and wounded.

By midday the Germans were across the river, marching in the direction of the valley of the Aire, a tributary of the Aisne, between it and the Meuse, with the object of crossing it to attack General Sarrail in the Forest of the Argonne. The position was critical, and for the French airmen, who could see what was happening and gave due warning in different directions, must have been intensely interesting. There seemed a good chance that the Germans might really carry out the complete investment of Verdun, which their newspapers had already announced as an accomplished fact, and join hands at last with the army of the Crown Prince. Driven northwards by General Sarrail after the Battle of the Marne, past St. Menehould on the Aisne and Clermont on the Aire, left and right of the Forest of the Argonne, that army, which consisted of the XVIth, XVIIIth, and XXIst Army Corps, now occupied a position extending from Varennes (also on the Aire and the east side of the forest) eastwards in a flattened arc rather less than a semicircle which passed about ten miles north of Verdun and then curved down to the east of it in the direction of Fresnes. Opposite to the Crown Prince across the forest from the Aisne towards the Meuse was General Sarrail with the VIth and VIIIth Army Corps. Behind him, falling back from the Meuse on his protection, was the Territorial battalion, which during the night had prevented the Metz army from crossing the river below St. Mihiel, and behind them again, hot on their heels, the pursuing Germans, with a body of cavalry, detached by General Sarrail to head them off, advancing to meet them, and, though at a considerable distance, another French force, the XXth Army Corps, hurrying as fast as they could from the Moselle to overtake them from behind. Meanwhile, the Toul garrison army, which had advanced from the fortress, was keeping up the lateral pressure on the stationary German force along the Rupt de Mad.

In contrast with the state of comparative immobility to which the campaign was shortly afterwards reduced, the manœuvres of the two forces were for the moment particularly lively. Looked at as a war game played on a chess-board, the position was more or less as follows: The French (White) had moved most of their pieces of value up towards the top left-hand corner of the board, where they had the Germans (Black) pretty well penned in front of them along the two back rows. Black, however, was still able to threaten an attack on White's King (Verdun) at about the centre of their fourth row, though it was defended by a few white pawns (its garrison army). Two rows lower down in the centre a black castle (the Metz army at St. Mihiel) was only prevented from checking White's King by some white pawns (the southern forts of Verdun) and, at the same time, threatened a move across the board to the left in order to get behind the main mass of White's pieces. To remove this danger, and to guard a pawn (the Territorial battalion) to the left of Black's castle, White moved back one of his knights (Sarrail's cavalry) from the left-hand top corner, moved up one of his castles (the Toul garrison force) from his back row, and brought across his Queen (the XXth Army Corps) from the lower right-hand corner of the board, where it had been trying to check Black's King (Metz). As the result of these three moves he was able to force Black's castle back to its original position near the centre of the board.

When the news of the occupation of St. Mihiel reached Lorraine the XXth Army Corps, which had barely finished its work there of checking a German advance from the direction of Metz, were at once ordered back to the Meuse, and the advanced guard of their cavalry by a forced night march managed to cross it at Lérouville just below Commercy, only five hours behind the German army, and got in touch with them shortly afterwards in the valley of the Aire. The dragoons at once engaged them with machine-guns, and held them till first the artillery and then the infantry of the corps came up and the battle became general. The Metz force made three separate attacks on the position which the French had taken up on the heights of the Aire, but were repulsed each time with heavy losses, and during the night they fell back on the Meuse, still, however, retaining a footing on the left bank of the river in the western suburb of St. Mihiel and the barracks of Chauvoncourt. After their battle of the day before in Lorraine the forced night march of the XXth Corps and their successful engagement on the Heights of the Aire were a magnificent performance, which had the satisfactory effect of putting an end to the bold effort of the right wing of the Metz army to effect the longed-for junction with the Crown Prince. What it unfortunately did not do was to relieve St. Mihiel. As soon as the Germans got back there they proceeded to entrench themselves strongly, and from a position near the town began to bombard the French forts in the Camp des Romains with their Austrian mammoths.

Concerning this artillery position M. Lamure was told an instructive little story on one of the rather adventurous expeditions which he made to the neighbourhood of St. Mihiel some weeks after the German occupation had begun. So many stories of the same kind (including one, I believe, about a tennis-court at Tooting) were published in the first part of the war that one became rather shy of believing them, but I have my reasons for thinking that this one is probably true. Anyhow, here it is.

Two years before the war a German company, formed for the manufacture of chemical produce, rented a large plot of ground close to St. Mihiel for a term of thirty years. It was a big company and it had need of big buildings with solid foundations. So a floor about two hundred and fifty feet long by thirty wide was laid down in reinforced concrete. Then the company, after announcing that its money had come to an end, and that it could not proceed to put up the proposed buildings, was dissolved. But the plot of ground and the concrete floor, which, before the workmen left, was tidily covered up with a loose coating of earth, still belonged to it. When the army of Metz arrived on the scene some one had the curiosity or the intelligence to inquire what might be hidden under this covering of earth, which was accordingly removed. And there, by the greatest good luck in the world, they discovered not only the concrete floor, but a number of holes in it which proved to be admirably adapted for emplacements for the Austrian guns.

On the whole, I am inclined to back the story of the St. Mihiel concrete floor against the Tooting tennis-court, though in any case it would only add one more to the long list of undoubted cases in which German settlers were planted in the Woevre district in order to render valuable services to the Fatherland either before or during the war. The main point is that from some position near St. Mihiel, whether prepared beforehand or not, the big Austrian howitzers in a very short time silenced the guns and smashed up the turrets and bastions of the Camp des Romains fort, until at last the plucky garrison had no guns left to shoot with, and were finally smoked out after trenches had been pushed up close to the fort. When the asphyxiated survivors had recovered enough to march out the Germans presented arms in recognition of the fine courage they had shown in the defence, and though they were naturally made prisoners the officers were allowed to keep their swords. The destruction of Troyon, les Paroches, and the Camp des Romains was followed, a day or two later, by that of Liouville, where the damage done was particularly extensive. The holes ploughed by the big shells were the largest I have seen, and for acres round the fort almost every square yard of ground is littered with scraps of shell casing and rusty iron.

As for the Camp des Romains, it was so badly hammered that the Germans could not use it, even when they had taken it, and were obliged to construct a new fort close to it. From that time all the subsequent efforts of the French to dislodge them have been unavailing. Although with St. Mihiel it is the only point which they have captured in the line of the river forts between Toul and Verdun, and although since the end of September, 1914, they have never advanced one foot beyond it, its possession has been extremely useful to them, and a nasty thorn in the side of the French. For though in position the Camp des Romains fort is only the apex of the St. Mihiel triangle, it is in effect its base and sides and area, since, without it, the triangle would not exist.

CHAPTER XIX
THE "SOIXANTE-QUINZE"

The capture of St. Mihiel and the Camp des Romains was the last real triumph—I had almost said the only real triumph—that the Germans won in the east of France. For the scene of their other great positive success was not in France but in the annexed part of Lorraine, even though as the result of it they still hold one corner of the Department of the Vosges. But there, as everywhere else, since the end of September, 1914, they have not only made no progress, but have been on the whole driven further back. That is an obvious fact, but it is one which no one who studies the course and the probabilities of the war can afford to overlook. It is true that the French in all that time have made very little appreciable advance. Measured by distance the ground they have recovered is nothing in comparison with the number of lives that it has cost. But the sacrifice of lives must be made. It is the only way of deliverance, and every yard of blood-drenched soil that France has won back from the invader brings one step nearer the victory of freedom over oppression and of right over wrong.

Also it must never be forgotten that few though the steps have been every one of them has been away from Paris and towards Berlin. The Germans began the war. For more than forty years they had been preparing for it. In spite of all the warnings they gave us of what we had to expect, England and France and Russia were not prepared. From one point of view that is a good thing. It throws the onus of the crime against humanity on to the right shoulders, and at the same time exposes the grotesque absurdity of the German fiction, intended chiefly for home and neutral consumption, that it was merely the instinct of self-preservation which forced them against their will to take up arms, and that they attacked their neighbours only to secure themselves against annihilation.

Of all the people whom the annihilation lie was intended to influence—and did influence—by far the most important was the Emperor William himself. Englishmen must always remember that he is the son of an English mother, and that at heart he is a pacifist and a Christian, even though the God in whom he quite sincerely believes is the God of the Old Testament. But he is also a hegemonist. He constantly sees (or saw) himself and his country and his army playing the big *rôle* on the world's stage, and the cunning and unscrupulous advisers by whom he is surrounded took advantage of that weakness in his nature to make him believe that Germany's salvation could only be secured by Germany's domination of Europe. Themselves they never made any secret of their determination to bring about the war, nor of their object in doing so. Wretched creatures like Bernhardi and Tannenberg frankly proclaimed that they were out for plunder—the plunder of the world;

that they could only secure it by crushing the rest of Europe in a world's war; and that in order to bring about and win that war Germany would deliberately refuse to fetter her actions by the universally accepted canons of right and wrong. The whole scheme was so monstrous that in spite of the nakedness of these threats—and God knows they were numerous enough—very few Englishmen or Frenchmen could bring themselves to believe that they were made in earnest, and the result was that, sheltered behind the prevailing feeling of incredulity excited in other countries by the utterances of the Pan-Germanist extremists, the rest of the war-party were able to go on quietly with their preparations for war without calling into being any corresponding activity on our part. And then, when at last the moment for which they had all been waiting had arrived—as soon, that is to say, as the men appointed for the task had convinced the Kaiser that Germany was in mortal danger—the war was declared.

After that only one more step was necessary to complete his downfall. Being a man of humane instincts and not a degraded savage like some of his advisers, he had to be persuaded—and he has allowed himself to be persuaded—that the surest means of shortening the war, and therefore of curtailing as far as was possible its inevitable horrors, was to make it more horrible still by instituting the Hunnish system of terrorism—of which the examples given in this book can convey only the very feeblest impression.

There is nothing immoral in a fight between an elephant and a tiger, or even in a leopard's pursuit of goats and other small deer—the neutral states and the helpless villagers of the jungle. The lions roaring after their prey do seek their meat from God. Attila and the Huns, whose methods the Kaiser ordered his soldiers to imitate in the war in China—even then the poison was working in his mind—were not, like the Emperor William and the Germans, an enlightened and semi-civilized state. The cruel ferocity of the modern Huns is infinitely more cruel and criminal than theirs was, because they call themselves Christians and have undoubtedly got a kind of Kultur. Every vile thing that they have done they have done deliberately and with their eyes open, and for that reason sooner or later their punishment is sure. For nations, like men and women, cannot for ever continue to sin with impunity against the light.

Still, at the beginning, because they were ready and also unscrupulous and we were neither, they scored a great advantage over us, and it was only because we and the French had the enormous moral stimulus that we were fighting for the right that we were able to throw them back from the Marne and the Grand Couronné. For the inequality of men and material—but especially material—was still great, and I take it that if the positions had been reversed, if the Allies had been the aggressors and Germany the object of our iniquitous invasion, we could not have made nearly as good a showing as they did. The positions being, however, as they were, we were the better men, and, with the single exception that they were allowed to push forward the St. Mihiel salient through the gap between the armies in the Woevre, everywhere in the west we drove them many miles back from the advanced positions which they had reached at the end of their first irresistible rush.

Then, along the whole line, including the two sides of the St. Mihiel triangle, we were brought up short by far the strongest and most elaborate system of earth entrenchments that the world had ever seen. It was a perfectly legitimate means of making war, and although, like every other step in the campaign, it had been devised by the enemy as part of their grand plan for destroying the French, from a military point of view they deserved every credit for having thought it out. They were the first people to see that no soldiers could stand up for any length of time in the open, or with only the protection of the shallow ditches which used to be called trenches, against modern weapons. Thanks to their foresight they had invented or perfected a simple means of defence infinitely stronger than the strongest and most modern fortress. We all know now that compared to a properly constructed trench with well-disposed shell-proof shelters the bastions and casemates and cupolas of such places as Toul and Verdun, which till the war was well under way were considered the *dernier cri* in fortifications, are as flimsy as a Gladstone bag compared to a fire-proof safe. But it was the Germans who taught us, and all that we could do—but we did it—was to set to work resolutely to play them at their own game.

Not, unfortunately, to fight them with their own weapons, or at least with their own shells. It took us all, especially our own country, which has always borne a strong family resemblance to its ancient King Ethelred, a very long time to learn that particular lesson. The French were quicker and more adaptable. Their main difficulty, thanks to shortsighted and ignoble political squabbles before the war, was that when war began they were very short of big guns, as a consequence of which in the earlier engagements their pieces were constantly outranged, sometimes by as much as two miles, by those opposed to them. But they had, and still have, one gun which, for its size, was far superior to any possessed by Germany, though they had produced a colourable imitation of it.

To every French civilian, and to every French soldier, no matter to what arm of the service he belongs, the Soixante-Quinze is the real hero of the war. And in one sense they are not far wrong. For without it not the most splendid courage and most dashing exploits of the chasseurs-alpins, chasseurs-à-pied, and all the splendid French and African regiments of their armies could have held out against the German advance, much less have rolled it back.

In the year 1894, in the month of July, the then German Military Attaché in Paris, Colonel Schwartz Koppen, was for some time considerably worried and puzzled during his morning rides in the Bois de Boulogne by the frequency of the reports of artillery fire, which he heard coming from the direction of Mont Valérien. He would have been still more worried if he could have looked into the future and seen what those sounds betokened for his countrymen twenty years ahead. They were due to the experimental firing of the new gun invented by Colonel Duport (who, like most inventors, got nothing for his trouble), which was being put through its paces under the auspices of General Mercier, the Minister of War, largely owing to the public-spirited action of another Minister, now President of the Republic. For it was M. Raymond Poincaré, at that time Minister of Finance, who proposed in the Chamber a vote of credit for "Repairs to artillery material," which really meant (as the members of the Chamber were well aware) the construction of twenty-four guns of 75 millimetres calibre, the first of their race, and the actual disturbers of Colonel Schwartz Koppen's morning peace of mind.

How long it was before he found out that his ears, though not his eyes, had assisted at a first appearance of some military and historical importance, I do not know, but at all events the Germans were at the time so much occupied with the subject of their own new 77 mm. field-gun that the genesis of its slightly smaller rival apparently escaped their notice.

After that, in spite of the efforts of General Deltoye, nothing further was done about the Soixante-Quinze for two or three years, when General Billot, Minister for War in the cabinet of M. Méline, took the matter in hand, and enough money was voted for their manufacture on a large scale. But once that was done no time was lost, and in 1897 the first Soixante-Quinzes, considerably improved by Colonel Sainte-Claire Deville and Colonel Rimailho, the inventor of the 155, were served out to the artillery of the army corps of the north-east. Apparently the moment chosen for their *début* could not have been more happily timed: the revival of the Dreyfus case had just suggested to the minds of the war-party in Germany that the golden opportunity for declaring war, while France was torn by internal strife, had arrived, and it is said that it was only the reports of the foreign military attachés on the great superiority of the 75 mm. to the 77 mm. in stability and rapidity and precision of fire that caused them to change their minds. Since then they have been able to introduce certain improvements into their own gun, modelled on the chief features of the Soixante-Quinze, but it still remains an inferior weapon.

I need not go into technical details about the French gun, though naturally all its secrets, including that of the famous liquid substance in its hydropneumatic brake, are well known to the Germans. For English readers it is enough to say that its muzzle diameter (75 mm.) is a trifle more than 3 inches, or one-thirty-third of its length, which is therefore just under 9 feet, that it fires two kinds of shells, a shrapnel shell of about 16 pounds, containing 300 balls, with a muzzle velocity of 1735 feet, and a high explosive shell of 11 pounds, containing 30 ounces of melinite, with a muzzle velocity of 1915 feet. These shells can be fired at the rate of thirty a minute, or about twice the rate possible for the 77 mm.

Its further superiority over the German gun the Soixante-Quinze owes, partly to the excellence of its *débouchoir* (the instrument by which the bursting point of the fuse is automatically regulated before the shell is put into the breech) and partly to the control of its liquid brake, which causes the gun to return after the recoil as nearly as possible to its exact original position. The Germans use a hand-*débouchoir*, which takes longer to manipulate and gives less accurate results, and because of its less powerful brake the aim of the 77 mm. has constantly to be readjusted.

The other chief French field guns are the 155 *court*, called the Rimailho after its inventor; the 120 *long*, a siege gun converted into a field gun; the 120 *court*; the 105, which is like a larger 75, and fires a shell of thirty-six pounds; and the 65, a mountain gun, which can be carried in four pieces on the backs of mules, and has done excellent work in the fighting in the Vosges. In English measurements the diameters of the shells fired by these different pieces are approximately: 65 mm., 2½ inches; 75 mm., 3 inches; 105 mm., 4¼ inches; 120 mm., 4¾ inches; and 155 mm., 6 inches.

Before they knew by actual experience what the Soixante-Quinze could do the Germans nicknamed it "the cigar-holder." Now it has become (it was what they called it in Lorraine when we were there) "a barbarous and disgusting engine of war," and the French artillerymen "the black devils." Learn a lesson from the German gunner. Whereas he complains of "barbarous engines" and "black devils," the French soldier greets his various projectiles as *la grosse* or *la petite marmite*, or "the slow-coach," or "the whistler," or "the train," just as our own men talk of Black Marias and Jack Johnsons. The contrast is significant. For it means that the Germans fear the French shells more than the French fear theirs. If the difference in the mental attitude is well founded, hardly anything could augur better for our eventual success. And it is. The ideal of Krupp, as of all Greater-Germanists, is the Kolossal. But the Frenchman is the better gunner. He not only has in the Soixante-Quinze a finer weapon, with better-regulated fuses, but he is incomparably quicker in serving it, and has a disconcerting way in hot actions of placing his battery in position (in an incredibly short space of time), firing the appointed number of rounds of spreading or direct fire, and then limbering up and departing to fresh woods and pastures new before the Germans have discovered where he is.

It is not a bad thing to have a gun which hits as hard and as quick as Bombardier Wells, and battery commanders as elusive as the Scarlet Pimpernel. For the combination means that the Soixante-Quinze and its sister field guns do the maximum of damage to the enemy with the minimum risk of destruction for themselves. No wonder the French people are proud of their artillery and work for it with unbounded enthusiasm. And no wonder—for a different reason—that the British Mission which went to France towards the end of 1915 to study the production of ammunition were greatly impressed by the state of things which they found in the French workshops. There was, they reported, no loss of time, no trade-union restrictions, no limitation of profits, no objections raised by the workpeople, no difficulties created by the introduction, in practically all cases, of female labour, and no restrictions on the women working the same hours as the men "with a good-will which is most impressive," and, in short, everything done to increase production. "As the war has proceeded," says the report of the Mission, "the French nation has settled down with determination and a feeling of set purpose to the fulfilment of the task allotted to it. There is no question but that the nation is at war, and the dominant sentiment, not only of the men but also of the women, is to carry the war to a successful termination. Everything else is subordinated to this determination."

In that spirit the French nation and the armies of the east settled down to the second period of the war—the struggle of the trenches. It was not so picturesque as what had gone before, not so pregnant with possibilities of thrilling victories or saddening but stimulating defeats, not so anxious, not so inspiring. It was utterly foreign to the genius of the French soldier. Morning after morning the official communiqués hardly ever varied. *Rien de nouveau sur le front occidental.*

And yet, though there was nothing new there was always the same thing—always suffering and exposure and wounds and death, and always fresh names added to the roll of honour. And sometimes, though one never knew any of the glorious details till even the men who had taken part in them had almost forgotten about them, there were more decided efforts to make headway and bloodier encounters than the minor struggles to gain a hundred yards of trench, wasting and deadly as that daily routine was bound to be. When the historians get to work they will give us, I suppose, a real record of all this trench warfare. They will tell us how the different battalions and regiments fared on different parts of the line, how one charged brilliantly across fifty yards of open ground and barbed wire and drove the enemy out of the opposite trench, only to be enfiladed by a murderous fire of mitrailleuses and forced to retire to their old trench, leaving half their men behind them, and all for nothing. They will tell of how another repelled a night attack with such gallantry and vigour that they drove the enemy helter-skelter before them and occupied after half an hour's work a position which they had been sitting in front of for months, harassed all the time by the daily wastage caused by snipers, gas attacks, hand-grenades, bombs of all kinds, trench mortars, Minenwerfers, and all the other improved prehistoric death-dealing devices which have sprung into being from the mud and chalk and solid rock of the trenches. Then we shall know the names of the gallant living and the gallant dead, and many other details of intense interest which at present it is impossible to know and still more to realize.

But for a general description I doubt if any of them will give us anything much better than the following account, written by a German journalist, of the wearing monotony of the life of the men at the front. I give it partly for that reason, but chiefly because I think it is useful for all of us to realize that French and English soldiers are not the only ones who, however brave and however cheerful they are, must sometimes be appalled by the unendingness of the struggle. There are two sides to the nightmare of the trenches, just as there are to the moral effect of shell-fire and the horror of the horizon. And sometimes non-combatants—I do not say the soldiers—are apt to forget the way in which it may be and must be affecting the enemy. Let them listen to this German, writing from the other side of the line:—

* * * * * *

"And the siege goes on.

"Along the whole front, hundreds of miles long, from the North Sea to Switzerland, the faithful soldiers are posted in the trenches.

"In Flanders the water reaches to their knees. The pumps are working, but without much success. In spite of cement and joists and props, the trenches fall in every day, and the sandbags have to be renewed with infinite trouble every minute. When they leave the trenches the soldiers march through water for miles. In Champagne they are white with chalk, in the Argonne and the Vosges they are coated with mud up to their forage-caps. There, too, the pumps are working to get the mastery over the water.

"It pours with rain, it snows, the wind blows. When our soldiers go to their quarters to rest, many of them support themselves with sticks; for the water and the cold have stiffened their legs. No army of ancient days could have shown such energy as this. Even Napoleon would never have dared to ask of his armies, though they were used to hardship, such prodigious efforts. At the present time the willingness of the men is tenfold. The soldier marches in blood up to his ankles, the blood of the enemy, and the blood of the comrade he loved; but his brow is crowned with laurels.

"The soldier stands there, in the mud and the water, among the wet sandbags pierced with bullets, in the narrow labyrinths of the trenches, behind crumbling walls and among shattered tree-trunks. And that is seen from the seashore where the waves break on the beach to the Swiss frontier where the mountains rise. A hundred thousand men, at this moment, are there, every ten paces, searching the horizon. Behind the sandbags machine-guns are on the watch day and night. In these damp shelters their comrades are sleeping curled up, but ready to dash out and risk their lives at the sentinel's first alarm, as they have done for seventeen months. Water oozes from the walls. They are silent; their eyes are looking for the Fatherland. They are lying down in their dirty overcoats, they are asleep or thinking of nothing. When the sentinel calls them, they start. They eat their soup while the water trickles down between the sacks, and they are wet through with rain.

"Rusting iron covered with mud, shell-holes filled with slimy water, scattered bundles of clothes, half buried in the earth, dead bodies which have lain there for weeks, and which it has been impossible to bury, and just over there, thirty or forty or a hundred yards away, the enemy.... That is all that the soldiers see, that is their horizon, that is their world. Hundreds of thousands of vigorous men are perishing there, though their destiny was to perpetuate the human race. Death has done good business this year. Already the rats are coming from the destroyed villages and hunting about in the ground. Near Souchez, a prisoner tells me, they are arriving in formidable swarms. The crows are croaking greedily. But there is no fear and no giving way. No soldier who is at the front, right at this point, has not the right to tremble. The war is pitiless. For, by God, it is not demanding too much to ask people who are in safety to look death in the face! A dead man is a dead man, and at this moment there are much more horrible things than death. Many French and English, whose nerves have given way, have jumped on the sandbags and asked death to set them free.

"And death is everywhere. It is everywhere, the whole length of the front, from the sea to the snow-mountains. Bullets whistle, mines and hand-grenades fly about, shells fired a long distance off plough into the ground with terrific explosions, a bit of trench trembles and flies into the air. Death takes officer and man without distinction. It is in the destroyed villages where the soldier is trying to rest, in the forests, in the thickets, and in the shelters where the cannons thunder, above in the air, below under the earth, everywhere.

"Honour to the brave men who fall in these days.

"Death, which stalks across Belgium, France, Alsace, has its special quarters, its craters which are always boiling over, to burst out every now and then and vomit blood and fire. The Yser canal, Souchez and Vimy, Berry-au-Bac, Tahure, the hills of Champagne, the Argonne, the heights of Vauquois, which have swallowed up thousands and thousands of men, Bois le Prêtre and

Hartmannsweilerkopf—all these places and others still are the craters which boil without ceasing. All of a sudden the air shrieks and shells arrive in swarms. Like heavy hammers in a smithy for hours at a time they hammer violently on the trenches and reduce everything to fire and blood.

FRENCH ATTACK FROM CEMETERY OF REHAINVILLER NEAR LUNÉVILLE. From "En Plein Feu." By kind permission of M. Vermot, Rue Duguay-Trouin, Paris.

"An attack. The trench is turned inside out and left defenceless. The enemy comes. The air shrieks again as our shells soar off towards the enemy, leaving behind them a curtain of smoke, gases, and scraps of iron which cover the lost trench. No one can cross that zone.

"It is impossible for the enemy to bring up reinforcements. A counter-attack. The reserves advance, the enemy falls exhausted, and the trench is ours again. It is always the same thing, always as savage and always as heroic. France is besieged, and she keeps trying and trying to burst the girdle that surrounds her. The insignificant breach that her shells have made is closed again at once. It was like this in the month of May and in June on the heights of Lorette. This is just what happened, too, in September near Loos and Vimy and in Champagne. The French launched asphyxiating gases and bombs and millions and millions of shells against the ramparts of their besiegers, but it was in vain. Her regiments, though they were heroic and daring, broke themselves up without gaining any success. Our rampart resisted. Joffre and French, who had tried everything, recognized the impossibility of destroying this rampart, and retired despairing and worn out from the theatre of the war.

Will Castelnau be able to discover the secret which Joffre and French have not been able to discover?...

"Telephones, automobiles, railways, long-range guns, and incalculable supplies of munitions have completely changed the methods of attack and defence. This war is less a war of men against men and courage against courage than a war between two industries. It is iron-mines, coal, chemical factories, huge furnaces, that conduct the war, and also the brains of inventors and manufacturers. The soldier of to-day is a courageous and intelligent machine who, with the life that he risks, works for this giant industry of the nations. Newer and more ingenious methods would be needed to destroy these dreadful engines. The enemy have not discovered them so far....

"A trench is taken and lost again, and that is all. Nothing important in the west. And the siege goes on. The rifles crack in the trenches, the revealing Bengal lights soar up into the thick night, the search-lights explore the darkness. The sentinels are crouching in the saps and look-outs. The aeroplanes fly and the batteries destroy each other. The pioneers work underground and the mines explode.

"The German soldier will stay at his post in spite of it all, faithful and magnificent. He will stay there as long as his country has need of him, or till he falls for her. Never, at any hour of the day or night, must we forget our valiant and wonderful soldiers."

I think we most of us have an idea by now of what trench-life is like, even though we may not have seen it. Even if we have seen it we should find it difficult to better that description of the sameness and the horrors of it. There are points in it which are naturally coloured by the imagination and predisposition of the writer. Joffre and French have not retired, despairing and worn out, from the theatre of the war. Nor is France besieged. That is the grand mistake that he makes. By rights it should be, since Germany was the attacking party. But with the one exception of the abortive attempt to attack Calais, which was foiled by French's contemptible little army, ever since the Germans were driven back to their trenches from the Marne to the Aisne, and from Nancy to the Seille, it is the Allies who have been the assailants. They have been met by a marvellous defence. There have been countless desperate sallies. But gradually, steadily, little by little, line upon line, trench by trench, they are sapping their way up to the earthen walls defended by the beleaguered garrison.

And the end is sure. The German garrison, for all their brave deeds and all the brave words of their Xenophon, are obviously getting downhearted. When you have spent a few hours in the trenches, with your head always below the level of the ground, with nothing above you but the sky and nothing in front of you or behind you but endless lines of mud or chalk, like the earth thrown up by the side of a newly-made grave, you can understand the wonderful descriptive truth of those four words, "That is their horizon." To live for days and nights at a time—to live for long months with scanty intervals of cave-dwelling in holes scooped out in the sides of hills—down there in the newly made grave, on a floor of mud between walls of mud, with tiny loopholes for your only windows, through which you see a narrow segment of the landscape (always with another mud-bank in front of you) between the stalks of the grasses, with your eye on a level with their roots— that, quite apart from the question of shells and fighting, has been the life and the outlook of our men and the French soldiers at the front, ever since they began fifteen weary months ago to be a besieging force. But, as I have tried to show earlier in this book, the French do not think about their life as this German and his compatriots in the trenches obviously do—for the simple but all-sufficient reason that they are the besiegers and not the besieged.

For the French and the English, though for them, too, "that is their horizon," can see beyond it, not perhaps the Angles of Mons, but decidedly the Angel of Victory.

CHAPTER XX
SIEGE WARFARE

The kind of modern siege in which the Allies are engaged, unlike the bombardment of a modern fortress, but like the sieges of old times, is bound to be a protracted affair. Still it is not likely that Germany will hold out as long as Troy did. From her geographical position, nearly surrounded by the host of enemies that her arrogance and self-seeking have arrayed against her, she was bound sooner or later to be the besieged party, unless she succeeded in crushing one or more of them by her first impetuous rush. It was not enough to drive them back. She had to annihilate them or at least to bring them to terms at the outset, and that she failed to do. Now, for the time being, she has created troublesome diversions in the Balkans and other parts of the world outside the main field of action, and has even opened a sally-port in the direction of Constantinople. But everywhere else her exits, and to a certain extent her entrances, are barred, north and south by the fleets of the Allies and the hitherto no-man's land of two neutral states, on the east by the armies of Russia, and on the west by lines of trenches every bit as strong as her own.

It is on this side that the pressure of the siege bears most heavily upon her, and that in all probability the breach in her defences will be made. But, as has been ably pointed out in *The Times* by Colonel Repington, whose military judgment carries more weight in France than that of any other English writer on the war, that breach will only be made by an even and continuous distribution of the pressure exerted along the whole of the western line, simultaneously with a sustained attack on the eastern front. It will not be effected by local offensives, however carefully prepared and however gallantly carried out. The day of brilliant cavalry charges on a grand scale is over. Even combined advances of infantry are a form of tactics that must be used as sparingly as possible, because of the enormous waste of life which under present conditions they necessarily entail. The slight advantage gained by the English last September at Loos and the French in Champagne was far too dearly earned. It was magnificent, but it was not siege tactics, and it is only by acting on the principle that the war, more particularly in the west, is not a series of battles but a siege, that it can be won. The time has come when it must be realized that partial offensives of this kind, carried on over a minute section of the front, are not worth the cost. The advance must be made by continuous sapping, that is to say by hammering away with artillery, and, so far as is possible, with nothing but artillery, along the whole line of the enemy's trenches at the same time, without giving them any rest or any chance of shifting reinforcements from one part of the line or from one front to another.

During the months of comparative stagnation which are now, it may be hoped, drawing to a close, this policy has not been adopted, partly, no doubt, because it could not be. There were not enough guns and not enough high explosive shells. Once or twice they have been massed in huge quantities at some given point, as on those twenty-five miles between Auberives and Massiges in the Champagne country, and they have shown what can be done—provided that too much is not attempted. Our one object is to drive the enemy back. We have to oust them from the ground which they now occupy. That is what is going finally to break the *morale* of Germany and the German army. We shall never do it, except at a prohibitive cost, as long as in our attacks we sacrifice length to depth. It is far more valuable to us, and far surer and less costly, to gain say one hundred square miles of ground by advancing a quarter of a mile along a front of four hundred miles than to win back the same acreage by pushing the enemy back five miles along a front of twenty.

But all this is in the future, and is the business of strategists and generals, and not of a newspaper correspondent, who may, after all, be completely wrong in his ideas. All that he can usefully do is to try to give his personal impressions of the way in which the present (or the old) plan has worked. Up till now it has in all probability been the only method that could be adopted, because of the lack of the guns and munitions necessary for a more comprehensive plan of action. It is commonly supposed that in this respect the French have been better off than the English. But in any case they, too, have been hampered in their general scheme of attack by a similar necessity for a sparing use of artillery ammunition, and it is this shortage which has principally dictated their conduct of the war of the trenches ever since it began.

At certain points all along the line, from the Channel to Verdun and from Verdun to the Vosges, there are what the German journalist quoted in the last chapter called "Craters of Death," where, as the siege has progressed, both French and English have, so to speak, brought their battering-rams to bear on the defences. These points have not been chosen because they are the weakest, for there are no weakest points in continuous lines of trenches. One part of the system is as strong as another. But there are, though it sounds paradoxical to say so, strongest points, where the enemy, either because he is particularly well served by lines of communication behind, or because he is particularly anxious for strategical reasons to break through in front, has for months past concentrated greater numbers of guns and men. And since these strongest points have no "weakest" points on either side of them by which they might be turned, it is precisely there that the besiegers have been obliged to concentrate their attack. At the same time any attempt to rush the less thickly manned lines of trenches in between them has been rendered practically impossible by the fact that owing to aeroplanes and telephones and motor-traction any given part of the line can be very quickly strengthened, even to the extent of bringing fresh bodies of troops halfway across Europe for the purpose. Under these conditions the position of stalemate to which both besiegers and besieged have very nearly been reduced was practically unavoidable.

This second stage of the war, that is to say the whole wearisome period of the fighting in the trenches, I do not propose to follow at all closely. Even in the struggles round the "craters of death" there was, except on rare occasions, a sameness and a lack of dramatic incident which would be bound to depress the spirits of the general reader. As regards its bearing on the final issue, by far its most important feature is that it has not depressed the spirits of the French soldiers. Even more remarkable than the heroism which from time to time they have shown in making or repelling attacks on a more or less extended scale is the extraordinary cheerfulness with which they have accepted the dreary monotony as well as the wearing daily attrition imposed upon them by the stagnant immobility of the trenches. I have spoken already of this remarkable buoyancy of spirits, which so far as I have seen is characteristic of the whole of the French armies, and need not enlarge upon it again, except to remark that it is one of the most valuable assets upon which the Allies are able to count.

But there is one special aspect of it about which I should like to say a word or two, though it deserves a whole volume to itself. Because the Army of the Republic is a national army, there is no trade or calling or profession which is not represented in its ranks. France not only expects but requires that every able-bodied man of military age shall do his duty in the defence of his country, unless she has other work to put into his hands. Amongst the rest she calls upon the clergy, and with one consent these men of peace, instead of beginning to make excuse, have answered to the call with a fervour of patriotism which is excelled by no single class of their fellow-countrymen. Before the divorce between Church and State, garrison chaplains, bearing duly specified military grades, were part of the regular equipment of the army. When the State refused to recognize them any longer as functionaries, all priests became at once liable along with the laymen of their own year to ordinary military service. Consequently in the present war, either as men on the active list or as reservists or territorials, thousands of *abbés* and *curés*, besides monks, novices, choristers, lay brothers, and other servants of the Church, are now serving with the colours.

As far as possible they are employed in the non-combatant ranks, but large numbers of them, both as officers and privates, serve shoulder to shoulder in the trenches and on the field of battle with the other fighting-men. As a body they seem to be inspired, even more than most soldiers, by the courage which springs from contempt of death. In nearly all the countless stories that are told of their heroism the dominant note is the same. Having once, in the pronouncement of their clerical vows, laid down their lives in the service of God, they are always ready to lay them down again in the service of their fellow-soldiers, whenever and wherever the need arises, without for one moment counting the cost. Time after time, like the many humble village *curés*, too old or too weak to serve their country in arms, who have nevertheless gone to meet the barbarians and death without flinching, they have shown to the enemy and to all the world that France has no more gallant sons and soldiers than her priests.

But they have done something more than that. Though they have become the soldiers of France they have remained the soldiers of Christ. Here is one of many instances that come crowding into my mind. A private soldier, badly wounded, was lying in one of the military hospitals, and, believing that he was on the point of death, asked anxiously for the services of a priest. At the moment none was to be found. The man in the next bed, with his thigh hideously shattered by a shell, was lying almost unconscious in a state of partial coma. Gradually, however, he realized what the doctor and the nurses of the ward were talking about. Weak and exhausted as he was, he managed to make one of them understand that he was himself a priest, and would pronounce the absolution of his fellow-soldier if she would hold up his hand; and then, as he whispered the words that brought to the other the comfort that he wanted, his own soul passed away.

That story is typical of the kind of lives which numbers of these men in their double capacity have led and are leading at the present moment. In out-of-the-way corners of the field, far from any church or chaplain, it is an everyday occurrence for some private soldier, with his clerical robes hastily thrown over his uniform, to celebrate mass for the men and officers of his regiment before the battle begins; or, when it is over, with the grime and the blood of it still thick upon him, to hear the confessions of the dying and give them the last consolations of their faith. Undoubtedly the influence of these soldier-priests and the influence of the religion for which they stand have had a large share in maintaining the wonderful *morale* of the French troops. Even the *franc maçons*, consciously or unconsciously, are affected by it. The war has brought the whole nation as well as the armies face to face with the realities of life and death. They have this enormous advantage over the Germans, that for them the war they are engaged in is a holy war. They are not fighting for what they can get. They are fighting to defend and to free their homes, and therefore they feel and know that they are on the side of freedom and justice and right. In their trouble and peril they have turned instinctively to the consolations and the sustaining strength of what through long ages was their national as well as their personal religion. They have returned to the faith of their fathers. Not only individual soldiers and civilians but the authorities of the State themselves have awakened to the fact that in the great crises of life men and women have a natural craving for something spiritual, something outside of and higher than themselves.

Right at the beginning of the war the official rulers of the State and the Army did a wonderful thing. They took the step of reappointing regular *aumoniers*, or military chaplains, to the troops of the Republic; that is to say, they had the courage to undo their own work by deliberately revoking part of the anti-clerical legislation which, some years before, the Government had imposed on the country. In the autumn of 1914 I saw in a town near the eastern frontier a remarkable example of this same disposition on the part of the officials of the State to close, at all events to some extent, the breach between State and Church. In the cathedral of the town (a favourite target for the bombs of German aeroplanes), a solemn service was being celebrated in memory of the soldiers who had fallen during the war. And inside the rails of the chancel, on a chair placed opposite to the throne of the Archbishop and by the side of the General commanding the district, was seated the Prefect of the Department. It was the first time for fifteen years that a Prefect of France, acting in his official capacity and wearing his official uniform, had attended any form of public religious service. To the congregation, therefore, his presence at that solemn moment, while the thunder of Beethoven's funeral march on the cathedral organ was almost drowned by the thunder of the guns on the heights outside the town, was a fact of the deepest significance. It was the outward and visible sign of the spirit of national unity and brotherly love which sprang into life all over France at the moment when war was declared. It was one of many proofs that for France and her highest interests the war has not been fought and the dead have not died in vain.

* * * * * *

Before I was carried away into this digression by the admiration which every one must feel for these brave soldier-priests of France, I was talking of the way in which, on the eastern half of the front, the chief energy of the war of the trenches has been concentrated at certain definite points or "craters of death." West of the Vosges these points are all in the plain of the Woevre and the Hauts de Meuse, that is to say, along the sides of the St. Mihiel salient. The chief of them are at Les Eparges, on the north side of the angle, in the Forest of Apremont at the angle itself, and near Pont-à-Mousson at the eastern extremity of its southern side. At, and to a lesser extent between, these points the French and the Germans have now been at it, hammer and tongs, for more than a year. I use the expression "hammer and tongs" designedly, because I can think of no other that so well expresses the position. St. Mihiel and the Camp des Romains are situated at the hinge of the tongs, Les Eparges and Pont-à-Mousson towards the extremities of the two legs. With the object of squeezing the legs closer and closer together, so as to crush the German forces between them or at least to force them to retire on Metz, the French have been hammering away at these places for months past, in accordance with sound dynamic principles. At the same time from the Forest of Apremont they have pounded even more vigorously at the Camp des Romains. Dynamically the process of applying the force of the hammer at the St. Mihiel end of the tongs is not so advantageous, but it is, as I have tried to show, necessary. Force must be met by an equivalent force if it is desired to prevent motion in a particular direction, and they have at least so far succeeded in their object as to produce a state of equilibrium.

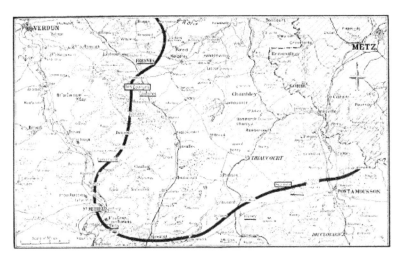

LA WOEVRE.

The position is one of great interest. What the Germans were trying to do at the end of September, 1914, they were still aiming at a year later, and, for all that one can foresee, the situation may be unchanged up to the time when this book is published, or even later. They wanted, and they still want, to cross the Meuse at St. Mihiel and in a sense complete the investment of Verdun. At any time since their first attempt at this manœuvre failed they might have repeated it, or would have repeated it if they could. If they had succeeded the consequences for the French and the whole of the Allies' line would have been just as serious as at the beginning. Never was there a clearer case of "As you were," and the fact that the point of danger for the French and the point of opportunity for the Germans was at the angle of the salient has made the situation there more pregnant with possibilities than at almost any other part of the front. The unsatisfactory side of it for our Allies is that because of their failure to turn the enemy out of the Camp des Romains they have not been able to put an end to the occupation of the Woevre, and that to a certain extent the menace of a forward movement still exists. On the other hand, the menace has always been held well in check, and the legs of the tongs are sensibly nearer to each other than they were fifteen months ago.

Through the closing months of 1914 and the whole of the following year a steady pressure was kept up on both sides of the salient by part of the Verdun garrison force and of the Third Army on the north side, that is to say, from the Meuse eastwards, and by part of the Toul garrison and of the Second Army operating from the south towards the Rupt de Mad. As the result of this general pressure, supplemented by occasional offensive movements in greater force, the enemy were driven back slightly on both their fronts.

The first of these offensive movements was made directly on St. Mihiel from the west. An attack was made on the German troops occupying the left bank of the river, and at first it had every appearance of being successful. The enemy were driven out of the suburb and barracks of Chauvoncourt and retired across the Meuse. Following in hot pursuit, the leading French troops took possession of the barracks—and fell into a trap. The ground had been mined by the Germans before their retreat, and the French paid the consequences of their impetuous advance. Practically the whole of the force that had entered the barracks was destroyed, and in the confusion the enemy successfully counter-attacked and remained masters of Chauvoncourt, which they still hold.

The next attack, a much bigger and brilliantly successful affair, was made at Les Eparges, twelve or thirteen miles north of St. Mihiel and the same distance south-east of Verdun. One of its objects was to defeat the enemy's project of investing Verdun by driving him further back in the direction of Vigneulles, which lies about mid-way between the two fronts of the salient, and at the same time to threaten his position in the Forest of La Mortagne, to the west of the road from Vigneulles to Les Eparges. The operations, which began on February 17th and lasted till April 10th, were carried out with great determination by the French, and in the end they not only pushed their trenches forward a considerable distance, but were able to occupy a much safer and more commanding position. Before the advance was made the Germans had constructed a very strong redoubt, to the east of the village of Les Eparges, which was the main objective of the attack. After a careful preparation first by saps and mines, and then by sustained artillery fire, it was gallantly stormed and then evacuated and finally retaken, after a fierce hand-to-hand struggle, on February 19th. For the next six or seven weeks there was continual fighting on more or less the same ground till, at the beginning of April, the Crown Prince, who had returned from one of his prolonged and mysterious absences to the command of the Fifth Army, had the mortification of adding yet another to the list of his failures, and the French finally and conclusively gained the upper hand. They had fought with extraordinary dash and courage, and had suffered severely. But the result was well worth the cost. The position which they now hold commands a wide view northwards and eastwards over the plain of the Woevre. From the east side of the Forest of Amblonville, in which they have their main cantonments, the ground falls with a fairly steep descent till it rises again to the long bare spur of Les Eparges, over a thousand feet high, looking out over the plain. They are no longer exposed to the risk of an unexpected attack, as it is impossible for the enemy to concentrate troops in the ravines and behind the slopes which separate the forest from Les Eparges without being seen. The other main advantages which the French have gained on this side of the wedge are that they have made some advance on the two main roads, six or seven miles apart, which run between Verdun and Metz, one along the valley of the Orne past Etain, the other from Fresnes in the direction of Mars-la-Tour. They have also made a slight move forward on the centre of the German line at Lamorville, a few miles to the north of St. Mihiel.

On the southern side of the wedge the chief French efforts have been made at the two extremities of the line, at the Bois d'Ailly and the Bois Brulé, in the Forest of Apremont, and, fourteen and twenty-one miles further east, at the Bois de Mort-Mare, directly south of Thiaucourt, and the Bois le Prêtre, a little to the west of Pont-à-Mousson. The approach to the Forest of Apremont from the Meuse is one of the many places on this part of the front where the French side of the low hills behind the trenches are for miles honeycombed with cave-dwellings. They have been there so long now that they have become part of the landscape and look as if they had always belonged to it. I suppose when the war is over they will still be left for the edification of the cheap trippers and tourists of the world. What will not be left for them to see, for it is gone already, is the Bois Brulé. In the height of summer you can walk for hours along the trenches, through acres of what was once a green forest, and see never a leaf. Nothing is left of the trees but shattered stumps, cut clean off by the shells close to the ground. That gives one some idea of the severity of the endless duel of the guns. At the east end of the wood the hill on which it stands drops down sharply into the plain, and through the loopholes in the front trenches (where you do not linger for more than a few seconds at a time) you look down on the brown roofs of the village of Apremont, three or four hundred feet below you. It is full of Germans, though they never show themselves. But their advanced trenches are much closer than that, on the top of the reverse slope of the hill, in some places at the regulation nearest distance of about fifteen yards. Behind the hill, that is to say, on the south or French side of it, and as far as one can see to the east, the plain stretches out flat and unbroken (except by the lines of

French and German trenches cut across it), backed on the south by a series of long, straight, level-topped hills, écheloned one behind the other, and ending far away to the right in the blue haze where the heights of the Moselle begin. That is where Pont-à-Mousson lies, and Bois le Prêtre, the greater part of it another dreary forest of stumps, through which the battle raged backwards and forwards again and again for months—or is it centuries?—till at last the whole of it was won and kept for France by her splendid soldiers.

And that is what they are doing all along the line. The progress is slow, but what changes there are in the position of the trenches are in favour of the French. Foot by foot they are winning back the land which was ravished from them at the beginning, and the longer the struggle for the possession of the Woevre goes on the surer it becomes that the occasional offensive movements of the French are assaults and those of the German attempts at sallies. The St. Mihiel salient is still a nuisance, but it has almost, if not quite, ceased to be a danger, and sooner or later it is practically certain that the prolonged attempt to cross the Meuse will have to be abandoned, and that not a single German will be left in France from Verdun to the Vosges.

In the Vosges themselves and in the Sundgau, ever since the retirement from Mulhouse, there has been continual fighting, sometimes of the most violent description, in which the Chasseurs Alpins and the Chasseurs-à-pied, splendidly supported by the French field artillery (supplemented during the latter part of last year with guns of heavier calibre), have done wonderfully fine work. They have not only successfully carried out their main task, which was to prevent the enemy from setting foot on the western slopes of the Vosges, but in the valleys of the Thur and the Doller and at other points along the line have gained a considerable amount of valuable ground. Further north, in the district of Senones, though they have not succeeded in penetrating again into the valley of the Bruche, they have kept the enemy well in check, and at the extreme right of the line, towards the Swiss frontier, have established themselves in a very strong position from which they are able to keep a watchful eye on Altkirch and Mulhouse, and at the same time to guard effectively against any attempt at either a straightforward or a roundabout attack on Belfort.

The main fighting has centred round Thann, Hartmannsweilerkopf, Cernay, Steinbach, the Ballon of Guebweiler, the valley of the Fecht, Reichackerkopf, and the valley of Münster, but from the Donon to Pfetterhausen on the Swiss frontier, especially on the southern section of this front, there is hardly any ground that has not been the scene of repeated combats, the net result of which is that the French have almost everywhere made slight advances. The summit of Hartmannsweilerkopf in particular, because it guards the entrance to the valley of St. Amarin, has been bathed in blood over and over again.

Four or five times it has been taken and retaken, with dogged perseverance and extraordinary heroism, first by the French and then by the Germans, and the struggle for its possession still continues, though at present it is in the hands of the French. For both sides this famous mountain-top has been one of the most deadly of all those terrible "craters of death."

Beyond this short general statement I shall not for the present attempt to follow the ins and outs of the campaign on this part of the line. Its strategical importance has been far greater than has appeared, and, once the weather conditions permit, there is always a chance of its developing into an attempt at a big offensive movement by one side or the other. But as regards the story of those heroic struggles we have had, I think, our fill of fighting. In the daily engagements on the plain of Alsace and among the fir-clad mountains of the Vosges the men of the armies of the east have shown the same enthusiastic devotion to their country, the same quiet disregard of danger and death, and the same cheerful endurance and unfailing confidence in the final triumph of right as their brother-soldiers who fought and died for the safety of Epinal and Nancy and Verdun and Toul. Higher praise than that they cannot have. The soldiers of France are the fearless sons of a great-hearted nation.

As I draw near to the end of this imperfect attempt to show the greatness of the debt which England owes to France, one other thought about them comes to me with increasing force. The French have played the game: they have fought the good fight like knights and gentlemen. That, more than almost anything else, is the reason why Englishmen have come to look upon them as something much more than Allies. Because of it they have forged a bond with us and our children's children which Time itself will hardly be able to weaken. They are our brothers, not only in arms, but in all that civilization stands for. The Germans are—different. They are our enemies, not only because they are fighting against us, but much more because of the way in which they have fought. As a state, and, in cases that cannot be numbered, as individuals they have turned their backs upon principles and ideals by which all honourable nations and men must strive to rule their lives. Their scutcheon is blackened with arson and murder and pillage and rape. Their hands are red with the blood of the innocent. To the ends of the earth and of time they have made their name a byword and a reproach. But—worse than all this—they glory in their shame. They claim that their dishonour is honour and their wrong the right. Their eyes are holden that they cannot see. Some day they will be opened and they will see themselves and their crimes in all their revolting ugliness. For it is unbelievable that a whole nation of ordinary men and women can continue to allow themselves to be blinded by the false and cruel and iniquitous standards of a few devils in human form. But for the present all their sense of right and wrong is being eaten away by a foul and malignant cancer. Till that cancer has been cut out of their being by the sword they are a deadly danger to the whole world, for their success would infallibly spread its poison into every country on which, in their present condition, they were able to lay their hand. Till the sword has done its work, as firmly and as thoroughly as the surgeon's scalpel, there is not one of the allied nations which can or will think of peace. Then and then only will come the end of the war.

CHAPTER THE LAST

GERMANY AND THE ALLIES

Once upon a time, in the careless, happy days before the war, a Royal Scotch Princess was married one fine morning to a Royal Irish Prince in a Royal English chapel. The chapel was ancient and small, and the young pair had so many friends that though not nearly all of them could be invited to the ceremony, they filled it to overflowing. Besides the Sovereign Head of both their houses and the State, there were present two Queens (I had almost said two fairy Godmothers) who walked down the chapel hand-in-hand looking as sweet and almost as young as the bride herself, I forget how many other princes and princesses, and scores and scores of the great lights of the land and especially of the legal profession (for where the country-to-be-ruled is there will the lawyers be gathered together). There were not many young people—the occasion was too important and the seats too few—and, except for the brothers and sisters and cousins of the two principals nearly all the guests were married and arrived in couples (like the animals coming into the ark out of the rain) dressed in their finest and full of their own or their ancestors' importance. For to be there at all, you understand, you had to be SOMEBODY, or at least to the third and fourth generation SOMEBODY'S offspring, unless you belonged to that mischievous but necessary profession the British Press, the representatives of which, the only blot on this brilliant assembly, were crowded together in a narrow position of vantage so close to the highest and furthest back row of the seats of the mighty that the shadows of the aigrettes in front quivered and danced upon their note-books.

To the strains of the organ, appropriately tender and jubilant by turns, the chapel gradually filled with its distinguished audience, and almost the last to arrive before the Royal party were an old old servant of the State and his matronly spouse, who took their places on two of the gilded chairs immediately below the Press box. Before she shook out the folds of her dress for the last time the lady turned round and, staring straight into the face of the newspaper man behind her, at a range of about two feet, said to her husband in a loud, clear voice (he is rather deaf), "Oh, it's only reporters."

Until you have tried it you have no idea of the degree of polite contempt which can be put into that last word. And even when you have tried, and tried your hardest, you will still, if you are only an amateur at the game, fall far short of the dizzy height of scorn reached by this professional expert without any conscious effort at all. For pride of rank and contempt of her inferiors had become to her second nature.

Once upon a time the same great lady (or perhaps it was another) was on her way to the gilded chamber to which her husband had been raised, chiefly by his own forensic skill, but partly by the nimble pencils of the men who recorded his eloquent speeches for the public press. In the square outside there was a large and excited crowd, some sympathetic, some jeering and hostile, and for a moment her carriage was stopped while the police arrested a pale-faced, elderly woman who had been trying to exercise what she believed to be her legal right of asking for an audience with the representatives of her sovereign. Once more in the same high-pitched voice and with an even deeper tinge of scorn, she explained the situation to her companion: "It's only one of those wretched suffragettes."

This book is not a suffragist or anti-suffragist pamphlet. It is an attempt to describe a single phase of the war, and at the same time to consider some of its actual and possible effects. Still, it seems to me worth saying that in England before the war there was in all classes far too much of the spirit expressed in the thoughtless and belittling "only" of these simple little true stories, and that is why I have told them. We were much too fond of using such phrases as "only a woman" or "only a parson." There were cases before the war when the keepers of public restaurants refused to serve a fellow-subject with food and drink because he was only a soldier—wearing the King's uniform. That sounds odd to-day. There have been times in our history, and not so very long ago either, when "only a Frenchman" (with or without a qualifying adjective) was the regulation way of speaking of our present Allies and tried and trusty friends, not only because they wore the wrong collars and hats, but because we were generally inclined to believe that an Englishman could tackle at least three of them with his left hand.

The unwholesome part of this particular form of national pride has, we may hope, left us for good. (It has now, incidentally, infected the Bulgarians, who say to-day that the Western nations can only fight in the trenches, and that in the open field one Bulgar is equal to five French or English.) We began to learn the folly of it even before the war. Sous-lieutenant Carpentier, of the French air-service, taught us a few lessons. So did Jack Johnson—though he was only a nigger. So did the football teams from Africa and New Zealand, though they were only Colonials, and so did our competitors in the Olympic Games, though they were only foreigners. But more than anything else, it is the war that has been and must be still our tutor. It is teaching us the lesson which cock-sure St. Peter (who must surely have had English blood in his veins) learnt long ago at Joppa—that nothing is common or unclean. It is teaching us that we must get rid of the kind of Lucifer pride that goes before a fall. It is teaching us to respect not only our Allies and our foes, but each other. We have found out that the whole of Europe can fight. As a body of soldiers, General French's contemptible little army, which was sent to fill the gap at Mons, was probably the finest fighting force, regimental officers, non-commissioned officers, and men, that ever stepped on to a field of battle. But it was we non-combatants who wore most of their laurels. At the beginning of this war and in all previous wars, in our complacent English way, we have always thought and talked of our regular army (when any part of it was at war) as though it were actually the nation, instead of only a minute fraction of it, as though it was we ourselves who were doing the fighting. We have a better right to our national pride now that the Government of the nation has decided and the nation (or most of it) has willingly agreed that at least all its unmarried men of military age shall be trained not only to defend their country but to take their stand beside the other allied nations in their battle for something that is far greater and more sacred and more important than the very greatest of them.

Photograph by Libert-Fernand, Nancy.

CHURCH AT DROUVILLE—MEURTHE ET MOSELLE

I take back nothing of what I have written earlier in this book about our refusal as a nation to bring ourselves in this respect in a line with our Allies. Our consent is not even now completely whole-hearted. For seventeen months we did so refuse, and during that time not all the magnificence of our unparalleled voluntary effort was magnificent enough to banish from the minds of our Allies the consciousness, however politely they might conceal it, that we were lagging behind in the struggle for the freedom of the world. But while we lagged behind—great as our contribution was even then to the common cause—we were learning. Outside our own country we have seen the splendid courage of tiny states like Belgium and Serbia, as well as the wonderful soldier-like qualities of the huge national armies of France and Russia and Italy and Germany. From our own people (and from those others as well) we have learnt that priests and parsons and men of every profession and trade and class and condition, however insignificant we used to think them, can endure hardness as good soldiers, and that women, if they cannot fight, can (besides knitting socks, which was all that they were supposed to be good for before the war began) do almost everything else connected with the war which is commonly regarded as men's work. Now that we have mastered these elementary principles we shall, if we let the war teach us all that it can, go on to the obvious corollary that no nation and no man and no woman has the right to despise another, and that pride and prejudice are the root of nearly all evil.

The war itself is the strongest possible evidence of that truth. For it was the pride of Germany that made the war—not her fear of being strangled by the surrounding nations, not her need of finding colonies for her surplus population, not her desire for a place under the sun, not her passionate longing to ensure for the world the liberty of the seas, not even her jealousy of England, but her overweening pride.

Between the pride of England and the pride of France there are certain well-marked differences. But both, because of their ancient histories, have pride of race, wholesomely tempered by the consciousness that *noblesse oblige*. Germany has the much more aggressive pride of the successful *parvenu*. Having made herself, within the memory of people now living, she looked upon her work with all the pride of the self-made man, and saw that it was good—after its kind—and straightway aspired to re-make the whole world after her own image and according to her own material conceptions. To do that she thought, quite wrongly, that it was necessary first to subdue it by the sword. She would have been wiser to keep it in its sheath. Her peaceful invasion was far more penetrating and far more likely to compass the end she had in view of making her the dominating nation of the earth. All the world takes her Kultur now at its proper value. But long before the war, up to the very eve of its declaration, German influence, and above all German finance and commerce, had been permeating all the nations now at war with her, as well as all the neutral states, like bindweed and Virginia Creeper running riot in a suburban garden. If the war had not come the independent existence of some of them—Switzerland, for example—would certainly have been choked. Even the larger countries were beginning to suffer. In England the phrase, "Made in Germany," first an economic measure of self-protection, then a rather feeble joke, and then a byword, was fast becoming a serious menace—if one accepts as just the principle of England for the English—to the real interests of the country. In France, in England, and in other countries there were too many commercial houses and too many people and too many opinions made in Germany, if those countries were to retain their national characteristics and national liberty of thought and action. The seriousness of the mischief in its gravest form all the world has seen lately in the United States, where the Government have had to struggle hard, and not always with success, against the crippling influence of the fear of the German vote, even though, happier than the neutral states of Europe, they were entirely free from the parallel influence—the fear of the German sword.

The process of Germanization was, in fact, as events move in history, rapid and almost universal. But, fortunately for the world, it was not rapid enough for German pride. So the war was made by the rulers of Germany to hurry forward the spread of German Kultur and all that the word implies, or—was permitted by the higher forces or Powers that rule the evolution of the world, in order to check it. To the Allies, who did not begin the war, but did everything in their power to prevent it, the only possible view is that the Powers or rather the Power that rules the evolution not of Germany alone nor of France nor of England, but of the whole world, is a greater and higher power than the rulers of Germany. That is the confidence in which we are fighting. We do not look upon ourselves as the Chosen People, with a special claim on the mercy of God. We have no special form of culture which we think or pretend it is our duty to impose on the rest of the world. We have no need and no right because our cause is a holy one to invent a special unholy code of the rules of war, and of might and right, in order to secure its triumph. These are forged credentials and counterfeit excuses, and not all the ingenuity of the false prophets who plunged deluded Germany into this war can make them pass as genuine. The prophets and the professors prophesied falsely, and the people, whether they loved to have it so or not, must suffer the consequences.

As for ourselves, we believe, rulers and people, that we went into this war with clean hands and clear consciences. But that is no proof that we are right. The Germans, or the majority of them, no doubt think the same of themselves and their country. At the bar of the nations we must be judged, when the war is over. But meanwhile, while it is still in progress, we can get some idea of the way in which the other nations regard us from the opinion of the neutral states and even of our Allies. *Fas est et ab amicis doceri.*

Since the war began I have watched it and England's share in it from Belgium, Holland, France, Italy, and German and French Switzerland, and have talked about it with the inhabitants of various other countries, including Serbs, Greeks, Russians, Swedes, Montenegrins, and Americans. Never once have I heard it said, though I have seen it hinted in print—in German print—that we came into the war from anything but disinterested motives. And that is the one thing that matters. I was once called upon, when the war was less than a year old, to speak about it at a large meeting of French and German Swiss, specially arranged as a meeting of neutrals. Strictly speaking, it was neutral only in name and on the surface, in the sense that the men composing it were persuaded that their highest duty was to stand together for a United Switzerland, and to sink their differences and individual opinions for the sake of their common country. But the differences and individual opinions were there. Every man in the room, whatever his politics (they were mostly Socialists), consciously and strongly wanted one side or the other, France or Germany, to win. But the very fact that as individual jurymen they were not impartial made their verdict, provided that it was unanimous, all the more convincing. It was in the days when every one in Switzerland was still discussing the rights and wrongs of the war—and before a German airman had dropped bombs on that particular Swiss town. Having explained that I personally was not a neutral (an obvious remark which was greeted with loud laughter, as a characteristic specimen of English humour), I went on to the further statement, not necessarily quite so obvious to the whole of that particular audience, that England had come into the war because Germany had been guilty of the violation of Belgium's neutrality, and that if we had not done so we could never have looked the other nations in the face again. Before the words were out of my mouth they had given their verdict in a unanimous burst of applause. Every man of them, and not only those who naturally sympathized with the Allies, showed as clearly as possible that on that point they needed no persuasion. Germany was guilty, and England had done the one thing possible. And that, as far as my observation goes, is the general opinion abroad, not only in Switzerland (in spite of the natural predisposition of many of the inhabitants to think well of Germany as well as to fear her) but in Holland, the Americas, Sweden, and practically the whole of the neutral world.

As for our Allies the French, we have fought side by side for a year and a half, and each of us knows by now of what mettle the other is made. They started the war with two fixed ideas about us—that we were not a military nation (which, if you compare the relative size of our two armies at the beginning, was, from their point of view, perfectly true), and that, conscious of the might of our fleet and lulled to a state of careless repose by the sense of our island security, it would take us a long time to wake up to the real seriousness of the war. Looking back on what has passed, it is not easy to say that they were wrong. Some of us—millions of us—realized it from the first. But very many did not. Long after the war had begun there were people in England who held that we were doing more than our share and more than enough, because, as was true, we were doing far more than we had promised.

There were even some so foolish and so selfish as to say that our soldiers in Flanders were fighting the battles of France, and not the battles of England, since England had not been and never could be attacked. The French were more generous than these narrow-minded myoptics (who, after all, were only a small minority), and at the same time more clear-sighted. Frankly and with deep gratitude they owned that but for the help of England France must have been crushed. But they also believed that when that had happened our turn would inevitably have come next, and that the only hope for England and the world was that France and England should face the foe together with every ounce of their united strength. Small blame to them, then, if they were seriously concerned when they saw that in England alone of all the combatant nations—Germany excepted—the enervating evil of strikes and labour threats could still exist. Small blame to them if they sometimes wondered how long it would be before, for our own security, we overcame our timid objections to the principle of national service.

But they always felt sure, I think, that the time would come—as it has come, in the last days of 1915—when England would face the necessity of putting her whole strength into the field in order to bring the war to a triumphant conclusion, and to complete what a friend of mine, a high official of France, spoke of in a letter which he wrote to me last May, as "le grand œuvre de la guerre, c'est à dire la Rédemption."

"C'est bien en effet de rédemption qu'il s'agit," he went on, "la rédemption du monde. L'humanité voit aujourd'hui, elle voit de ses yeux, ce qu'elle serait devenue si les Boches avaient triomphé, imposant au monde leur loi morale. Pour moi je suis tenté parfois de remercier les Boches d'avoir complété ma vie morale: ils m'ont appris la Haine, la haine forte comme l'Amour, qui emplit le cœur, le réchauffe, le brûle parfois, qui décuple les forces, qui tranforme la vie. C'est le rôle que les Boches joueront désormais dans le monde civilisé; ils auront pour fonction d'être un objet de haine. A cette idée l'Angleterre vient peu à peu. Elle n'est pas encore au point, puisque les ouvriers de tramways de Londres ont fait grève: j'ai vu à l'hôpital un petit chasseur-à-pied, amputé du bras droit, qui en lisant cette nouvelle dans le journal s'est mis à pleurer. Mais le Boche commetra bien encore quelques infamies nouvelles, et l'Angleterre tout entière 'haïra' d'une haine active et féconde."

I doubt myself whether we shall ever quite reach that point. The very sound of the phrase, "Redemption by Hate," is rather strong meat for English minds. We have not got that Latin fervour of expression, and we have not seen a tithe or anything like a tithe of what the French have seen of the abominable works of the Boche, especially in the eastern provinces. I have heard it rumoured that the British soldier—the British Tommy, that is to say—is by way of thinking and saying that brother Boche is not such a bad fellow after all, and that he would not mind making friends with him. At the present moment and until the war is won anything approaching that frame of mind, if it were at all widespread, would be a calamitous and fatal mistake. The British soldier, especially the British soldier of the new armies, has seen, or at least has fought against, the Germans on the fields of battle and in the trenches, where they are at their best. For no one can deny their fighting qualities. He has not seen "with his eyes" what they did behind the present lines of trenches, when they had to deal not with soldiers, but with defenceless civilians. He is a light-hearted and forgiving individual, and does not realize that what they did then they will do again in this war if ever they get the chance. He cannot be expected in the trenches to grasp the far graver general danger of the poisonous influence which was being exercised on the world and on Germany before the war by the whole rotten system of German Militarism and German Kultur, bolstered up by German pride. He has no time while he is fighting our battles to reflect that that influence will infallibly begin its corrupting and deadening work again after the war, and will spread with far greater rapidity, unless the Militarist party is beaten to its knees.

But, even admitting that here and there in the ranks there may be some of this quasi-friendly feeling towards "brother Boche," the fact, if it is a fact, need disturb no one. We may not have in England the Latin quickness and fervour of the French, but what we have got is the bulldog grip. Once we have taken hold, though we may be slow in starting, we do not let go. Now that our teeth are set we will hold on to the end—and God defend the right!

But what is the right? The proud German dream of a Greater Germany? I think not. I doubt if even the Germans themselves can think so, if they look at it dispassionately as it was presented—three years before the war began—by the Pan-Germanist prophet, Otto Richard Tannenberg. We certainly cannot complain that they did not give us fair warning.

The gist of his country's dream can be given quite shortly in his own words. "Greater Germany," he wrote, "can only be made possible by a struggle with Europe. Russia, France, and England will oppose the establishment of Greater Germany. Austria, feeble as she is, will not weigh heavily in the balance. The Germans will not march against Germany. The basis of our enterprise must be the Pan-Germanist principle.

"Some one must make room, either the Slavs of the West or of the South, or else we ourselves! As we are the strongest the choice will not be difficult. We must give up our attitude of modest expectation. There can be no question of remaining without stirring at the point where we stand to-day.... Since 1871 our neighbours have often enough given us chances of appealing to the decision of the sword. Only the wish has been lacking to us. After all, every war can be avoided. But it is also easy to find motives, when one wants to....

As for us, there is no need to hunt for one in the vicissitudes of the relations between the various Courts; one fact is enough for us, that since the foundation, the consolidation, and the expansion of our empire the Germans are being harassed and oppressed in all countries. In Russia, in Austria, in England, in America we have seen a feeling of hatred against Germany develop which we cannot tolerate much longer without losing our standing in those countries."

That was written, remember, not during the war, nor on the eve of it, but in 1911. We have seen since then how the Pan-Germanist principle that "after all, every war can be avoided, but it is also easy to find motives, if one wants to" was carried out. What we will not see and will not tolerate is the establishment of Greater Germany. For it means amongst other things, according to the prophet Tannenberg, not only that Ireland will become independent of England, and that Austria-Hungary will be incorporated in the German Empire, but that the neutral states of Holland, Luxembourg, Switzerland, and Belgium, neutral no longer, will disappear completely from the map of Europe and lose their identity and their freedom in the maw of the same all-embracing and all-devouring organization.

What need have we of further witness? Out of their own mouths the Germans are condemned, for the thousandth time. The war was deliberately provoked, though "like any war," it might have been avoided. The excuse for it, invented long beforehand, that it was to put an end to the alleged oppression of Germans in Russia, Austria, England, America, and all other countries, was as false as the pretence that any such oppression existed. The real object, the aggrandizement of Germany, not only by the oppression but by the suppression of all the weaker Latin and German races of Europe, was exhibited naked and unashamed, for all the world to see, long before the would-be oppressor drew the sword. It remains to-day more than ever the real object of the war, now that it is unsheathed. No possible special pleading can maintain, much less prove, that the suppression of Belgium, Holland, Luxembourg, and Switzerland (to say nothing of the partial suppression of France, England, Russia, Italy, and Servia), is right. The mere suggestion of such an idea is an abominable wrong, which God will not defend, and because of it Great Britain will not tolerate, in any shape or form, the establishment of a Greater Germany. We are going to win this war. But let every man of the Allies and above all every Englishman, reflect on this undoubted fact. Because it is a war between right and wrong, between the powers of light and the powers of darkness, we shall not win it until we have learnt its great lesson, until we know as a nation—and we do not know it yet—that its particular message to our own country is the duty of self-sacrifice.

* * * * * *

It is the first day of the New Year. Last night the Old Year, the saddest and most terrible that the world has ever seen, came to its appointed end.

Five or six miles from where I am writing French and Germans were facing each other in unwonted silence under the dark night in the unending vigil of the trenches. A few days and nights ago the roar of the guns at Hartmannsweilerkopf, at Thann, at Altkirch, at Pfetterhausen, at Moos, was more violent and more continuous than anything that has been heard here since the war began. Now there was not a sound. Only in the last few minutes of 1915 a sudden squall of wind and rain swooped down from a cloudless sky. Moaning and weeping like a suffering child that cannot sleep, like a broken-hearted old man worn out by the anguish of life, the Old Year passed away to make room for the New. To-day in a glorious burst of sunshine, the New has come—and every second the air quivers to the shock of the heavy guns. For the weary fight has begun again. The end is not yet. Perhaps even here, through this peaceful valley, so little removed from the actual field of battle, the German hosts may make their last despairing unavailing effort to reach the heart of France. But they will never reach it. The way is barred by the dead, the uncounted glorious dead whose graves stretch from here to the English Channel in an unbroken line. For their sakes, and the sake of all they fought and died for, France and England can never put up the sword till the victory is won. "Then shall be brought to pass the saying that is written, Death is swallowed up in victory. O death, where is thy sting? O grave, where is thy victory? The sting of death is sin, and the strength of sin is the law. But thanks be to God, which giveth us the victory through our Lord Jesus Christ."

DELÉMONT,

January 1st, 1916.

EPILOGUE

By Monsieur Léon Mirman,

Prefect of the Department of Meurthe et Moselle.

[M. L. Mirman, who is a Fellow of the University of Paris and was a Mathematical Lecturer at the Lycée of Reims, was elected Deputy for Reims in 1893. He represented the city in Parliament till 1905, when he resigned his post as Deputy to become *Directeur de l'Assistance et de l'Hygiène Publiques*. Interesting as this office was in time of peace, it did not agree in time of war with his ideas of active work, and at the beginning of the month of August, 1914, he was appointed, at his own request, to the frontier post of Prefect of Nancy.—G. F. C.]

Nancy, February 2nd, 1916.

My dear Campbell,

You wrote the last words of your book on the 1st of January, 1916, at Delémont. I am very sorry that you did not open the year 1916 where you began the year 1915, among your friends at Nancy. You would have witnessed there a fresh crime, bearing the unmistakable hall-mark of "Kultur."

Nancy—as you proved for yourself *de visu*, and as you state in the course of your book—is a *ville ouverte*, without any fortifications. It does not contain a single military establishment. The barracks, which are full of soldiers in time of peace, were emptied on the first day of the war, and were all converted either into hospitals or else into homes of refuge for women and children, refugees whom I gathered in from the destroyed communes. Not one cannon, not one shell, not one soldier is housed in the town. And yet, by means of a long-range gun, mounted at a distance of about 33 kilometres, the Boches are sending us shells of 800 kilos., which fall from a height of 8000 metres and crush a house like a walnut. They have no military objective. What, then, is their purpose? Their intention is twofold. In the first place they wish to "terrorize"; these people are fools, they will never understand that they inspire not fear but horror, and that by acts of this kind they are sowing not terror but hatred. In the second place, they hope to kill, in this great industrial town, a few women and children. This object they can obviously attain more easily than the other; it lies within the reach of every artilleryman, however poor a gunner he may be, who takes a large town as his target.

So far this statement tells you nothing that you did not know before. It is a long time since the Boches gave us their first samples. Every one is acquainted with their methods. To-day it is only of set purpose that it is possible to ignore them. The bombardment, without any military reason, of open towns with no garrison, has become, on the part of the Germans, an everyday affair. But these last bombardments of Nancy show a particularly studied nicety, full of the most delicate refinement.

These heavy guns began to fire on our beloved city of Lorraine in the dawn of the new year, on the sunny morning of the 1st of January, 1916. Picture to yourself, *cher ami*, on the evening of that 1st of January, the family hearth of a German intellectual, a chemist, a philosopher, a historian, or an artist. Herr Doktor is surrounded by his children, they are celebrating the feast of the New Year by eating sausages and jam, or black puddings and sugar. The evening paper arrives. The family stop talking. Herr Doktor unfolds the sheet, and reads aloud the stop-press news: "To-day, January 1, twelve shells of 800 kilos, were fired on Nancy. Several houses were reduced to dust. Two old men were buried under the ruins of one of them. The explosion of a shell killed a child of fifteen months in the arms of its grandmother...." Herr Doktor exclaims: "Wife, children, stand up! We must celebrate this victory on our feet. Hoch! Hoch! Hoch! The children of Nancy have received some New Year's presents, some kolossal presents, explosive sugar-plums weighing 800 kilos. The year 1916 has opened magnificently. This victory of Nancy will fill with pride and enthusiasm all the sons of Great Germany. Let us thank our old German God for having granted it to us. Let us praise our mighty Emperor. Hoch! Hoch! Hoch!"

As for us we buried our dead, poor innocent victims, in silence. We washed the pavement red with blood. We put down this new crime in the list of accounts that has to be settled. And we set ourselves again to our work, with our spirits not cast down but invigorated by the ordeal.

German crimes! You have seen some of them, my dear Campbell, in Lorraine. A day will come when we shall have to make a complete list of them, for the instruction of future generations. There will be some of us, I hope, who will devote ourselves to this task. It would be too monstrous that the veil of oblivion should be drawn over all these crimes.

It is imperative that we should know, that the whole world shall recognize, that our school-children shall learn all the evil that the German has done to mankind. At the head of these plain statements—all the more terrible indictments for the dryness of the official reports—we will place the following declarations, the authors of which are classed amongst the most notorious German writers:

"There is nothing in common between them (Kultur and Civilization). The war which is being waged is that of Kultur against Civilization. Kultur, the spiritual (!) organization of the world, which does not exclude bloody savagery—Kultur which is above morals, reason, science; Kultur, die Sublimerung des Dämonischen." This unforgettable profession of faith appeared under the signature of Thomas Mann in the *Neue Rundschau*, in the number of November, 1914.[A]

A. This quotation is second-hand; I have taken it from the *Au-dessus de la Mélée* of Romain Rolland. We know that he belongs to the small number of those men, if I may dare call them so, who at the moment when their family is massacred, their house set on fire, their old father shot, their sister violated, isolate themselves in a tower of ivory, from the top of which, looking on at these crimes, and striving to hold an even balance between the assassins and the victims, they proclaim themselves "Above the conflict."... This state of mind is at least a guarantee to us of the accuracy of the expressions which he quotes from the profession of faith of his "brother" Thomas Mann.

And this criticism, addressed by Maximilian Harden to the German Government, after having treated as lies their distracted efforts to excuse the violation of Belgium neutrality:—

"What is the use of all this fuss?... Might creates right for us. Does a strong man ever submit to the foolish pretensions or the sentimentality of a band of weaklings?"

You know, my dear Campbell, the spirit in which we began this war—the same spirit as that of our English friends. For our part we were governed by respect for treaties, for international agreements, for the laws of war, for the rights of nations, for everything by which men, in their bloody struggles one against the other, had tried to raise themselves little by little above the level of wild beasts. Since the war had come, since it had been forced upon us by the enemy—who, after an elaborate preparation, had chosen his own time— we wished, while engaging in it and carrying it through, to minimize its calamities as much as possible, by strictly observing the articles of agreement by which the nations had mutually bound themselves to consider the wounded as *res sacra*, not to maltreat civilians, not to bombard open towns, and so on. We have paid dearly for the chivalrous illusions which we had at the outset.

Let me give you two examples of the state of mind which prevailed in France at that moment.

The Boches—I say it not to justify but to explain their acts of murder— pretended, as you remind us in the course of your book, that civilians had fired upon them. It is a cynical falsehood. Since the beginning of August,

1914, I have administered the Department of Meurthe et Moselle, and I have made a searching investigation in all my communes. I affirm that no non-combatant, no man not regularly classed in the ranks of the army, has ever fired on the enemy. Never? I exaggerate. There has been one case. One day, in 1914, a German aeroplane flew over the plains of Lorraine; it dropped murderous bombs at random on the peaceable population of certain rural communes. On seeing this, the Mayor of one of these communes, close to Nancy, lost his sangfroid, armed himself with an old fowling-piece, and began to fire at the aeroplane. There was certainly some excuse for him, was there not? But I considered that he was at fault. Assassins must not be killed by passers-by; it is the business of the gendarmes to arrest them. In war it is the army's business—it is strong enough for the job—to punish the enemy. Consequently the action of this mayor called for censure. I did not hesitate to make an order against this honest but over-strung magistrate; in virtue of the powers conferred upon me by the law, I suspended him from his functions. This order was universally approved; it interpreted the unanimous wish of all civilians not to provide any pretext for German brutality.

I take another example of our standard of behaviour from the story of Badonviller. This Lorraine commune was one of the first that suffered the horrors of Kultur. It was entered by the Germans at the beginning of the month of August. Because our troops had met them with a stubborn resistance which cost them dear, they were mad with fury when they entered the little town; it was there that they first used the special implements with which their soldiers had been supplied for methodical and "scientific" house-burnings; they destroyed, with fire applied by hand, half the commune. That was not enough for them; they shot down the people in the streets like rabbits, they killed women and children on the threshold of their doors. The mayor, M. Benoit, a much-respected business man, saw his young wife assassinated before his eyes; he saw his house burnt, and was himself the object of the worst forms of violence. These scenes of outrage only lasted for a short time. On the next day the French troops retook Badonviller by a vigorous effort, and, after a hot pursuit, made a number of prisoners. These prisoners were brought to the square in front of the Mairie. They were some of the brute-beasts with human faces, who, a few hours before, had burnt the commune and bathed it in blood. The houses to which they had set fire were still smoking. The bodies of their innocent victims were not yet buried. A crowd of infuriated peasants gathered round them, shaking their fists at them, and abusing them with angry cries. The situation was becoming awkward, when the mayor arrived. M. Benoit had just seen his poor wife placed in her coffin. He had no longer a home. His house was a mass of smoking ashes. He was ruined. His heart was broken. He drew near the scene. The prisoners thought that their last hour had come, and turned livid with terror.

But M. Benoit is a Mayor of France. He knows the traditions of our country. He respects the law. He forced a way through the crowd. With a single gesture he called for silence. He reminded them that these men were prisoners, that prisoners were protected by international agreements, and that no one had a right to lay a finger on them—no, not even on them. He put himself in front of them. He made a rampart for them with his body. He declared that while he lived not a hair of the head of one of these prisoners of war should be touched. And the peasants, mastered by their sense of duty, stifled their cries of anger, unclenched their fists, and respectfully moved away and went into their houses.

The Bavarian assassins were decorated by the Kaiser, for their crimes, with the Iron Cross. The French Government at my request granted to M. Benoit the Cross of the Legion of Honour, and a few days later I presented it to him with my own hands.

Those are the principles with which, on one side and the other, we began the war, and these two incidents, taken at random from a hundred of the same kind, seem to me to show accurately the difference between the two methods, the difference between the Civilization on which Thomas Mann heaps his contempt, jeering at its "reason, its gentleness, and its emancipation," and the Kultur which, according to him, is "above morality, reason, and science," the Kultur which he hails as "die Subliemerung des Dämonischen."

Have these principles been modified? Those of the Germans, no; our own, yes. The Germans have systematically continued the practical application of their gentlemanly instincts. After the crimes of Lorraine and Belgium came the unpardonable outrage of the *Lusitania*, followed by others so numerous and so varied that I must give up the idea of finding room for them in this letter; a whole volume would not be long enough to give a full list of them.

If the principles of the Boches have remained the same and have incited them every day to the commission of fresh outrages, ours—I say it frankly—have changed.

We want three things—to-day reprisals of defence—to-morrow compensations—finally, to save the future, punishment.

Reprisals? Most certainly. There are two kinds of reprisals, those of vengeance and those of defence. The first I reject; the second I demand. I should be proud if French soldiers and their brothers-in-arms kept their hands clean when they penetrate into Germany. I swear that no violence could have stained them if the Boches had not been piling up provocations for months and months. In any case I am quite sure that if, contrary to my hopes, they were to give way to these provocations, our dear soldiers would never commit a tenth part of the acts of violence which have been suffered by our unhappy populations; they would dismiss with horror the idea of setting fire to ambulances, or of massacring old men and women and children.

But there are reprisals of defence. These I hope for, and our Nations demand them. We have got to defend our soldiers and our civilians. To reply, in the trenches, to grenades with oranges, to gases which kill with gases which make the eyes smart, to liquid fire with cold water, would not only be idiotic, it would be criminal. In battle, an eye for an eye, a tooth for a tooth. Abel must fight with the same weapons as Cain. However varied the forms of human folly may be, I imagine that no one will dispute this necessity. If, however, any soft-hearted philanthropists raise a protest and entreat us not to answer gas by gas and fire by fire, it would be easy to form a few gangs of them and place them in the front-line trenches, with instructions, when asphyxiating gases of the enemy arrive, to disperse the clouds by blowing upon them, and to put out the flames of the liquid fire with their gentle tears.

We have also got to defend civilians. Intoxicated by their philosophers the Boches can only understand the arguments of force. They laugh ponderously at our protests in the name of right. Blows are the only things that they can feel. We ought thoroughly to convince them that every time that one of our open towns is bombarded by cannon, by Zeppelin, or by aeroplanes, one of our aeroplanes, while we are waiting for something better, will bombard one of theirs. An excellent effect was produced by the operations at Carlsruhe and Stuttgart. Let us equip hundreds of aeroplanes for purposes of bombardment, and let each outrage of the Boches on our towns be followed by an immediate riposte, frankly announced in the newspapers to the whole world. Is that cruelty? I would accept that reproach from no one. I have immense pity in my heart—pity for our children and our women who are the victims of German assassins, pity for our children and our women whom it is our duty to protect, and whom we can protect in this way only! That, I repeat, is not a reprisal of vengeance, but a reprisal of defence. The people who protest against the use of such means ought not to remain far from the danger zone. Let them go—not alone, that would be too easy, but with their family, their old mothers, their wives, their children—let them go and take up their abode in the open towns which serve most often as targets, to Reims, to Pont-à-Mousson, to Nancy, to Dunkerque; let them go and live there in the houses of the poor, which are crushed like walnuts by big shells and split from top to bottom by Zeppelin bombs, or else let them take a berth for a few months on a transatlantic steamer; when they have been there long enough, when they have observed at close quarters the acts of the Boches, when they have seen some loved one fall by their side, when they have felt on their own brow the wind of a Camarde, then, if they still demand that the Allies should not engage in reprisals of defence, their advice, though it may not be wise, will at least be worthy of respect. In the meantime, in the name of the women and children already assassinated, and that the list of these pitiable victims may not be lengthened, those people had better be silent who, from the asylum of their safe and comfortable homes, invite us to reply to crime by diplomatic notes or by prayers, and to counter actions that kill with words that lull to sleep!

I said that from to-day our wish is for reprisals of defence, and that to-morrow we shall want compensation and punishment.

One word only about *compensations*. It is not enough that everything which has been destroyed and can be paid for shall be paid for. Those who have wilfully set our villages on fire must be compelled to rebuild them; we shall, I hope, requisition in "Boche"-land enough manual labour to repair all that can be repaired of their crimes. When they have not destroyed our manufactories they have pillaged them, stealing raw material, manufactured articles, and machines; I sincerely hope that they will be compelled to restore our plant to us in good condition, that in case of need, while we wait for better, we shall not hesitate to take theirs in place of our own, which they have no doubt broken up, and that we shall have the sense to impose upon them a whole category of economic measures calculated to restore those of our industries which they have deliberately ruined.

And I imagine also that in the domain of art, compensations will be put down in settling up the accounts. We will leave them all their own public monuments, in the clumsy bad taste of which they take such pride. But there are in the German and Austrian museums masterpieces of art—not of German art, but of Flemish or Italian, Dutch or French, Russian or English. The Boches will entertain profound respect for us if we collect all these works, which in any case they do not understand, and form with them in beautiful maltreated towns such as Louvain, Ypres, Reims, and Arras, museums of the Great War. If we do not act in this way they would feel no gratitude towards us, but would treat us simply as imbeciles, and for once I should be of their opinion.

But to come to a graver question: the necessity for punishment. It will not be enough that the material and economic damage which they have done shall be repaired, it will not be enough that the Monster which has steeped the whole world in blood shall be struck down and rent limb from limb, and placed for ever in a condition in which it can do no harm. The outraged conscience of humanity demands personal decrees against the assassins.

Ah! If the sponge were to be passed over all the crimes that have been committed, over all the outrages and all the violations of the rights of nations, if this war were to be ended by an ordinary treaty modifying the frontiers, and stipulating for financial and economic conditions and nothing more, and if, after this treaty, wearied of hating and giving in to a great craving for moral peace, the hostile Nations were to blot from their memories the recollection of the Evil accomplished, and were to throw themselves into each other's arms and exchange a mighty kiss of concord and of love—let us take every precaution against such a possibility! A misfortune would overtake humanity far more serious for it than all the catastrophes which it has suffered in the course of its sorrowful history. I say that if we do not strike at the head of the most exalted, the most powerful among the responsible authors of these crimes—those who let loose the war, those who gloried in tearing up treaties like "scraps of paper," those who ordered the sinking of the *Lusitania* and the *Persia* and their thousands of passengers, those who first bombarded open towns, those who for the first time launched aeroplanes and Zeppelins over our industrial cities on both sides of the Channel (to speak only of our own front) those who burnt Louvain, who murdered the Cathedral of Reims, those who gave the order for the first acts of incendiarism and pillage and assassination, those who splashed the statue of Charity with the noble blood of Miss Cavell, those who started the *régime* of asphyxiating gases and liquid fire, and all who have placed themselves beyond the pale of the law, and of humanity—if the sword of the law does not fall on all these men personally, this is what will happen: man will no longer believe in honour, he will no longer believe in right, he will no longer believe in justice, he will no longer believe in anything. His faith in a better future will vanish and be dispelled for ever, along with the beautiful dreams which—whether they were realizable or not—were our joy, our hope, and our pride, in which we were constructing, on the foundation of Law and of Right, better national and international organizations than those by which man up to our day had protected himself. If the criminals do not bear the punishment of their crimes the principle of responsibility gives way, carrying with it all our codes and laws. It will remain a settled principle that only Force counts. The force of Germany will not have triumphed this time, but its hateful doctrine will remain all-powerful, and that would be for humanity a terrible moral relapse.

The Germans have taught us to hate—and perhaps that is their greatest moral crime. To this new passion, but lately still unknown to us, we had for long ages closed our hearts. We should not have allowed it to enter them, if, whether as conquerors or conquered, we had been challenged by our enemies to an honourable combat. Under the repeated blows of their outrages our hearts ended by giving it admittance; hatred has entered into them, it has settled itself there, and taken up its abode. It will stay there till justice has been done. Our soul will not be freed from hatred till the day when the expiation of the chief culprits has been carried out. Then, and then only, humanity will be able to resume its enthusiastic and yet halting march in the direction of Progress.

These are not the extravagant visions of a solitary dreamer. You recognize these sentiments, friend Campbell. You have felt how strongly they were imposed upon upright consciences, however enamoured of the ideal, by the stern contact with realities. No one can remain a stranger to that fact who has made the melancholy pilgrimages which you have in the murdered lands,—for example, in the wasted fields of Lorraine or Champagne—if, in the cities of Reims or of Pont-à-Mousson, in Sermaize or Clermont en Argonne, in Nomeny or Gerbéviller—and all the other places, alas! where innocent blood has flowed—he can hear and remember with a brotherly heart the cries of the martyrs, as he passes through the midst of the ruins.

Is it impossible to realize these projects? Is it an idle fancy to talk of such conditions and to demand such punishments, while the enemy is still burrowing in trenches dug in our soil? No! No! Whatever trials we may still have to submit to, whatever long sufferings we may still have to endure, in France, as in England, in Russia, in Italy, in Belgium, and in Servia, we all know perfectly well—as the rest of the world is beginning to know—that absolute victory, with the conditions dictated by us, will without any doubt be the prize of our efforts, if we pursue those efforts with enough resolution and method, that is to say if we are determined to have it, if our determination and our actions are in proportion to the importance of the object we have to attain. And you, friend Campbell, will have the honour of being of the number of those who, from the first hour, have had a clear vision of the future, of those who have taught your noble Nation to *understand* and to be *determined*. And so with all my heart I give you my hand.

Yours truly,

LÉON MIRMAN.

Milton Keynes UK
Ingram Content Group UK Ltd.
UKHW020828231024
450026UK00004B/464